I0181032

Breaking Open the Word

AN OCIA GUIDE TO SUNDAY SCRIPTURE

MARY KATHARINE DEELEY

Liguori
PUBLICATIONS
A Redemptorist Ministry

Imprimi Potest: Stephen T. Rehrauer, CSsR, Provincial, Denver Province, the Redemptorists

Imprimatur: "In accordance with CIC 827, permission to publish has been granted on April 15, 2021, by the Most Reverend Mark S. Rivituso, Auxiliary Bishop, Archdiocese of St. Louis. Permission to publish is an indication that nothing contrary to Church teaching is contained in this work. It does not imply any endorsement of the opinions expressed in the publication; nor is any liability assumed by this permission."

Published by Liguori Publications.
Liguori Publications, a nonprofit corporation, is an apostolate of the Redemptorists.
To learn more about the Redemptorists, visit Redemptorists.com.
To order this book, visit Liguori.org or call 800-325-9521.

Library of Congress Cataloging-in-Publication Data
Names: Liguori Publications. Title: Breaking Open the Word: An OCIA Guide to Sunday Scripture during Year C of the Catholic Church. Description: First edition | Liguori: Liguori Publications, 2023| Includes index | Contents: Year C | Identifiers: LCCN 2020018311 |
ISBN 9780764828171 (paperback) | Subjects: LCSH: Church year meditations | Catholic Church— Prayers and devotions. | Catholic Church. *Ordo lectionum Missae* (2nd ed., 1998). English.
Classification: LCC BX2170.C55 B735 2020 | DDC 242/.3—dc23 |
LC record available at lccn.loc.gov/2020018311

Printed in the United States of America | 27 26 25 24 23 / 6 5 4 3 2

The process by which adults are initiated into the Catholic faith throughout the United States is now called the OCIA—the Order of Christian Initiation of Adults. "Order" is a clearer translation of the Latin term for the process formerly known as the RCIA—the Rite of Christian Initiation of Adults. People preparing for baptism and reception into the Church celebrate several rites as part of the order to which those rites belong—an order whose mission is to journey in the faith. The US Conference of Catholic Bishops adopted the name change in 2021, with American dioceses introducing the name thereafter. For more information, please contact your local diocese.

Contents

Overview

What is Breaking Open the Word?

The *Lectionary for Sunday Mass* forms the basis for the OCIA process. This is most appropriate since the Scriptures tell the story of the faith experienced by the people of God: the relationship between the Chosen People and Yahweh, and the relationship between the early Christian community and Jesus of Nazareth, the Son of God. As we reflect upon these faith stories, our own stories of how God has impacted our lives become more clearly perceived and articulated. Because the Scriptures convey the stories of a community, they are meant to be encountered in community as we gather to worship and celebrate together. It is also fitting that the catechumens and candidates gather in community to break open God's word and apply it to their own lives in the here and now.

In their reflection and linking of the Scriptures to their own lives, the early Christians began to develop official summaries and teachings about the meaning of their communal religious experiences. Since these doctrines and dogmas were born of theological reflection grounded in Scripture, the Church now ties these teachings to Scripture in the OCIA process. Therefore, the sessions begin with Scripture reflection and move toward an encounter with Catholic belief. Since it is primarily through the Sunday liturgy that the community hands on its traditions and beliefs, this is also the most opportune time for the catechumens and candidates to be formed by the community. Beginning with the period of the catechumenate, it is urged that they be dismissed from the liturgy following the Prayers of the Faithful to reflect together upon the word of God and the teachings of the Church.

How to use Breaking Open the Word

Breaking Open the Word is intended for use by team leaders of Christian initiation groups (adults, adolescents, and children). It can also be used as a separate resource: Whether you are planning homilies, leading or participating in faith-sharing groups, or searching for further enrichment through the Sunday readings, *Breaking Open the Word* will make it easier.

Available for each liturgical year (A, B, and C), *Breaking Open the Word* contains the readings for every Sunday of each year. The readings are arranged so there are twenty-eight weeks between the first Sunday of Advent and Pentecost, and there are twenty-eight weeks between Trinity Sunday and Christ the King.

The reflections, themes, and prayers in this book are aids to lead inquirers, catechumens, candidates, and neophytes. To better anticipate and stimulate questions and discussion, familiarize yourself with these resources. Leading others to Christ is the most important work you will do in your life; your personal preparation for this work is important.

Themes that emerge from the readings and reflections are listed at the end of each commentary with references to *Journey of Faith* materials. This includes lessons related to the theme, as well as at least one lesson that ties most closely to the Scripture readings. Incorporating these lessons ensures that you cover all *Journey of Faith* lessons in the liturgical year.

Sundays between the first Sunday of Advent and the eighth Sunday in Ordinary Time refer to the Catechumenate period; Sundays between the first Sunday of Lent and Easter refer to the Enlightenment period; Sundays between the second Sunday of Easter and Pentecost refer to the Mystagogy period. Because the twenty-eight weeks between Trinity and Christ the King may be used either for continuing mystagogy or for beginning a new group of inquirers (or both), the Sundays between Trinity and Christ the King refer to materials from both Mystagogy and Inquiry.

Included in Breaking Open the Word

➤ Readings for all Sundays of the liturgical year (A, B, or C), Advent through Christ the King

➤ Readings for the Easter Triduum

➤ Year A readings for the third, fourth, and fifth Sundays of Lent

➤ Readings for those occasional Sundays that supersede Ordinary Time Sunday readings

➤ Scripture commentary for every set of readings

➤ Discussion and/or reflection questions for every set of readings

➤ Readings are cross-referenced to the catechetical materials associated with Liguori Publications' *Journey of Faith* program.

➤ A brief collection of short gathering prayers and dismissal prayers for each phase of the initiation process

➤ A thematic index

All readings are taken directly from the Lectionary for Mass *for use in the dioceses of the United States of America, second typical edition © 2001 Confraternity of Christian Doctrine Inc., Washington, DC.*

Suggested Agenda for a Sunday Session

The readings are taken directly from the *Lectionary* text used during Mass—a reflection of the *New American Bible Translation*. Since May 19, 2002, the revised *Lectionary*, based on the *New American Bible (NABRE)* is the only English-language *Lectionary* that may be used at Mass in the dioceses of the United States, except for the current *Lectionary for Masses with Children* which remains in use. Below is a suggested timeline for holding a Sunday session:

30 minutes	Liturgy—all gather in church. Dismissal after the Prayer of the Faithful.
10 minutes	Refreshments and settling in.
15 minutes	Prayer and reflection— Where are we at this moment?
45 minutes	Reread, reflect upon, and share the readings of the day—either all or the one chosen for this session. Spouses and sponsors can join this session after Mass.
10 minutes	Evaluation and prayer— How are we going to live the Scriptures this week?

Note: During Precatechumenate (Inquiry) or Mystagogy, this format may be adapted for either a Sunday morning after Mass or for a weekday evening session.

I thank God every time I remember you, constantly praying with joy in every one of my prayers for all of you, because of your sharing in the gospel from the first day until now...And this is my prayer, that your love may overflow more and more with knowledge and full insight,...having produced the harvest of righteousness that comes through Jesus Christ for the glory and praise of God.

Philippians 1:3, 4, 5, 9, 11
New Revised Standard Version

Enjoy!

READING 1, JEREMIAH 33:14–16

The days are coming, says the LORD, when I will fulfill the promise I made to the house of Israel and Judah. In those days, in that time, I will raise up for David a just shoot; he shall do what is right and just in the land. In those days Judah shall be safe and Jerusalem shall dwell secure; this is what they shall call her: "The LORD our justice."

PSALM 25:4–5, 8–9, 10, 14

READING 2, 1 THESSALONIANS 3:12—4:2

Brothers and sisters: May the Lord make you increase and abound in love for one another and for all, just as we have for you, so as to strengthen your hearts, to be blameless in holiness before our God and Father at the coming of our Lord Jesus with all his holy ones. [Amen.] Finally, brothers and sisters, we earnestly ask and exhort you in the Lord Jesus that, as you received from us how you should conduct yourselves to please God and as you are conducting yourselves you do so even more. For you know what instructions we gave you through the Lord Jesus.

GOSPEL, LUKE 21:25–28, 34–36

Jesus said to his disciples: "There will be signs in the sun, the moon, and the stars, and on earth nations will be in dismay, perplexed by the roaring of the sea and the waves. People will die of fright in anticipation of what is coming upon the world, for the powers of the heavens will be shaken. And then they will see the Son of Man coming in a cloud with power and great glory. But when these signs begin to happen, stand erect and raise your heads because your redemption is at hand. Beware that your hearts do not become drowsy from carousing and drunkenness and the anxieties of daily life, and that day catch you by surprise like a trap. For that day will assault everyone who lives on the face of the earth. Be vigilant at all times and pray that you have the strength to escape the tribulations that are imminent and to stand before the Son of Man."

The Days Are Coming

It seems strange to have celebrated the triumph of Christ the King last week and find ourselves beginning a new year in our Church. "New year" suggests a time of new commitment and an anticipation of good things ahead. Jeremiah thought about that when he preached about the fulfillment of God's promise. Likewise, Paul holds out hope of grace and love for the Thessalonians, urging them to live the Christian life ever more deeply. Only in the Gospel do we get a glimpse that these coming days will not be easy ones, and even at that, Jesus exhorts his listeners not to be weighed down with worry or wild partying for they have the means to escape the dark days and stand before the Son of Man. These messages may seem to be different, but are they?

The Heart of God's Promise

By the time Jeremiah spoke his prophecy, The Israelites had already experienced a history of hardship and conquest. God had promised to make Abraham's descendants as numerous as the stars, but a famine drove those descendants into Egypt. Enslaved there, the people called out, and God raised up Moses to help lead the people out of Egypt and into the Promised Land. When Moses died, God promised to raise up a prophet like Moses when the people needed it. Later, Assyria and then Babylon laid waste to the northern and southern kingdoms of Israel and Judah. Where was the promised prophet like Moses? God also promised to be with the House of David forever. Where was God in all this tragedy? Jeremiah says, "Wait—the days are surely coming." But notice he doesn't say that everything will be fine, and everyone will be happy. Rather, God promises that this righteous branch will execute justice and righteousness, after which everyone can live in safety.

A Path through the Storm

In other passages of 1 Thessalonians, Paul talks about vigilance, warning that the day of the Lord will come like a thief in the night. He counsels steadfast faith in the meantime (see chapter 5). In our passage for today, Paul's beautiful prayer to God to increase the love Christians have for everyone reminds us that we are given the grace and strength to continue walking on the path toward God. Jesus does not sugarcoat the difficulty of transforming the world. When the day of the Lord comes, there will surely be distress among the nations and the people. Justice and righteousness demand that no one person or group of people holds

all the power. Those in power might beg to differ. Jesus offers a different perspective to his followers: "stand erect, raise your heads because your redemption is drawing near." Jesus' vision of the Son of Man coming in a cloud recalls the words of the prophet in Daniel 7:13–14. Daniel refers to someone who looked like a human being, so "son of man" is not capitalized. Jesus is referring to himself ushering in the end times.

Good News for All of Us

In our homes, the beginning of Advent also heralds the coming of Christmas. Dutifully, we open the little doors on our Advent calendars, searching for the one precious gift. For many people touched by war, famine, poverty, or injustice, or those who are in a difficult time in their lives, God's promise to come seems far away. Our readings today tell us that God remembers his promises and we have been given the way to live through the darkness. We are asked to increase our love and stand firm in faith always—in good and bad times. We can turn to our mentors and teachers in faith for guidance. We can ask our friends for help. We can become mentors ourselves, walking with others toward the one precious gift that is Jesus himself.

Questions for Reflection and Discussion

➤ How does God's justice differ from the world's idea of justice? Why is the day of the Lord so often depicted as a frightening time?

➤ Who has taught or is teaching you how to live and please God? Who are your mentors in faith?

Related Journey of Faith Lesson

Q4, "Who Is Jesus Christ?"

Themes

End Times
    Q4, "Who Is Jesus Christ?"
Hope
    C6, "The Sacrament of Penance and Reconciliation"
    C7, "The Sacrament of Anointing of the Sick"
Persecution
    C10, "The People of God"
    C11, "The Early Church"

Second Sunday of Advent, Year C

READING 1, BARUCH 5:1–9

Jerusalem, take off your robe of mourning and misery; put on the splendor of glory from God forever: wrapped in the cloak of justice from God, bear on your head the mitre that displays the glory of the eternal name. For God will show all the earth your splendor: you will be named by God forever the peace of justice, the glory of God's worship. Up, Jerusalem! stand upon the heights; look to the east and see your children gathered from the east and the west at the word of the Holy One, rejoicing that they are remembered by God. Led away on foot by their enemies they left you: but God will bring them back to you, borne aloft in glory as on royal thrones. For God has commanded that every lofty mountain be made low, and that the age-old depths and gorges be filled to level ground, that Israel may advance secure in the glory of God. The forests and every fragrant kind of tree have overshadowed Israel at God's command; for God is leading Israel in joy by the light of his glory, with his mercy and justice for company.

PSALM 126:1–2, 2–3, 4–5, 6

READING 2, PHILIPPIANS 1:4–6, 8–11

Brothers and sisters: I pray always with joy in my every prayer for all of you, because of your partnership for the gospel from the first day until now. I am confident of this, that the one who began a good work in you will continue to complete it until the day of Christ Jesus. God is my witness, how I long for all of you with the affection of Christ Jesus. And this is my prayer: that your love may increase ever more and more in knowledge and every kind of perception, to discern what is of value, so that you may be pure and blameless for the day of Christ, filled with the fruit of righteousness that comes through Jesus Christ for the glory and praise of God.

GOSPEL, LUKE 3:1–6

In the fifteenth year of the reign of Tiberius Caesar, when Pontius Pilate was governor of Judea, and Herod was tetrarch of Galilee, and his brother Philip tetrarch of the region of Ituraea and Trachonitis, and Lysanias was tetrarch of Abilene, during the high priesthood of Annas and Caiaphas, the word of God came to John the son of Zechariah in the desert. John went throughout the whole region of the Jordan, proclaiming a baptism of repentance for the forgiveness of sins, as it is written in the book of the words of the prophet Isaiah: A voice of one crying out in the desert: "Prepare the way of the Lord, make straight his paths. Every valley shall be filled and every mountain and hill shall be made low. The winding roads shall be made straight, and the rough ways made smooth, and all flesh shall see the salvation of God."

Homecoming

When I was a young adult, I eagerly anticipated Christmas because it meant going home for a week or two. Our families came together by traveling from the next town over, Colorado, and Illinois to spend the holidays with our mother, each other, and—later—our stepfather. We caught up on family news, exchanged presents, and sat up late talking as only families can. These days, I am "home" for my sister and her children and, every other year, for my children, their spouses, and my grandchildren. (I have to share them with their in-laws, which is hard but understandable.) I love it when they come home.

In the readings today, we read God's vision of homecoming. Baruch's prophecy speaks of the end of exile when all those who were scattered from Israel will return by the hand of the Lord. Paul talks to the Philippians about the good work that is going on in them even now and preparing them for the day of the Lord. And Luke sets the stage for the coming of Christ by telling the beginning of the ministry of John the Baptist, who heard the word of God. That ministry would be an invitation to all people to come home.

You Will Be Led with Joy

At the end of the Babylonian exile, the kingdom of Judah was destroyed. The Babylonians had taken most of the men back to Babylon, leaving the women, children, and elderly to fend for themselves. Israel had no ruler, no temple, and no land of their own to speak of. Clinging to faith was certainly difficult and returning to "normal" seemed impossible. Into the despair of the people, Baruch speaks of a beautiful vision of God bringing the exiles back—not as a ragged band but in glory, walking safely through the land, shaded by the trees. For a people hungry for a word of hope, this must have been like a drink of cool water.

Saint Paul opens his Letter to the Philippians by giving thanks for them and their work. But his eye is on the coming day of Christ (which Paul thought would arrive very soon.) Thus, Paul focuses on the good work God has begun in the Philippians and prays that their love will continue to grow so that when Christ comes and sees them, he will welcome them even more joyously than my mother did when we, her kids, returned home at Christmas.

From Prophecy to Fulfillment

Luke is rarely given to exaggeration. The beginning of his Gospel is a historian's record of who watched over the temple. But the word of God does not come to the powerful or to those in charge. It comes to John, son of Zechariah, the man we know as the forerunner of Jesus, but who is nobody to the powerful. His message, though, calls people's attention to their own sinfulness; it preaches repentance—a change of heart—that their sins might be forgiven. According to Luke, this is all done to fulfill God's command in Isaiah. "Prepare the way of the Lord, make straight his paths." Of course, when the path to God is straight, in the world or in our hearts, it is easier for us to get to God as well.

Good News for All of Us

How do we make a home for God in our hearts? How do we prepare to go home to God when that day finally comes? The answers to those two questions may be the same. We open our hearts to love for God, ourselves, all people, and all creation. We let love overflow and discern the action that will keep us on the path to God. We harvest justice and righteousness in our thoughts and actions. Is it easy? Absolutely not. But as Christians, we have been given the gift of God's grace and the prayers of Paul and all the saints to help us on our way. We can also start small, finding just one more prayer, thought, or action that will advance us in our journey.

Questions for Reflection and Discussion

➤ *Name one prayer, one thought, and one action that will help you make a home for Christ in your heart.*

➤ *Is there something that keeps you from being fully open to Christ? If so, have you been able to talk to anyone about that?*

Related Journey of Faith Lesson

C3, "The Sacrament of Baptism"

Themes

Baptism
   C3, "The Sacrament of Baptism"
Confirmation
   C4, "The Sacrament of Confirmation"
Repentance
   C6, "The Sacrament of Penance and Reconciliation"

READING 1, ZEPHANIAH 3:14–18A

Shout for joy, O daughter Zion! Sing joyfully, O Israel! Be glad and exult with all your heart, O daughter Jerusalem! The LORD has removed the judgment against you he has turned away your enemies; the King of Israel, the LORD, is in your midst, you have no further misfortune to fear. On that day, it shall be said to Jerusalem: Fear not, O Zion, be not discouraged! The LORD, your God, is in your midst, a mighty savior; he will rejoice over you with gladness, and renew you in his love, he will sing joyfully because of you, as one sings at festivals.

ISAIAH 12:2–3, 4, 5–6

READING 2, PHILIPPIANS 4:4–7

Brothers and sisters: Rejoice in the Lord always. I shall say it again: rejoice! Your kindness should be known to all. The Lord is near. Have no anxiety at all, but in everything, by prayer and petition, with thanksgiving, make your requests known to God. Then the peace of God that surpasses all understanding will guard your hearts and minds in Christ Jesus.

GOSPEL, LUKE 3:10–18

The crowds asked John the Baptist, "What should we do?" He said to them in reply, "Whoever has two cloaks should share with the person who has none. And whoever has food should do likewise." Even tax collectors came to be baptized and they said to him, "Teacher, what should we do?" He answered them, "Stop collecting more than what is prescribed." Soldiers also asked him, "And what is it that we should do?" He told them, "Do not practice extortion, do not falsely accuse anyone, and be satisfied with your wages." Now the people were filled with expectation, and all were asking in their hearts whether John might be the Christ. John answered them all, saying, "I am baptizing you with water, but one mightier than I is coming. I am not worthy to loosen the thongs of his sandals. He will baptize you with the Holy Spirit and fire. His winnowing fan is in his hand to clear his threshing floor and to gather the wheat into his barn, but the chaff he will burn with unquenchable fire." Exhorting them in many ways, he preached Good News to the people.

Renewed in God's Love

In their long relationship with God, the people of Israel moved from faithfulness to sinfulness and back to faithfulness in a cycle I think we know well. At that time, the Israelites saw tragedies, like the exile to Babylon, as judgments on their sinfulness. Today many Christians might find that odd, but we must remember that the Israelites did not have a concept of heaven and hell. Rather they believed that punishment and reward were played out in the arena of this world and in the generations to come. Faithfulness was rewarded to the thousandth generation. Sin was punished to the third or fourth generation.

When Zephaniah writes his prophecy, the best king since David was on the throne. Josiah is widely credited with discovering the book of the Law, Deuteronomy. He instituted reforms that helped the people stay faithful. Zephaniah's prophecy rejoices that the Lord has taken away the judgments against the people. The message is: "Do not fear; the Lord is in your midst." Those must have been welcome words indeed.

The Peace of God

Saint Paul echoes Zephaniah's joy. Our second reading includes probably one of Paul's better-known quotations. "The Lord is near....Make your requests known to God." At the end of this short passage, Paul mentions one gift by which we know God is active in our lives. "...The peace of God that surpasses all understanding will guard your hearts and minds in Christ Jesus...." In John's Gospel, Jesus wishes the disciples peace— "...My peace I give to you. Not as the world gives do I give it to you" (John 14:27). Peace is also one of the fruits of the Holy Spirit named in Galatians (5:22). For Christians everywhere, an abiding sense of peace is a sign that the living God is present in the life of an individual or a community.

Preparing for a Baptism by Fire

At first hearing, the listener might think that our Gospel is talking about Jesus, so closely do John the Baptist's words echo Jesus' commands. The crowds listening to John were seeking a path to follow and a new way of life. John reminds them that change begins with their own actions. To the crowds, he advocates sharing possessions and food with the poor. To the tax collectors, he reminds them not to collect more than what is prescribed by law. Soldiers are told in no uncertain terms not to intimidate those they are guarding, but rather to be satisfied with their wages.

The people heard in John's words a different way to live. It is no surprise that they wondered if he was the Messiah. John's answer makes it clear. He is merely getting them ready for the Messiah whose baptism will be by the Holy Spirit and fire. For John, the path to following the Messiah will require all of what he said and more. John's message is a little uncomfortable. That's because true change of heart is a lifelong project. And John is just trying to prepare us for that part of the Good News.

Good News for All of Us

It is likely that few of us realize how many of our colloquial phrases come from Scripture. We use "baptism by fire" to mean someone who has had to learn a job or situation much faster than normal or under stressful or harrowing circumstances. It's helpful to know the context in these readings. After the death and resurrection of Jesus, the Holy Spirit came in wind and fire and filled every disciple with an urgency to preach the Good News. It wasn't an easy time. Early Christians risked ridicule, imprisonment, and death. But our colloquial phrase leaves out the reference to the Holy Spirit, and the disciples of Jesus in the early days recognized the Spirit as Christ alive in their midst. Somehow it made the journey a little easier. The Spirit does that for us as well.

Questions for Reflection and Discussion

> *Saint Paul tells us to make our requests known to God in prayer. What was the last request you made of God?*

> *John the Baptist suggests one action each person can take in his or her own life to prepare for the Messiah. What is your one action this Advent?*

Related Journey of Faith Lesson

C2, "The Sacraments: An Introduction"

Themes

Joy
    C2, "The Sacraments: An Introduction"
Mercy
    C16, "Social Justice"
Ministry
    C13, "Christian Moral Living"

Fourth Sunday of Advent, Year C

READING 1, MICAH 5:1–4A

Thus says the LORD: You, Bethlehem-Ephrathah too small to be among the clans of Judah, from you shall come forth for me one who is to be ruler in Israel; whose origin is from of old, from ancient times. Therefore, the Lord will give them up, until the time when she who is to give birth has borne, and the rest of his kindred shall return to the children of Israel. He shall stand firm and shepherd his flock by the strength of the LORD, in the majestic name of the LORD, his God; and they shall remain, for now his greatness shall reach to the ends of the earth; he shall be peace.

PSALM 80, 2–3, 15–16, 18–19

READING 2, HEBREWS 10:5–10

Brothers and sisters: When Christ came into the world, he said: "Sacrifice and offering you did not desire, but a body you prepared for me; in holocausts and sin offerings you took no delight. Then I said, 'As is written of me in the scroll, behold, I come to do your will, O God.'" First, he says, "Sacrifices and offerings, holocausts and sin offerings, you neither desired nor delighted in." These are offered according to the law. Then he says, "Behold, I come to do your will." He takes away the first to establish the second. By this "will," we have been consecrated through the offering of the body of Jesus Christ once for all.

GOSPEL, LUKE 1:39–45

Mary set out and traveled to the hill country in haste to a town of Judah, where she entered the house of Zechariah and greeted Elizabeth. When Elizabeth heard Mary's greeting, the infant leaped in her womb, and Elizabeth, filled with the Holy Spirit, cried out in a loud voice and said, "Blessed are you among women, and blessed is the fruit of your womb. And how does this happen to me, that the mother of my Lord should come to me? For at the moment the sound of your greeting reached my ears, the infant in my womb leaped for joy. Blessed are you who believed that what was spoken to you by the Lord would be fulfilled."

A Prophetic Voice

In the Scriptures, the prophet's job was not to predict the future. Rather, it was to see where God was active in the world and to call attention to what God was saying to the people. The messages varied, as did the methods, but every prophet saw things through God's eyes, even if their visions were not welcome.

In today's Gospel, Elizabeth takes on a prophetic role that Luke signals, saying, "Elizabeth was filled with the Holy Spirit...." Her message is welcome. She sees immediately where God is active in the world and recognizes Mary as the Mother of the Lord. She echoes Gabriel in calling Mary "blessed" not only because of the honor God bestowed on her, but also because she believed the Lord would fulfill his promise.

Elizabeth is mentioned only here in Luke's Gospel. But her prophetic voice and joyful recognition of God's presence in the world proclaims the Good News to all of us this close to Christmas.

He Shall Be the One of Peace

Throughout the Bible, God shows up in unexpected places and uses unexpected people to fulfill his plan for the world. From the burning bush (Exodus 3:1–6) to a voice in the night (1 Samuel 3:2–9) to a vision of heaven (Isaiah 6:1–3)—just to name a few—God has made his presence known. God also called those who couldn't speak well (Moses), who were sinners (Isaiah and Peter), who were foreigners (Ruth) or who were just too young (Jeremiah). Is it any wonder that Micah comments on Bethlehem as a "clan" from whom God's promised one will come? The Israelites thought the Messiah would be a great warrior from the mighty lineage of a king. But we remember that this king, David, was Jesse's youngest child and merely a shepherd boy. The Messiah would come from David's birthplace, Bethlehem, and not the city in which he ruled, Jerusalem. Any power the Messiah has belongs to God. And where God reigns, there is peace over the whole earth.

A Perfect Offering

Who is Jesus for us? Most of us could answer within a minute or two: Messiah, Lord, Brother, Master, Teacher. All those answers are right. The Letter to the Hebrews takes us a bit deeper than that. Jesus is the one who gives himself wholeheartedly to God, freely and in love for the sake of the world. Jesus offers his body to the Father as the perfect sacrifice, and thus we are sanctified by his offering. What a wondrous gift—to lay down your life for your friends.

Good News for All of Us

God used Jesse's youngest son, who was born in a little town and whose great-grandmother was a foreigner from Moab (Ruth), to work out the divine promise for a Messiah. God used a young woman to bring the Messiah into our world so he could show us what we can be: the children of the living God. He died to make that a reality.

It is comforting to know that God can also use our strengths, our weaknesses, our lives to fulfill his purpose in the world. If we give our lives to him and are open to his voice, God can do wonders in this world and lead us home, following the Good Shepherd who gives his life for the sheep.

Questions for Reflection and Discussion

➤ *What gifts has God given you and how do you think God is using, or could use, them?*

➤ *Each of us has a unique relationship with God. Elizabeth named Mary's relationship. Who names yours? Who helps you know your true self and calls you to account for it?*

Related Journey of Faith Lesson

C10, "The People of God"

Themes

Mary
    C10, "The People of God"
Messiah
    Q4, "Who Is Jesus Christ?"
Waiting
    C11, "The Early Church"

Feast of the Holy Family, Year C

READING 1, SIRACH 3:2–6, 12–14

God sets a father in honor over his children; a mother's authority he confirms over her sons. Whoever honors his father atones for sins and preserves himself from them. When he prays, he is heard; he stores up riches who Reveres his mother. Whoever honors his father is gladdened by children, and, when he prays, is heard. Whoever reveres his father will live a long life; he who obeys his father brings comfort to his mother. My son, take care of your father when he is old; grieve him not as long as he lives. Even if his mind fails, be considerate of him; revile him not all the days of his life; kindness to a father will not be forgotten, firmly planted against the debt of your sins—a house raised in justice to you.

PSALM 128:1–2, 3, 4–5

READING 2, COLOSSIANS 3:12–17

Brothers and sisters: Put on, as God's chosen ones, holy and beloved, heartfelt compassion, kindness, humility, gentleness, and patience, bearing with one another and forgiving one another, if one has a grievance against another; as the Lord has forgiven you, so must you also do. And over all these put on love, that is, the bond of perfection. And let the peace of Christ control your hearts, the peace into which you were also called in one body.

And be thankful. Let the word of Christ dwell in you richly, as in all wisdom you teach and admonish one another, singing psalms, hymns, and spiritual songs with gratitude in your hearts to God. And whatever you do, in word or in deed, do everything in the name of the Lord Jesus, giving thanks to God the Father through him.

GOSPEL, LUKE 2:41–52

Each year Jesus' parents went to Jerusalem for the feast of Passover, and when he was twelve years old, they went up according to festival custom. After they had completed its days, as they were returning, the boy Jesus remained behind in Jerusalem, but his parents did not know it. Thinking that he was in the caravan, they journeyed for a day and looked for him among their relatives and acquaintances, but not finding him, they returned to Jerusalem to look for him. After three days they found him in the temple, sitting in the midst of the teachers, listening to them and asking them questions, and all who heard him were astounded at his understanding and his answers. When his parents saw him, they were astonished, and his mother said to him, "Son, why have you done this to us? Your father and I have been looking for you with great anxiety." And he said to them, "Why were you looking for me? Did you not know that I must be in my Father's house?" But they did not understand what he said to them. He went down with them and came to Nazareth and was obedient to them; and his mother kept all these things in her heart. And Jesus advanced in wisdom and age and favor before God and man.

All in the Family

Since the mid-twentieth century, Catholics have referred to the family as the "domestic Church." The phrase itself is old, dating from the early first century. The Church fathers used the word *ecclesiola*—literally translated as "little church." Vatican II recovered the phrase and recognized the family as the place where faith is first practiced and taught, values are formed, and the love of God is evident in the relationship between parents and children.

The readings today celebrate both the domestic family and the family of the Church. As members of both, we strive to live in the love of God and conduct ourselves as befitting the children of God. Our first reading lays out the expectations for parents and children. Children are to honor and respect their parents as an obedience to the Lord. In exchange, God promises a long life and joy in their own children.

The Letter to the Colossians turns to the Church family. All believers should adopt the characteristics and behaviors that will identify them as members of the same faith. The list serves nicely as an examination of conscience: Every time I come to one I know I haven't practiced (often due to a lack of patience), I stop and ask God to give me the grace to do better.

Paul's vision of how Christians should be continues to guide us today. In our day-to-day interactions, the peace of Christ should rule our hearts. When we teach or admonish one another it should be out of love. The most important consideration is last: "...do everything in the name of the Lord Jesus." Keeping Jesus in front of us will always remind us of who we are called to be.

The Boy Jesus

We don't know much about the childhood of Jesus. Luke's story, in some ways, seems to contradict the Old Testament reading. Jesus stays behind in Jerusalem; he doesn't tell his parents; they have to come looking for him; and then he seems to give them a little sass when they call him out. We're told that Jesus was about twelve, and nearly everyone will tell you that twelve is the beginning of a difficult period in the parent-child relationship. Children are trying to discover who they are apart from their parents and parents still want to protect and control their children's immature responses. Jesus had been led by God to the temple to listen and ask questions. It was part of his preparation for what was to come. His parents didn't know what he meant when he spoke of being in "his Father's house." Nevertheless, Jesus submits to Mary and Joseph and returns with them to Nazareth. Luke records his obedience and the way he grows in wisdom and in years. Mary kept this experience and everything else about Jesus in her heart. We get the impression that Sirach would have been proud of Jesus at this point. Certainly those around him were, as was his Father in heaven.

Good News for All of Us

Family life isn't always easy. Long days, sometimes longer nights, and time that either stands still or passes all too quickly are part of the territory. Family life forms us, becomes part of our development, and ultimately influences how we will make our own families. That's why it's so important to talk about how we grew up and what expectations we might bring into a marriage as we do in Pre-Cana. Not to do so would be to fly blind. In the same way, our Church family forms us. When something goes wrong in a parish, it can take a long time to restore the community to wholeness. When everything goes right, the community is vibrant and caring—eagerly worshiping together and serving one another.

Think about your families, the one you live with and the one you worship with. Where does love and grace abound? Where is there a need for healing? How can the Holy Family be a model for all of us?

Questions for Reflection and Discussion

➤ *Which Christian characteristics in the list from Colossians would help you most in living with your family (either in the domestic Church or in the worshiping Church)?*

➤ *Sometimes it's children who must take care of aging parents. Sirach gives some good, (though not always easy) advice for that. What helps ease our path as parents get older?*

Related Journey of Faith Lesson

C13, "Christian Moral Living"

Themes

Family Life
    C13, "Christian Moral Living"
Marriage
    C8, "The Sacrament of Matrimony"
Values
    C15, "A Consistent Ethic of Life"
    C14, "The Dignity of Life"

READING 1, ISAIAH 60:1-6

Rise up in splendor, Jerusalem! Your light has come, the glory of the LORD shines upon you. See, darkness covers the earth, and thick clouds cover the peoples; but upon you the LORD shines, and over you appears his glory. Nations shall walk by your light, and kings by your shining radiance. Raise your eyes and look about; they all gather and come to you: your sons come from afar, and your daughters in the arms of their nurses. Then you shall be radiant at what you see, your heart shall throb and overflow, for the riches of the sea shall be emptied out before you, the wealth of nations shall be brought to you. Caravans of camels shall fill you, dromedaries from Midian and Ephah; all from Sheba shall come bearing gold and frankincense and proclaiming the praises of the LORD.

PSALM 72:1-2, 7-8, 10-11, 12-13

READING 2, EPHESIANS 3:2-3A, 5-6

Brothers and sisters: You have heard of the stewardship of God's grace that was given to me for your benefit, namely, that the mystery was made known to me by revelation. It was not made known to people in other generations as it has now been revealed to his holy apostles and prophets by the Spirit: that the Gentiles are coheirs, members of the same body, and copartners in the promise in Christ Jesus through the gospel.

GOSPEL, MATTHEW 2:1-12

When Jesus was born in Bethlehem of Judea, in the days of King Herod, behold, magi from the east arrived in Jerusalem, saying, "Where is the newborn king of the Jews? We saw his star at its rising and have come to do him homage." When King Herod heard this, he was greatly troubled, and all Jerusalem with him. Assembling all the chief priests and the scribes of the people, He inquired of them where the Christ was to be born. They said to him, "In Bethlehem of Judea, for thus it has been written through the prophet: And you, Bethlehem, land of Judah, are by no means least among the rulers of Judah; since from you shall come a ruler, who is to shepherd my people Israel." Then Herod called the magi secretly and ascertained from them the time of the star's appearance. He sent them to Bethlehem and said, "Go and search diligently for the child. When you have found him, bring me word, that I too may go and do him homage." After their audience with the king, they set out. And behold, the star that they had seen at its rising preceded them, until it came and stopped over the place where the child was. They were overjoyed at seeing the star, and on entering the house they saw the child with Mary his mother. They prostrated themselves and did him homage. Then they opened their treasures and offered him gifts of gold, frankincense, and myrrh. And having been warned in a dream not to return to Herod, they departed for their country by another way.

Come to the Light

At various points in Isaiah's prophecy, he describes what will happen when the day of the Lord comes. At one point, he tells of a great banquet with wine and feasting (Isaiah 25:6–7). In another, he pictures a desert blooming with flowers and trees (Isaiah 41:18–20). In our first reading, he pictures the restored city of Jerusalem shining on a hill with the glory of the Lord spreading its light over the earth. "Nations shall walk by your light and kings by the radiance of your dawning." The gathering of the nations into unity with Israel was not always a part of Israel's expectation. The promised Messiah was to gather the twelve tribes of Israel into one flock with one shepherd. There was some sense that the nations would know that the Lord was king over the land, but Isaiah presents a very real vision of the world's rulers bowing to the Lord, praising him, and bringing their offerings. In the kingdom of God, all things were possible, even the idea of the nations worshiping God together with the Jews.

Good News for the Gentiles

In Jesus' time, the thought that Jews and Gentiles might worship together seemed absurd. The early Christians were Jews and insisted that the Gentiles must convert to Judaism before they could be baptized. Yet Jesus talked to the Samaritan woman (John 4), healed the child of the Syrophoenician woman (Mark 7:26–30), and told the scribes and Pharisees that the people of Nineveh would rise in judgment against them (Matthew 12:41). In each of these instances, the non-Jewish nations were granted favor by God. If we were to reread the Book of Jonah, we would find that Jonah had a hard time thinking that God could be "slow to anger and abounding in steadfast mercy," even to the Gentiles. After Jesus' death, the argument about conversion continued until Peter had a vision (Acts 10) and the first Council of Jerusalem was called. In the end, Gentiles were welcomed into Christianity without having to convert to Judaism. Here in Ephesians, Paul proclaims that Good News. Jews and Gentiles are members of the same body and sharers in the same promise.

The Coming of the Magi

The Epiphany story is unique to Matthew. Nowhere else do we hear of the three wise men who follow a star. But we are caught in the fulfillment of Isaiah's prophecy. Three "kings" (as the tradition says) follow the bright light of a star and find not a shining city on a hill, but a baby in a manger. The gifts they present echo the gifts the nations bring to the city of God, the heavenly Jerusalem. The wise men add one gift, though. They bring a jar of myrrh, the perfume for burial. In honoring Jesus' birth, they also foreshadow his death. And being wise indeed, they avoid Herod by taking a different road home.

Good News for All of Us

While the Bible records that God chose the Jews and that Christians have a unique claim as children of God through Jesus Christ, we also know that God created and loved the whole world. Jesus came to redeem the whole world. Every person has dignity before God and can call on him for help. Isaiah's vision and the story of the Magi show the power of God's love and the Good News. These become a light shining into the world for all to see.

When Jesus tells the disciples to go into the whole world and preach the Good News, he commissions them to share the light of God's glory not just to neighboring towns and villages, but to all people. We are called to do the same.

Questions for Reflection and Discussion

➤ *Have you ever talked about your faith or about Jesus with anyone else? Tell that story.*

➤ *The Magi brought gold, frankincense, and myrrh to Jesus both because of his kingship and as a preparation for his death. What gifts would you bring to Jesus, Mary, or Joseph that would represent who Jesus is for you?*

Related Journey of Faith Lesson

C13, "Christian Moral Living"

Themes

Ecumenism
    C13, "Christian Moral Living"
Peace
    C14, "The Dignity of Life"
People of God
    C10, "The People of God"

READING 1, ISAIAH 42:1–4, 6–7

Thus says the LORD: Here is my servant whom I uphold, my chosen one with whom I am pleased, upon whom I have put my spirit; he shall bring forth justice to the nations, not crying out, not shouting, not making his voice heard in the street. A bruised reed he shall not break, and a smoldering wick he shall not quench, until he establishes justice on the earth; the coastlands will wait for his teaching. I, the LORD, have called you for the victory of justice, I have grasped you by the hand; I formed you, and set you as a covenant of the people, a light for the nations, to open the eyes of the blind, to bring out prisoners from confinement, and from the dungeon, those who live in darkness.

PSALM 29:1–2, 3–4, 9B–10

READING 2, ACTS 10:34–38

Peter proceeded to speak to those gathered in the house of Cornelius, saying: "In truth, I see that God shows no partiality. Rather, in every nation whoever fears him and acts uprightly is acceptable to him. You know the word that he sent to the Israelites as he proclaimed peace through Jesus Christ, who is Lord of all, what has happened all over Judea, beginning in Galilee after the baptism that John preached, how God anointed Jesus of Nazareth with the Holy Spirit and power. He went about doing good and healing all those oppressed by the devil, for God was with him."

GOSPEL, LUKE 3:15–16, 21–22

The people were filled with expectation, and all were asking in their hearts whether John might be the Christ. John answered them all, saying, "I am baptizing you with water, but one mightier than I is coming. I am not worthy to loosen the thongs of his sandals. He will baptize you with the Holy Spirit and fire." After all the people had been baptized and Jesus also had been baptized and was praying, heaven was opened and the Holy Spirit descended upon him in bodily form like a dove. And a voice came from heaven, "You are my beloved Son; with you I am well pleased."

A Covenant to the People

We have several examples of covenants throughout the Hebrew Scriptures. A covenant is an agreement or contract between two parties. God makes a covenant with Noah never to again destroy the earth with a flood. In the covenant with Moses, the people were to obey the Law (notably the Ten Commandments) as well as other laws and God promised to protect and care for them. God's covenant to David was one of everlasting love which would never be taken away, even if God had to discipline David's descendants for sinful behavior. We can imagine anyone of these being written down and the parties to the covenant being given a copy. But in Isaiah's prophecy, the servant of God himself is the covenant—someone who embodies God's promise of justice and righteousness. Notably, the servant is not a warrior, so many people would not think of him as the Messiah, but he is the one Israel waited for—the one who would help them see with new eyes and be released from whatever prison held them fast.

A Familiar Message

We heard a portion of the Gospel for today on the third Sunday of Advent. Then, as now, we are cautioned to prepare for a baptism by the Holy Spirit and fire. Today we continue the passage. The Holy Spirit in the form of a dove descends on Jesus himself. It is no accident that the voice that accompanies the Spirit speaks nearly the same words that open Isaiah's prophecy. But Luke makes a deliberate choice to substitute the word "Son," for "servant." We don't know who heard the voice; no reaction from anyone is recorded. But the people listening to the story would likely remember Isaiah's prophecy and wonder if this is the servant of God who will bring justice and righteousness. Luke's change of words would also suggest to them that the relationship between Jesus and the Father was deeper and more intimate than they may have imagined.

God Shows No Partiality

In the early days of the Church, the apostles felt compelled to preach the gospel to all they met. At the time it was argued that only those who were Jews and were circumcised could accept baptism. When Peter meets Cornelius, the question of interaction with Gentiles arises. Peter has a dream in which what is unclean is declared clean by God. Under that influence, Peter gives this great speech about his understanding that God shows no partiality. He doesn't draw this out of thin air. Both the Books of Deuteronomy (10:17) and 2 Chronicles (19:7) record that God neither shows partiality nor takes bribes. What makes Peter's declaration different is that it applies to the Gentiles as well as the Jews, so Peter can declare: "In every nation whoever fears him and acts uprightly is acceptable to him." Though there would be some controversy about this argument (and it will lead to the first Council of Jerusalem), Peter remains confident Gentiles will be accepted as converts. If we were to read further in Acts, we would see the Holy Spirit descending on Cornelius and his family even before they are baptized, as if in confirmation of Peter's understanding.

Good News for All of Us

As Catholics, we believe that the Church has the fullness of the means of salvation. We are so fortunate that grace, prayer, sacraments, liturgy, the examples of the saints, and so much more are available to us through baptism and the Church knows of no other entry in the Divine Life (*Catechism of the Catholic Church*, 1257). Our mission to share the Good News comes from this. We also know that our preaching and example is often flawed. So, the *Catechism* teaches that God is not bound to his sacraments and that every person who is ignorant of the Gospel of Christ and of his Church but seeks the truth and does the will of God in accordance with his understanding of it, can be saved (*CCC* 1260). Indeed, God's love abounds for all his creation.

Questions for Reflection and Discussion

> *Name one thing that is challenging and one thing that is comforting about being baptized.*

> *God's justice might seem far away. Assuming we are called to cooperate with God's will, name two things you would change to bring about a more just and holy world.*

Related Journey of Faith Lesson

C3, "The Sacrament of Baptism"

Themes

Conversion
    C3, "The Sacrament of Baptism"
Holy Spirit
    C4, "The Sacrament of Confirmation"
Justice
    C16, "Social Justice"
    C14, "The Dignity of Life"

READING 1, ISAIAH 62:1–5

For Zion's sake I will not be silent, for Jerusalem's sake I will not be quiet, until her vindication shines forth like the dawn and her victory like a burning torch. Nations shall behold your vindication, and all the kings your glory; you shall be called by a new name pronounced by the mouth of the LORD. You shall be a glorious crown in the hand of the LORD, a royal diadem held by your God. No more shall people call you "Forsaken," or your land "Desolate," but you shall be called "My Delight," and your land "Espoused." For the LORD delights in you and makes your land his spouse. As a young man marries a virgin, your Builder shall marry you; and as a bridegroom rejoices in his bride so shall your God rejoice in you.

PSALM 96:1–2, 2–3, 7–8, 9–10

READING 2, 1 CORINTHIANS 12:4–11

Brothers and sisters: There are different kinds of spiritual gifts but the same Spirit; there are different forms of service but the same Lord; there are different workings but the same God who produces all of them in everyone. To each individual the manifestation of the Spirit is given for some benefit. To one is given through the Spirit the expression of wisdom; to another, the expression of knowledge according to the same Spirit; to another, faith by the same Spirit; to another, gifts of healing by the one Spirit; to another, mighty deeds; to another, prophecy; to another, discernment of spirits; to another, varieties of tongues; to another, interpretation of tongues. But one and the same Spirit produces all of these, distributing them individually to each person as he wishes.

GOSPEL, JOHN 2:1–11

There was a wedding at Cana in Galilee, and the mother of Jesus was there. Jesus and his disciples were also invited to the wedding. When the wine ran short, the mother of Jesus said to him, "They have no wine." And Jesus said to her, "Woman, how does your concern affect me? My hour has not yet come." His mother said to the servers, "Do whatever he tells you." Now there were six stone water jars there for Jewish ceremonial washings, each holding twenty to thirty gallons. Jesus told them, "Fill the jars with water." So they filled them to the brim. Then he told them, "Draw some out now and take it to the headwaiter." So they took it. And when the headwaiter tasted the water that had become wine, without knowing where it came from—although the servers who had drawn the water knew—, the headwaiter called the bridegroom and said to him, "Everyone serves good wine first, and then when people have drunk freely, an inferior one; but you have kept the good wine until now." Jesus did this as the beginning of his signs at Cana in Galilee and so revealed his glory, and his disciples began to believe in him.

A New Identity

In the brief few weeks between the Christmas season and the start of Lent, our readings give us the opportunity to reflect on what the Incarnation means for us and the world. Isaiah tells us it means a new identity—we are no longer called "Forsaken," but we are called, "My Delight is in her." Reconciled to God through Jesus, we have been given a new life and God rejoices in his people. Isaiah's vision comes almost at the end of his prophecy and holds out the glorious day when the reign of God will come on the land. Jesus would have said, "The kingdom of God is at hand," but we also know that the fullness of God's kingdom has not yet been accomplished. Isaiah and the rest of the prophets announced its coming. Jesus, the Incarnation of God, was the beginning here on earth. When it will fully come, we do not know. But the words and actions of Jesus give us a path to follow while we await his coming in glory.

Making the Ordinary Extraordinary

In John's Gospel, Jesus begins his public ministry at a wedding feast. The story of what happened at Cana is unique to John and seems odd when compared with the cure of the demoniac (Mark), the healings of a multitude (Matthew), and the preaching in the synagogue (Luke). Changing water into wine (reluctantly, if his conversation with his mother is any indication) seems almost petty. But John takes great stock in these "signs." John remembers Moses' words, that God led the people out of Egypt with signs and wonders. Such signs were evidence of God's breaking into human history. The jars of water at the wedding were used for ceremonial washing and held between twenty and thirty gallons each. In an instant, Jesus produced 180 gallons of the best wine the guests had ever tasted. He changed something that was ordinary—water—into something extraordinary—wine. The abundance recalled the prophecies of a great banquet at the Day of the Lord (see Isaiah 25) in which all the nations would drink their fill. If Jesus can do that with water, what extraordinary thing might he make of us?

The Gifts of the Spirit

When Paul preached to the Corinthians, many of them embraced Christianity. But we know from Paul's letter that there were also divisions in the Corinthian community. It seemed that when they came together at the table of the Lord, there were arguments, drunkenness, and some members who felt superior to others. This was not the extraordinary life he thought Christians should be living. In this section of his first letter, Paul lays out the expectation that Christians will respect the gifts that each has been given, reminding them that they are gifts from God for the common good. Healing, discernment, miracles, prophecy, tongues, and interpretation are given according to the Spirit and no one member had a monopoly on those gifts. For Paul, the common good (and the will of the Lord) was served when all members of the community lifted up the gifts of their brothers and sisters and used their own gifts for one another.

Good News for All of Us

Jesus brought us the promise of salvation and showed us a new way of living. Made strong by the grace of God in baptism and reconciliation, we are capable of overcoming hate, greed, jealousy, and everything that gets in the way of living as God's children. That God loves us so much is nothing less than a miracle. It is our turn to show the world the evidence of God's love in what we say and do and to invite others to do the same.

Questions for Reflection and Discussion

➤ *Are there any gifts that you think the Spirit has given you? What do your friends say you are good at?*

➤ *Have you ever had an experience of an ordinary moment that has become extraordinary because of something that happened or something you felt?*

Related Journey of Faith Lesson

C2, "The Sacraments: An Introduction"

Themes

Celebration
    C2, "The Sacraments: An Introduction"
    C5, "The Sacrament of the Eucharist"
Covenant
    C8, "The Sacrament of Matrimony"
Relationships
    C10, "The People of God"
    C11, "The Early Church"

READING 1, NEHEMIAH 8:2–4A, 5–6, 8–10

Ezra the priest brought the law before the assembly, which consisted of men, women, and those children old enough to understand. Standing at one end of the open place that was before the Water Gate, he read out of the book from daybreak till midday, in the presence of the men, the women, and those children old enough to understand; and all the people listened attentively to the book of the law. Ezra the scribe stood on a wooden platform that had been made for the occasion. He opened the scroll so that all the people might see it— for he was standing higher up than any of the people —; and, as he opened it, all the people rose. Ezra blessed the LORD, the great God, and all the people, their hands raised high, answered, "Amen, amen!" Then they bowed down and prostrated themselves before the LORD, their faces to the ground. Ezra read plainly from the book of the law of God, interpreting it so that all could understand what was read. Then Nehemiah, that is, His Excellency, and Ezra the priest-scribe and the Levites who were instructing the people said to all the people: "Today is holy to the LORD your God. Do not be sad, and do not weep"—for all the people were weeping as they heard the words of the law. He said further: "Go, eat rich foods and drink sweet drinks, and allot portions to those who had nothing prepared; for today is holy to our LORD. Do not be saddened this day, for rejoicing in the LORD must be your strength!"

PSALM 19:8, 9, 10, 15

READING 2, 1 CORINTHIANS 12:12–30

Brothers and sisters: As a body is one though it has many parts, and all the parts of the body, though many, are one body, so also Christ. For in one Spirit, we were all baptized into one body, whether Jews or Greeks, slaves or free persons, and we were all given to drink of one Spirit. Now the body is not a single part, but many. If a foot should say, "Because I am not a hand I do not belong to the body," it does not for this reason belong any less to the body. Or if an ear should say, "Because I am not an eye I do not belong to the body," it does not for this reason belong any less to the body. If the whole body were an eye, where would the hearing be? If the whole body were hearing, where would the sense of smell be? But as it is, God placed the parts, each one of them, in the body as he intended. If they were all one part, where would the body be? But as it is, there are many parts, yet one body. The eye cannot say to the hand, "I do not need you," nor again the head to the feet, "I do not need you." Indeed, the parts of the body that seem to be weaker are all the more necessary, and those parts of the body that we consider less honorable we surround with greater honor, and our less presentable parts are treated with greater propriety, whereas our more presentable parts do not need this. But God has so constructed the body as to give greater honor to a part that is without it, so that there may be no division in the body, but that the parts may have the same concern for one another. If one part suffers, all the parts suffer with it; if one part is honored, all the parts share its joy. Now you are Christ's body, and individually parts of it. Some people God has designated in the church to be, first, apostles; second, prophets; third, teachers; then, mighty deeds; then gifts of healing, assistance, administration, and varieties of tongues. Are all apostles? Are all prophets? Are all teachers? Do all work mighty deeds? Do all have gifts of healing? Do all speak in tongues? Do all interpret?

GOSPEL, LUKE 1:1–4; 4:14–21

Since many have undertaken to compile a narrative of the events that have been fulfilled among us, just as those who were eyewitnesses from the beginning and ministers of the word have handed them down to us, I too have decided, after investigating everything accurately anew, to write it down in an orderly sequence for you, most excellent Theophilus, so that you may realize the certainty of the teachings you have received. Jesus returned to Galilee in the power of the Spirit, and news of him spread throughout the whole region. He taught in their synagogues and was praised by all. He came to Nazareth, where he had grown up, and went according to his custom into the synagogue on the sabbath day. He stood up to read and was handed a scroll of the prophet Isaiah. He unrolled the scroll and found the passage where it was written: The Spirit of the Lord is upon me, because he has anointed me to bring glad tidings to the poor. He has sent me to proclaim liberty to captives and recovery of sight to the blind, to let the oppressed go free, and to proclaim a year acceptable to the Lord. Rolling up the scroll, he handed it back to the attendant and sat down, and the eyes of all in the synagogue looked intently at him. He said to them, "Today this scripture passage is fulfilled in your hearing."

Fulfilled in Your Hearing

Luke shows a preference for "an orderly account" of Jesus' life, told as fully as possible. He states that in his prologue and demonstrates it in the beginning of his Gospel when he narrates the annunciation of John, Jesus, and then gives a full rendering of the birth itself as well as stories that are unique to Luke. Today we hear of Jesus' first public appearance in the synagogue. To Isaiah's wonderful words about opening the eyes of the blind and bringing out prisoners from darkness, Jesus adds: "...[The Lord] has anointed me to bring Good News to the poor." Throughout Luke, God's care for the poor is evident in what Jesus preaches and the way he restores those who are outcasts. I can only imagine the hope that he stirred in many when he says, "Today this scripture...is fulfilled in your hearing."

The Joy of the Lord Is Our Strength

When the people returned from exile in Babylon, they had been away from their homes for more than forty years. The land was no longer theirs, their temple was gone, they had not been allowed to practice their faith openly in that time. How does a group reestablish its identity when there is no physical sign of it? Ezra, who would lead the effort to rebuild the temple along with Nehemiah, exhorts people not to weep, but to celebrate and share with those who could not be at the feast. He knew it was God who had brought them home.

Many Members, One Body

Saint Paul lays out what may be his most famous analogy. The Church is the body of Christ, with Christ as its head. While no analogy can capture the fullness of God and God's relationship with the Church, the body of Christ speaks at once about a living entity whose members share in the gifts of the Spirit and carry on the mission of Jesus. Paul reminds us that no one part of the body is greater than any other part. Apostles, prophets, teachers, power, leadership, healing, and tongues are all gifts the Spirit gives as it wills. No one has all the gifts. And Paul has said that all gifts are for the common, not any individual's, good.

Good News for All of Us

We are the body of Christ. What an extraordinary gift God has given us. As members of his body, we each have something to give to every other member and something we can receive from every other member. When we share our gifts in love, we give witness that the words of Isaiah have been fulfilled in our hearing. Christ is among us in this body of the Church. That is Good News indeed!

Questions for Reflection and Discussion

➤ *In what ways does your church, town, or city reach out to the poor and marginalized? How do you participate in their actions?*

➤ *How important are the words and stories of sacred Scripture for you? If you didn't hear them for a year or more, what would you miss?*

Related Journey of Faith Lesson

C11, "The Early Church"

Themes

Church
    C11, "The Early Church"
    C12, "Church History"
Lay Ministry
    C10, "The People of God"
Ordained Ministry
    C9, "The Sacrament of Holy Orders"

Fourth Sunday in Ordinary Time, Year C

READING 1, JEREMIAH 1,4–5, 17–19

The word of the LORD came to me, saying: Before
I formed you in the womb I knew you, before you
were born I dedicated you, a prophet to the nations I
appointed you. But do you gird your loins; stand up
and tell them all that I command you. Be not crushed
on their account, as though I would leave you crushed
before them; for it is I this day who have made you a
fortified city, a pillar of iron, a wall of brass, against the
whole land: against Judah's kings and princes, against
its priests and people. They will fight against you but
not prevail over you, for I am with you to deliver you,
says the LORD.

PSALM 71:1–2, 3–4, 5–6, 15, 17

READING 2, 1 CORINTHIANS 12:31—13:13

Brothers and sisters: Strive eagerly for the greatest
spiritual gifts. But I shall show you a still more
excellent way. If I speak in human and angelic tongues,
but do not have love, I am a resounding gong or a
clashing cymbal. And if I have the gift of prophecy
and comprehend all mysteries and all knowledge; if
I have all faith so as to move mountains, but do not
have love, I am nothing. If I give away everything I
own, and if I hand my body over so that I may boast,
but do not have love, I gain nothing. Love is patient,
love is kind. It is not jealous, it is not pompous, it is
not inflated, it is not rude, it does not seek its own
interests, it is not quick-tempered, it does not brood
over injury, it does not rejoice over wrongdoing but
rejoices with the truth. It bears all things, believes all
things, hopes all things, endures all things. Love never
fails. If there are prophecies, they will be brought to
nothing; if tongues, they will cease; if knowledge, it
will be brought to nothing. For we know partially, and
we prophesy partially, but when the perfect comes, the
partial will pass away. When I was a child, I used to
talk as a child, think as a child, reason as a child; when
I became a man, I put aside childish things. At present
we see indistinctly, as in a mirror, but then face to face.
At present I know partially; then I shall know fully, as
I am fully known. So faith, hope, love remain, these
three; but the greatest of these is love.

GOSPEL, LUKE 4:21–30

Jesus began speaking in the synagogue, saying: "Today
this Scripture passage is fulfilled in your hearing."
And all spoke highly of him and were amazed at the
gracious words that came from his mouth. They also
asked, "Isn't this the son of Joseph?" He said to them,
"Surely you will quote me this proverb, 'Physician, cure
yourself,' and say, 'Do here in your native place the
things that we heard were done in Capernaum.'" And
he said, "Amen, I say to you, no prophet is accepted
in his own native place. Indeed, I tell you, there were
many widows in Israel in the days of Elijah when the
sky was closed for three and a half years and a severe
famine spread over the entire land. It was to none
of these that Elijah was sent, but only to a widow in
Zarephath in the land of Sidon. Again, there were many
lepers in Israel during the time of Elisha the prophet;
yet not one of them was cleansed, but only Naaman
the Syrian." When the people in the synagogue heard
this, they were all filled with fury. They rose up, drove
him out of the town, and led him to the brow of the hill
on which their town had been built, to hurl him down
headlong. But Jesus passed through the midst of them
and went away.

Before You Were Born, I Knew You

Every mother and father wonders who their child will
be and how they will grow up. We parents watch and
worry about who the kids are with, what they're doing,
and whether we're doing the right thing. When my
daughters graduated from high school, I thought, *I
hope I haven't messed this up too badly.*

When God called Jeremiah as a prophet, he told him
something that is true for all of us. "Before I formed
you in the womb, I knew you; before you were born, I
dedicated you." We can take comfort in knowing God
had us in the palm of his hand from the first moment.
And we know his goal for us is to become one with him
forever. God watches over us, maybe worrying when
he sees us doing something we shouldn't. But like many
parents, God allows us to make our own decisions and
stays [mostly] in the background. But he also offers us
gentle guidance back to the right path when we need it.

When Jeremiah heard God's words, he protested, "I am too young." God assured him that he would be there, placing the words in his mouth. Jeremiah's mission was not going to be easy, but the strength he needed would come from God who knew him best.

The Power of Love

Jesus, like Jeremiah, didn't always have an easy time with preaching. In today's Gospel, Jesus finishes preaching in the synagogue and "everyone was amazed." In the Gospels, "amazed" is a code for "they didn't get it." Immediately the people wondered how he could speak so eloquently: "Is not this Joseph's son?"

They thought they knew Jesus—a kid from the village. Of course, Jesus knows them far better. He reminds them that Elijah and Elisha, two Old Testament prophets, were recognized by foreigners long before their power was known by their own people. Suddenly, their awe and hope turned to anger. They could not see that he had to be about his Father's business. Nor did they have any idea of how he slipped away from them at the top of the hill. But we remember that God who knew us and loved us from conception also promised to accompany us on our journey through life. Jesus rested deeply in the Father's love. That gave him the strength to continue his own mission to the cross.

Good News for All of Us

God's love that gave Jesus the strength to preach when people were angry, to explain over and over when his followers didn't understand and, ultimately, to lay down his life for us, is the same love that gives meaning to every gift of the spirit we use, every impulse we have to serve others, and every prayer we utter in petition, thanksgiving, or contrition. Paul's passage from the First Letter to the Corinthians is often heard at weddings because it accurately describes what love is and the many ways we can fail at it. Paul is right when he says that without love, everything we do is a noisy gong and will come to nothing. God loved us from the beginning. Jesus is our model. We can only strive to emulate what our Lord has done because we do not have full knowledge of God. Paul acknowledges this, promising that we shall see God face to face and know and love him as fully as he knows and loves us. That will be a great day!

Questions for Reflection and Discussion

> *God called Jeremiah to be a prophet to the people. What do you think God has called you to be? How has he led you to that knowledge?*

> *Paul describes love as many things. Which of them best describes your love for your family or friends? Which ones would you like to work on?*

Related Journey of Faith Lesson

C2, "The Sacraments: An Introduction"

Themes

Love
    C2, "The Sacraments: An Introduction"
    C15, "A Consistent Ethic of Life"
Matrimony
    C8, "The Sacrament of Matrimony"
Vocation
    C10, "The People of God"

READING 1, ISAIAH 6:1–2A, 3–8

In the year King Uzziah died, I saw the Lord seated on a high and lofty throne, with the train of his garment filling the temple. Seraphim were stationed above. They cried one to the other, "Holy, holy, holy is the LORD of hosts! All the earth is filled with his glory!" At the sound of that cry, the frame of the door shook, and the house was filled with smoke. Then I said, "Woe is me; I am doomed! For I am a man of unclean lips, living among a people of unclean lips; yet my eyes have seen the King, the LORD of hosts!" Then one of the seraphim flew to me, holding an ember that he had taken with tongs from the altar. He touched my mouth with it, and said, "See, now that this has touched your lips, your wickedness is removed, your sin purged." Then I heard the voice of the Lord saying, "Whom shall I send? Who will go for us?" "Here I am," I said, "send me!"

PSALM 138:1–2A, 2B–3, 4–5, 7–8

READING 2, 1 CORINTHIANS 15:1–11

I am reminding you, brothers and sisters, of the gospel I preached to you, which you indeed received and in which you also stand. Through it you are also being saved, if you hold fast to the word, I preached to you, unless you believed in vain. For I handed on to you as of first importance what I also received: that Christ died for our sins in accordance with the Scriptures; that he was buried; that he was raised on the third day in accordance with the Scriptures; that he appeared to Cephas, then to the Twelve. After that, Christ appeared to more than five hundred brothers at once, most of whom are still living, though some have fallen asleep. After that he appeared to James, then to all the apostles. Last of all, as to one born abnormally, he appeared to me. For I am the least of the apostles, not fit to be called an apostle, because I persecuted the church of God. But by the grace of God, I am what I am, and his grace to me has not been ineffective. Indeed, I have toiled harder than all of them; not I, however, but the grace of God that is with me. Therefore, whether it be I or they, so we preach and so you believed.

GOSPEL, LUKE 5:1–11

While the crowd was pressing in on Jesus and listening to the word of God, he was standing by the Lake of Gennesaret. He saw two boats there alongside the lake; the fishermen had disembarked and were washing their nets. Getting into one of the boats, the one belonging to Simon, he asked him to put out a short distance from the shore. Then he sat down and taught the crowds from the boat. After he had finished speaking, he said to Simon, "Put out into deep water and lower your nets for a catch." Simon said in reply, "Master, we have worked hard all night and have caught nothing, but at your command I will lower the nets." When they had done this, they caught a great number of fish and their nets were tearing.

They signaled to their partners in the other boat to come to help them. They came and filled both boats so that the boats were in danger of sinking. When Simon Peter saw this, he fell at the knees of Jesus and said, "Depart from me, Lord, for I am a sinful man." For astonishment at the catch of fish they had made seized him and all those with him, and likewise James and John, the sons of Zebedee, who were partners of Simon. Jesus said to Simon, "Do not be afraid; from now on you will be catching men." When they brought their boats to the shore, they left everything and followed him.

Whom Shall I Send?

One of life's great questions is: "What am I here for? We all want to know if we will make a difference and how. To that end we choose majors, careers, places to live, and, to some extent, people to live with. Last week, our first reading described God's dedication of Jeremiah in the womb to his mission as prophet. How has God dedicated us?

Today we hear three different perspectives on God's call and our response. Isaiah sees a vision of God and believes he is lost because of sinfulness. God blots out his sin and asks a simple question: Whom shall I send? Isaiah eagerly proclaims, "Here I am, send me." Isaiah's fear of seeing God in a vision has long roots in Israel's history. In Moses' time, people believed they would die if any of them dared to see God face to face (Exodus 19:10–12). Only those who were set apart (sanctified) could approach the Holy One. But when God forgave his sins, he sanctified Isaiah and Isaiah's fear gave way to eagerness to respond. Isaiah didn't know what he was being sent for. His heart simply said yes when God asked the question.

The Least of the Apostles

Paul was a latecomer to God's call. His history was problematic because he had persecuted and killed Christians for years. But a vision of Jesus on the road to Damascus turned his life around. When Paul writes to the Corinthians, he tells them the Good News knowing that he is the least important of all those who saw Christ after the resurrection. It is only because of God's grace that Paul finds himself as a preacher for Christ. Maybe he worked harder than any of the others because he was trying to atone for his murderous past. While it sounds like he's almost bragging, he is quick to remind us that the change in him is not because of anything he did. Rather, his good work is due to the grace of God working in him so others might believe.

Into Deep Water

Our Gospel reading does not begin like the story of someone's call. Jesus wants to teach the crowd. There's a convenient boat. The boat owners had no way of anticipating what he would do after the lesson. And the call is indirect, as calls often are: "Put out into deep water." Simon Peter might be forgiven for wondering what Jesus was doing. After the miraculous catch of fish, Simon reacts as Isaiah did. "Get away from me: I am a sinful man." But here we have no angels with burning tongs, not even a word of forgiveness. Jesus regards Peter gently—I am sure he loves him. He doesn't tell Simon that he has to do better in his life; rather, he almost asks a mental question: "And your point is…?" Simon is the one Jesus wants, flaws and all. Maybe he knew him better than Simon knew himself.

Good News for All of Us

What is God calling me to do? What is my mission? God uses a variety of clues to tell us. There might be a clear vision, a gradual recognition, or an invitation from a friend or stranger who has seen something of value in us that we have missed. We may have to look back at our choices to see how we ended up in a particular place and see a pattern that draws us inevitably to a next step. Our imaginations can help—where do we see ourselves in the future? What gets us up in the morning? What would we die for? Good friends, good family, and spiritual mentors can help us. Of course, over all this is prayer and a growing relationship with God without which we might lose our way. The Good News is that God wants us for his own and can make the best of any bad or good decision we may make.

Questions for Reflection and Discussion

> ➤ *What does your current work or life situation tell you about your purpose in life? There may be clues in the work itself or in your dreams about the next step. What do you think God has to say about it?*

> ➤ *If Jesus did appear to you and ask you to do something without telling you exactly what it was, what would your response be?*

Related Journey of Faith Lesson

C13, "Christian Moral Living"

Themes

Call
    C13, "Christian Moral Living"
Spirit of God
    C4, "The Sacrament of Confirmation"
Trinity
    C2, "The Sacraments: An Introduction"

READING 1, JEREMIAH 17:5–8

Thus says the LORD: Cursed is the one who trusts in human beings, who seeks his strength in flesh, whose heart turns away from the LORD. He is like a barren bush in the desert that enjoys no change of season, but stands in a lava waste, a salt and empty earth. Blessed is the one who trusts in the LORD, whose hope is the LORD. He is like a tree planted beside the waters that stretches out its roots to the stream: it fears not the heat when it comes; its leaves stay green; in the year of drought, it shows no distress, but still bears fruit.

PSALM 1:1–4, 6

READING 2, 1 CORINTHIANS 15:12, 16–20

Brothers and sisters: If Christ is preached as raised from the dead, how can some among you say there is no resurrection of the dead? If the dead are not raised, neither has Christ been raised, and if Christ has not been raised, your faith is vain; you are still in your sins. Then those who have fallen asleep in Christ have perished. If for this life only we have hoped in Christ, we are the most pitiable people of all. But now Christ has been raised from the dead, the first fruits of those who have fallen asleep.

GOSPEL, LUKE 6:17, 20–26

Jesus came down with the twelve and stood on a stretch of level ground with a great crowd of his disciples and a large number of the people from all Judea and Jerusalem and the coastal region of Tyre and Sidon. And raising his eyes toward his disciples he said: "Blessed are you who are poor, for the kingdom of God is yours. Blessed are you who are now hungry, for you will be satisfied. Blessed are you who are now weeping, for you will laugh. Blessed are you when people hate you, and when they exclude and insult you, and denounce your name as evil on account of the Son of Man. Rejoice and leap for joy on that day! Behold, your reward will be great in heaven. For their ancestors treated the prophets in the same way. But woe to you who are rich, for you have received your consolation. Woe to you who are filled now, for you will be hungry. Woe to you who laugh now, for you will grieve and weep. Woe to you when all speak well of you, for their ancestors treated the false prophets in this way."

Be Like the Tree

If we were to take a long look at ourselves, we would undoubtedly find some attitudes and behaviors that are good and some that need work. If we look at the world, we will undoubtedly see some people who look only for themselves and some who serve others selflessly. Today's readings draw a sharp contrast between the two and, in the process, tell us something about God's choices. Jeremiah expands the images we hear in Psalm 1 (our psalm reading). The comparison between those who trust in mere mortals and those who trust in God echoes the psalm's emphasis on those who obey the Lord and the wicked. Jeremiah couldn't be clearer. The former will live in the wilderness, while the latter will be like trees planted by the water. The analogy was appropriate. Sixty percent of Israel is a desert. Plant life is rare. By contrast, the coastal regions and the areas bordering the Jordan River are rich with greenery. The trees that grow closest to the water sources are strong and healthy. Those who trust in the Lord are just like them.

In the Gospel, Jesus offers a contrast as well. This passage is called the Sermon on the Plain to contrast it with Matthew's Sermon on the Mount. We recognize the similar passages; "Blessed are you..." they begin. But Jesus lists only four types of people: those who are poor, hungry, weeping, or hated because of the Son of Man. What he promises is a reversal of their fortune by the grace of God. We heard a similar idea in the Magnificat—Mary's prayer after her visit with Elizabeth: "God will raise up the fallen," she says, "The hungry will be filled, and the rich will be sent away empty." When God comes, the status quo will be upended.

Jesus deviates from Matthew's pattern another way as well. He follows his four blessings with curses for those who are rich, full, laughing, and spoken well of. They will lose what they have. In the context of these readings, Luke seems to assume that those who are cursed got their wealth by taking advantage of the poor. When the Lord comes, his justice will set things right.

A Faith that Is Not in Vain

Saint Paul is dealing with a different problem altogether. Some people in the Corinthian community do not believe in the resurrection of the dead. That wasn't a problem for Judaism—it had never been a doctrine of the religion, but Paul wants them to understand that Christianity proclaims Christ risen from the dead. They believed that Christ was alive in the believing community through the power of the Holy Spirit, and that his followers would rise as well. If Christ wasn't raised from the dead, then such faith was in vain and any hope for something beyond this life was foolish. Paul concludes that Christ has been raised from the dead, and so shall we.

Good News for All of Us

We can certainly understand Jeremiah's message about trusting in the Lord and not just in people. Paul's certain faith that Jesus was raised from the dead also rings true for us. The Sermon on the Plain may be a little more difficult. Should we not ever be rich or full or laughing? Should we never have anyone speak well of us? Jesus' concern is not with wealth and fame per se. Rather, Jesus was concerned that the wealthy and powerful did not share their good fortune. The poor and marginalized were often looked down on or were berated by the more powerful. Some thought that being poor was a punishment for sin and being rich was a sign of God's favor. But throughout Israel's history, God showed a preference for the poor, choosing even to be born in poverty. Jesus preached a gospel in which rich and poor were equal; no one was better than anyone else. And all were called to live in solidarity with their brothers and sisters in Christ and to love them.

Questions for Reflection and Discussion

➤ *Give an example of a time when you trusted God more than someone else or yourself. If you can't think of one, then what would trusting in God look like?*

➤ *What was going on inside when you heard Jesus' words to the rich, full, laughing, and well thought of? Were you challenged, taken aback, irritated, or something else?*

Related Journey of Faith Lesson

C15, "A Consistent Ethic of Life"

Themes

Blessings
    C2, "The Sacraments: An Introduction"
Poor in Spirit
    C15, "A Consistent Ethic of Life"
    C14, "The Dignity of Life"
Salvation
    Q4, "Who Is Jesus Christ?"

Seventh Sunday in Ordinary Time, Year C

READING 1, 1 SAMUEL 26:2, 7–9, 12–13, 22–23

In those days, Saul went down to the desert of Ziph with three thousand picked men of Israel, to search for David in the desert of Ziph. So, David and Abishai went among Saul's soldiers by night and found Saul lying asleep within the barricade, with his spear thrust into the ground at his head and Abner and his men sleeping around him. Abishai whispered to David: "God has delivered your enemy into your grasp this day. Let me nail him to the ground with one thrust of the spear; I will not need a second thrust!" But David said to Abishai, "Do not harm him, for who can lay hands on the LORD's anointed and remain unpunished?" So, David took the spear and the water jug from their place at Saul's head, and they got away without anyone's seeing or knowing or awakening. All remained asleep, because the LORD had put them into a deep slumber.... David stood on a remote hilltop at a great distance from Abner, son of Ner, and the troops. He said: "Here is the king's spear. Let an attendant come over to get it. The LORD will reward each man for his justice and faithfulness. Today, though the LORD delivered you into my grasp, I would not harm the LORD anointed."

PSALM 103:1–2, 3–4, 8, 10, 12–13

READING 2, 1 CORINTHIANS 15:45–49

Brothers and sisters: It is written, The first man, Adam, became a living being, the last Adam a life-giving spirit. But the spiritual was not first; rather the natural and then the spiritual. The first man was from the earth, earthly; the second man, from heaven. As was the earthly one, so also are the earthly, and as is the heavenly one, so also are the heavenly. Just as we have borne the image of the earthly one, we shall also bear the image of the heavenly one.

GOSPEL, LUKE 6:27–38

Jesus said to his disciples: "To you who hear I say, love your enemies, do good to those who hate you, bless those who curse you, pray for those who mistreat you. To the person who strikes you on one cheek, offer the other one as well, and from the person who takes your cloak, do not withhold even your tunic.

Give to everyone who asks of you, and from the one who takes what is yours do not demand it back. Do to others as you would have them do to you. For if you love those who love you, what credit is that to you? Even sinners love those who love them. And if you do good to those who do good to you, what credit is that to you? Even sinners do the same. If you lend money to those from whom you expect repayment, what credit is that to you? Even sinners lend to sinners and get back the same amount. But rather, love your enemies and do good to them, and lend expecting nothing back; then your reward will be great, and you will be children of the Most High, for he himself is kind to the ungrateful and the wicked.

Be merciful, just as your Father is merciful. "Stop judging and you will not be judged. Stop condemning and you will not be condemned. Forgive and you will be forgiven. Give, and gifts will be given to you; a good measure, packed together, shaken down, and overflowing, will be poured into your lap. For the measure with which you measure will in return be measured out to you."

Love Your Enemies

I enjoy gathering with friends and people I know. We share common experiences and common interests, and we tend to see things in similar ways. I wouldn't hesitate to ask anyone for a favor, nor would they hesitate to ask me. There is nothing wrong with any of that. But Jesus asks us to do more with our love. He asks us to love those who don't share common interests or like the same things. He asks us to love people who might disagree with us on religious, political, or social issues. He asks us to expect nothing in return for what we give them. Do not expect them to love you back or to return a favor. For Jesus, such expectation is not the measure of love. Love is the giving of self without expectation. We are to love others because they are sons and daughters of God and are worthy of love. If love is tied to the expectation of a favor or limited only to those who will love us back, then our love is small.

There are two other pieces in today's Gospel that stand out. The first is one of the most quoted of phrases and has its counterpart in most of the world's religions: The words are: "Do unto others as you would have them do unto you." The second comes at the end as Jesus urges his followers not to judge or condemn, lest that happen to them. Rather, Jesus exhorts them to forgive and give to others. Jesus makes it clear that they will get back all they give and more and the more they give without expectation, the more they will receive from their Father in heaven.

A Cautionary Tale

In the history of the kings of Israel, Saul's place as the first anointed king is assured, but he is not very well remembered. The whole idea of a king was a controversial one, because the Israelites recognized the Lord as their ruler. But they yearned for a central leader to protect them from their enemies and govern them. The prophet Samuel anoints Saul, who ultimately disobeys God and descends into madness. The story in 1 Samuel tells us that God regretted making Saul

king and had Samuel anoint a young boy, David. Saul grew jealous of David's fame after David killed Goliath. Our reading today comes a little while after that event. We see that David had an opportunity to destroy his enemy by killing Saul, but he can't bring himself to do it because of his respect for the office of king. He announces his mercy from far away, perhaps expecting Saul to be in his debt. It doesn't turn out that way. Saul will be killed in battle and David will become king. As for Israel, their memory of Saul gradually fades from their story. By the end of the books of Samuel, Saul is not mentioned again.

David's refusal to kill Saul when he had the chance shows the impulse to love your enemies at work. David did not allow fear, power, or hatred to rule his actions. Rather, he let Saul know of his opportunity and the choice he made. It might not have been an entirely loving gesture, but we all start in small ways.

Good News for All of Us

Dr. Robert Enright of the International Forgiveness Institute is quick to point out that when we forgive someone, we freely give them gifts of generosity and love simply because we have chosen a path of mercy, even though they may not deserve it. To forgive is to free ourselves from anger, jealousy, and feelings of revenge. I think Jesus would agree with that and he would add that we are merciful because God has shown us mercy; we are loving because God first loved us; we forgive because we have been forgiven. It's not easy. But with a little soul work and a lot of prayer, we can reach out even to our enemies and become the image of our Lord who is in heaven.

Questions for Reflection and Discussion

➤ Think about the last time someone wronged you. Did you forgive that person? If so, how long did it take? If not, what has kept you from doing so?

➤ Have you ever been forgiven by someone for something that you did? What did that feel like?

Related Journey of Faith Lesson

C6, "The Sacrament of Penance and Reconciliation"

Themes

Anointed
    C4, "The Sacrament of Confirmation"
    C7, "The Sacrament of Anointing of the Sick"
Forgiveness
    C6, "The Sacrament of Penance and Reconciliation"
    Q4, "Who Is Jesus Christ?"
Judgment
    C13, "Christian Moral Living"

Eighth Sunday in Ordinary Time, Year C

READING 1, SIRACH 27:4–7

When a sieve is shaken, the husks appear; so do one's faults when one speaks. As the test of what the potter molds is in the furnace, so in tribulation is the test of the just. The fruit of a tree shows the care it has had; so too does one's speech disclose the bent of one's mind. Praise no one before he speaks, for it is then that people are tested.

PSALM 92:2–3, 13–14, 15–16

READING 2, 1 CORINTHIANS 15:54–58

Brothers and sisters: When this which is corruptible clothes itself with incorruptibility and this which is mortal clothes itself with immortality, then the word that is written shall come about: *Death is swallowed up in victory. Where, O death, is your victory? Where, O death, is your sting?* The sting of death is sin, and the power of sin is the law. But thanks be to God who gives us the victory through our Lord Jesus Christ. Therefore, my beloved brothers and sisters, be firm, steadfast, always fully devoted to the work of the Lord, knowing that in the Lord your labor is not in vain.

GOSPEL, LUKE 6:39–45

Jesus told his disciples a parable, "Can a blind person guide a blind person? Will not both fall into a pit? No disciple is superior to the teacher; but when fully trained, every disciple will be like his teacher. Why do you notice the splinter in your brother's eye, but do not perceive the wooden beam in your own? How can you say to your brother, 'Brother, let me remove that splinter in your eye,' when you do not even notice the wooden beam in your own eye? You hypocrite! Remove the wooden beam from your eye first; Then you will see clearly to remove the splinter in your brother's eye.

"A good tree does not bear rotten fruit, nor does a rotten tree bear good fruit. For every tree is known by Its own fruit. For people do not pick figs from thornbushes, nor do they gather grapes from brambles. A good person out of the store of goodness in his heart produces good, but an evil person out of a store of evil produces evil; for from the fullness of the heart the mouth speaks."

Speak from the Heart

The Wisdom literature (of which Sirach is a part) draws from life experiences for its advice and assumes that its audience makes God a part of it. In our first reading, the author cautions against making assumptions about the character of people until they speak. Ultimately their speech will lay bare any defects of their spirit. We see that when someone, out of anger or frustration, suddenly uses a racial slur, a particularly vulgar term, or a cutting remark that puts down an entire group of people. In the New Testament, James devotes an entire chapter of his letter to the power of the tongue for blessing and cursing (see James 3:1–12). Maybe we ourselves have done that. Those short outbursts betray a weakness of the soul that needs healing before we can grow deeper in faith.

Jesus continues his sermon in Luke's Gospel with a familiar analogy. We are quick to see the splinter in someone else's eye but fail to notice that we have a great wooden beam in our own eye. If we notice the beam in our own eye, we also must admit that we are not as good as we thought we were. If our speech can betray us in moments of stress, even more can our attitudes and actions betray us as we navigate our lives with others. Ultimately, if we strive to be good, more often than not we will do good and speak well. Whatever is abundant in our hearts, whether good or evil, will influence both what we do and what we say.

A Victory Over Death

As we continue with Paul's First Letter to the Corinthians, we hear a passage made famous by Handel's "Messiah." Those who are familiar with the music unconsciously hum along as we read familiar words, but even if you are not familiar with the music, the excitement of Paul's words comes across, "Death, where is your victory?" It's a rhetorical question. Death has been conquered by the resurrection of Jesus. Paul reminds us that the sting of death is sin. Every sin is a little taste of death whether it's speaking hurtful words, feeling superior to someone else, or doing something evil. We say God gave us victory over death through Christ. For those who believe, Christ has given eternal life that we might be one with Christ forever in heaven.

Good News for All of Us

At our baptism, we are anointed with the oil of the sacrament as part of the ritual of exorcism. The oil was, and is, a sign of God's grace and healing. The ritual reminds us that we are human beings with human weaknesses who might stumble and fall, but we are also human beings who have been given the grace to make different choices. We can make a choice to follow God and do the right thing in any given situation. We are freed from original sin to live our lives as children of God. We are free to speak lovingly, act with humility, and love God and neighbor. The sacrament of baptism frees us from death to follow Jesus.

Questions for Reflection and Discussion

➤ Is there someone in your life who is the epitome of a good person? What makes them so? What one trait of theirs would you like to emulate?

➤ What are one or two words of advice you would give someone based on your life experience? Is there a biblical story that illustrates that advice?

Related Journey of Faith Lesson

C6, "The Sacrament of Penance and Reconciliation"

Themes

Passion
   C10, "The People of God"
   C14, "The Dignity of Life"
Reconciliation
   C6, "The Sacrament of Penance and Reconciliation"
Service
   C16, "Social Justice"
   C15, "A Consistent Ethic of Life"

First Sunday of Lent, Year C

READING 1, DEUTERONOMY 26:4–10

Moses spoke to the people, saying: "The priest shall receive the basket from you and shall set it in front of the altar of the LORD, your God. Then you shall declare before the LORD, your God, 'My father was a wandering Aramean who went down to Egypt with a small household and lived there as an alien. But there he became a nation great, strong, and numerous. When the Egyptians maltreated and oppressed us, imposing hard labor upon us, we cried to the LORD, the God of our fathers, and he heard our cry and saw our affliction, our toil, and our oppression. He brought us out of Egypt with his strong hand and outstretched arm, with terrifying power, with signs and wonders; and bringing us into this country, he gave us this land flowing with milk and honey. Therefore, I have now brought you the first fruits of the products of the soil which you, O LORD, have given me.' And having set them before the LORD, your God, you shall bow down in his presence."

PSALM 91:1–2, 10–11, 12–13, 14–15

READING 2, ROMANS 10:8–13

Brothers and sisters: What does Scripture say? *The word is near you, in your mouth and in your heart—* that is, the word of faith that we preach—, for, if you confess with your mouth that Jesus is Lord and believe in your heart that God raised him from the dead, you will be saved. For one believes with the heart and so is justified, and one confesses with the mouth and so is saved. For the Scripture says, *No one who believes in him will be put to shame.* For there is no distinction between Jew and Greek; the same Lord is Lord of all, enriching all who call upon him. For "everyone who calls on the name of the Lord will be saved."

GOSPEL, LUKE 4:1–13

Filled with the Holy Spirit, Jesus returned from the Jordan and was led by the Spirit into the desert for forty days, to be tempted by the devil. He ate nothing during those days, and when they were over he was hungry. The devil said to him, "If you are the Son of God, command this stone to become bread." Jesus answered him, "It is written, One does not live on bread alone." Then he took him up and showed him all the kingdoms of the world in a single instant. The devil said to him, "I shall give to you all this power and glory; for it has been handed over to me, and I may give it to whomever I wish. All this will be yours, if you worship me." Jesus said to him in reply, "It is written: You shall worship the Lord, your God, and him alone shall you serve." Then he led him to Jerusalem, made him stand on the parapet of the temple, and said to him, "If you are the Son of God, throw yourself down from here, for it is written: He will command his angels concerning you, to guard you, and: With their hands they will support you, lest you dash your foot against a stone." Jesus said to him in reply, "It also says, You shall not put the Lord, your God, to the test." When the devil had finished every temptation, he departed from him for a time.

Called to Follow Jesus

While Ordinary Time after Christmas gives us a chance to reflect on what the Incarnation means for us, the season of Lent poses a single question: "Knowing that it might mean hardship, changing your priorities, and even changing your life, will you follow Jesus?" For six weeks we practice disciplining our bodies (fasting), training our heart to focus on the Lord (prayer), and caring for the least among us (almsgiving). The goal is not to get to Easter and think: Thank God that's over; now I can have all the chocolate I want. It is to undergo *metanoia*—a change of mind and heart. We are to use this time to make something more of ourselves with God's help so that when Easter comes, we can rejoice in the resurrection from a deeper understanding and a more faithful witness.

Just before the Israelites enter the Promised Land, Moses gives some final instructions. Our first reading today regards the offering of the first fruits of the harvest which the Israelites will offer in gratitude for the land God has given them. That offering is accompanied by a recitation. Each family recalls their ancestors, their sojourn and slavery in Egypt, and the miraculous defeat of the Egyptians as God freed the people from bondage. Moses wanted the people to remember who they were, where they came from, whose people they were. He wanted them to keep the covenant with God especially in the promised land where easier living might make them forget to follow the commandments and to make gods of other things.

If Jesus had forgotten who he was and whose he was in the wilderness, he would have been lost. The temptations of the devil played on the same weaknesses that Moses warned against. The devil tempts Jesus to use power to satisfy his body rather than trust in his Father. Unsuccessful, the devil lures Jesus by appealing to human greed and desire for power; again, he fails. Finally, he tries to sow doubt that Jesus is loved by the Father ("if you are the Son of God…") and suggests that Jesus put God to the test. Jesus never wavers from his commitment to his Father. Secure in the Father's love and grace, Jesus resists the devil and shows us that we can as well. Chillingly, Luke concludes that there will be another more favorable time for temptation.

Good News for All of Us

Paul's Letter to the Romans reminds us that God's word is on our lips and in our hearts. From baptism, we have been prepared to follow Jesus (God's Word, according to the fourth Gospel) until the very end when we shall see God face to face. During our lives, we stray off the path that Jesus has set, or we lose sight of Jesus altogether. Our temptations are many and they strike in our weak moments or at the weaknesses that are in our hearts—desire for wealth or power, doubt about whether we are loved, jealousy, greed. Even in small measure these weaknesses can lead to sin, and the evil one knows it. But Jesus sets us on the right path from the very beginning of Lent. And Paul is sure about the power of faith: "No one who believes in him will be put to shame…Everyone who calls on the name of the Lord shall be saved." Lent is the time to deepen that belief, say yes to following Jesus, and rest in the knowledge that we are God's children and loved by God.

Questions for Reflection and Discussion

> *Trace your faith journey. Where has God been active in your life? How do you understand your relationship with God?*

> *How would the devil have tempted you in the desert? What weaknesses would he have tried to exploit to get you to follow him?*

Related Journey of Faith Lesson

E2, "Living Lent"

Themes

Idolatry
    E4, "The Creed"
Prayer
    E6, "The Lord's Prayer"
Temptation
    E2, "Living Lent"

READING 1, GENESIS 15:5–12, 17–18

The Lord God took Abram outside and said, "Look up at the sky and count the stars, if you can. Just so," he added, "shall your descendants be." Abram put his faith in the LORD, who credited it to him as an act of righteousness. He then said to him, "I am the LORD who brought you from Ur of the Chaldeans to give you this land as a possession." "O Lord GOD," he asked, "how am I to know that I shall possess it?" He answered him, "Bring me a three-year-old heifer, a three-year-old she-goat, a three-year-old ram, a turtledove, and a young pigeon." Abram brought him all these, split them in two, and placed each half opposite the other; but the birds he did not cut up. Birds of prey swooped down on the carcasses, but Abram stayed with them. As the sun was about to set, a trance fell upon Abram, and a deep, terrifying darkness enveloped him. When the sun had set and it was dark, there appeared a smoking fire pot and a flaming torch, which passed between those pieces. It was on that occasion that the LORD made a covenant with Abram, saying: "To your descendants I give this land, from the Wadi of Egypt to the Great River, the Euphrates."

PSALM 27:1, 2–8, 8–9, 13–14

READING 2, PHILIPPIANS 3:17—4:1

Join with others in being imitators of me, brothers and sisters, and observe those who thus conduct themselves according to the model you have in us. For many, as I have often told you and now tell you even in tears, conduct themselves as enemies of the cross of Christ. Their end is destruction. Their God is their stomach; their glory is in their "shame." Their minds are occupied with earthly things. But our citizenship is in heaven, and from it we also await a savior, the Lord Jesus Christ. He will change our lowly body to conform with his glorified body by the power that enables him also to bring all things into subjection to himself. Therefore, my brothers and sisters, whom I love and long for, my joy and crown, in this way stand firm in the Lord.

GOSPEL, LUKE 9:28B–36

Jesus took Peter, John, and James and went up the mountain to pray. While he was praying his face changed in appearance and his clothing became dazzling white. And behold, two men were conversing with him, Moses and Elijah, who appeared in glory and spoke of his exodus that he was going to accomplish in Jerusalem. Peter and his companions had been overcome by sleep, but becoming fully awake, they saw his glory and the two men standing with him. As they were about to part from him, Peter said to Jesus, "Master, it is good that we are here; let us make three tents, one for you, one for Moses, and one for Elijah." But he did not know what he was saying. While he was still speaking, a cloud came and cast a shadow over them, and they became frightened when they entered the cloud. Then from the cloud came a voice that said, "This is my chosen Son; listen to him." After the voice had spoken, Jesus was found alone. They fell silent and did not at that time tell anyone what they had seen.

The Promise of God

In the Judeo-Christian tradition, the promises of God shaped generations who looked for signs that the promises would come to fulfillment. In the time of Noah, God promised never again to destroy the earth with a flood; in the time of Moses, God promised to remain with the people of Israel as their God; In the time of the prophets, God promised to send a messiah—someone to free the people. In today's first reading, God promises a childless old man that his descendants will be more numerous than the stars. Did it sound hard to believe? It probably did, but Abraham, who had been called by God out of his homeland, believed what God said and, as the Scripture says, "it was attributed to him as an act of righteousness." In difficult times in a land that was not his own, Abraham had to trust that God would keep his promise. Abraham's descendants grew into a people who obeyed the Lord—at least most of the time. And God never deserted them, even when they turned away.

The Fulfillment of the Promise

Before the events leading to the crucifixion, Jesus gave Peter, John, and James a glimpse of who he really was. The story of the transfiguration is found in Matthew and Mark and is always proclaimed on the second Sunday of Lent. That glimpse of glory was both energizing and unsettling. To see Jesus change before their eyes was dramatic enough. The appearance of Moses and Elijah who represent the Law and the Prophets (from which the evangelists draw most of their quotations for the Gospels) underscores Jesus' mission as the fulfillment of the word of God. Finally, the settling of the cloud and the voice which spoke out of it let them know that the Lord God was present just as it had on Mount Sinai. "This is my beloved Son," it says—a phrase we heard at Jesus' baptism. But the voice adds that Jesus is "…My chosen one. Listen to him." Peter, James, and John are afraid, as we might be, and they keep silence after God has spoken. More importantly, they don't leave Jesus. The command from the cloud to listen was so compelling, they continue to follow Jesus into Jerusalem as he goes to his death. The story of the transfiguration is for us, too. We are with the apostles on that mountain and we, too, hear the words of the Father calling us to listen. Will we do so?

Good News for All of Us

We may be tempted to think that the Letter to the Philippians was written with us in mind. Certainly, there are many distractions which turn us away from God and there are any number of false gods we can follow. Paul says that "many conduct themselves as enemies of Christ…" I think most people wouldn't think of themselves that way. They might say, "I don't believe in God," or "I know what's right for me." They might be guided by a desire for material possessions or power. For Paul, though, the enemies of the cross of Christ are those who easily dismiss the power of God and who tempt anyone to abandon their faith and follow their own path. Now God still loves them and wants them to be with him. To that end, we share the Good News and become witnesses to the faith. But the Scriptures are clear, God made a promise to send us a savior and has done so. God has made a covenant with us to be our God forever. The Incarnation is the best and truest expression of God with us. Will we keep our part of the covenant? Will we follow Jesus forever?

Questions for Reflection and Discussion

> Is there anything so compelling you would do it even if it meant certain hardship and maybe death?

> What are some of the false gods in our world today? What helps you stay in the way of Christ?

Related Journey of Faith Lesson

E1, "Election: Saying Yes to Jesus"

Themes

Crisis
    E2, "Living Lent"
Trust
    E1, "Election: Saying Yes to Jesus"

Third Sunday of Lent, Year C

READING 1, EXODUS 3:1–8A, 13–15

Moses was tending the flock of his father-in-law Jethro, the priest of Midian. Leading the flock across the desert, he came to Horeb, the mountain of God. There an angel of the LORD appeared to Moses in fire flaming out of a bush. As he looked on, he was surprised to see that the bush, though on fire, was not consumed. So Moses decided, "I must go over to look at this remarkable sight, and see why the bush is not burned." When the LORD saw him coming over to look at it more closely, God called out to him from the bush, "Moses! Moses!" He answered, "Here I am." God said, "Come no nearer! Remove the sandals from your feet, for the place where you stand is holy ground. I am the God of your fathers," he continued, "the God of Abraham, the God of Isaac, the God of Jacob." Moses hid his face, for he was afraid to look at God. But the LORD said, "I have witnessed the affliction of my people in Egypt and have heard their cry of complaint against their slave drivers, so I know well what they are suffering. Therefore, I have come down to rescue them from the hands of the Egyptians and lead them out of that land into a good and spacious land, a land flowing with milk and honey." Moses said to God, "But when I go to the Israelites and say to them, 'The God of your fathers has sent me to you,' if they ask me, 'What is his name?' what am I to tell them?" God replied, "I am who am." Then he added, "This is what you shall tell the Israelites: I AM sent me to you." God spoke further to Moses, "Thus shall you say to the Israelites: The LORD, the God of your fathers, the God of Abraham, the God of Isaac, the God of Jacob, has sent me to you. "This is my name forever; thus am I to be remembered through all generations."

PSALM 103:1–2, 3–4, 6–7, 8, 11

READING 2, 1 CORINTHIANS 10:1–6, 10–12

I do not want you to be unaware, brothers and sisters, that our ancestors were all under the cloud and all passed through the sea, and all of them were baptized into Moses in the cloud and in the sea. All ate the same spiritual food, and all drank the same spiritual drink, for they drank from a spiritual rock that followed them, and the rock was the Christ. Yet God was not pleased with most of them, for they were struck down in the desert. These things happened as examples for us, so that we might not desire evil things, as they did. Do not grumble as some of them did and suffered death by the destroyer. These things happened to them as an example, and they have been written down as a warning to us, upon whom the end of the ages has come. Therefore, whoever thinks he is standing secure should take care not to fall.

GOSPEL, LUKE 13:1–9

Some people told Jesus about the Galileans whose blood Pilate had mingled with the blood of their sacrifices. Jesus said to them in reply, "Do you think that because these Galileans suffered in this way they were greater sinners than all other Galileans? By no means! But I tell you, if you do not repent, you will all perish as they did! Or those eighteen people who were killed when the tower at Siloam fell on them—do you think they were more guilty than everyone else who lived in Jerusalem? By no means! But I tell you, if you do not repent, you will all perish as they did!" And he told them this parable: "There Once was a person who had a fig tree planted in his orchard, and when he came in search of fruit on it but found none, he said to the gardener, 'For three years now I have come in search of fruit on this fig tree but have found none. So cut it down. Why should it exhaust the soil? 'He said to him in reply, 'Sir, leave it for this year also, and I shall cultivate the ground around it and fertilize it; it may bear fruit in the future. If not you can cut it down.'"

Holy Ground

The encounter Moses has with God in our first reading tells us many things about God. Moses turns aside because he sees a bush that's burning, but not consumed. Some people think that belief in God means becoming a robot and doing only what God wants. God does not compete with us; God does not destroy our will or our humanness. When God dwells in our hearts, we burn with a light that others want to see. As well, God wants us to know him. When Moses asks what he should tell the Israelites when they ask who sent him. God gives a name that we loosely translate as "I AM." The Hebrew word has no exact translation but looks like a variation of the verb "to be." The Hebrew Scriptures never attempt to translate the name or say it. Instead, they write the name in Exodus and substitute another word when they say it—*Adonai*, the Lord. (When used in this way in most Bibles, this word is written in smaller capital letters: the LORD.) To give your name to someone is to move into a deeper personal relationship with them. God gave Moses and the Israelites the ability to call on him personally whenever they wanted and to trust that he would hear them. No wonder Moses took his shoes off. Wherever we meet God is holy ground indeed.

Sin and Self-Righteousness

The thought that God rewards the righteous and punishes sinners was attractive not only in parts of Israelite theology, but also in early Christianity. We see the remnants of that thinking today when individual preachers tell people that something like 9/11 happened because of the sin of certain groups of people in the nation. Such thinking allows people (usually those in power) to point a finger at a presumed sinner, while upholding the evidence of their own righteousness. They were not punished; therefore, they must be pleasing in God's sight. Jesus is quick to condemn such self-righteousness as its own sin. As he does in so many places in Luke's Gospel, Jesus tells the offenders that they are no better than the sinners they so eagerly point out, and he challenges them to repent, lest they suffer a similar fate. The parable of the fig tree underscores his challenge. There is time for the self-righteous to change their ways, but that time is limited. Jesus, the master gardener, will do what he can to save them, but if they don't bear fruit, they will be destroyed.

In our second reading, Paul reminds the Corinthians that it's easy to start on the right path, and it's difficult to stay the course until the end. When the Israelites were wandering in the desert, many were struck down for their wickedness and for their complaints. Like Jesus, Paul holds these people from the past as examples to encourage the early Christians not to fall into sin. His parting words are cautionary: "Therefore, whoever thinks he is standing secure should take care not to fall."

Good News for All of Us

Being a disciple of Christ is not a sprint; it's a marathon. We learn where we are likely to stumble, the easiest terrain to get across, and where we need to bear down and use every bit of strength to make progress. We learn to pace ourselves. Our readings today tell us that God runs with us and we can call on him by name. They also give us a graphic description of what happens when pride and self-interest get in the way. If we take the time, we have been given, we will make it to the end and we will be fruitful in our effort.

Questions for Reflection and Discussion

> *Are there any places that have been "holy ground" for you? These are places where you felt the presence of God or heard the words of Jesus so clearly, it stayed with you for a long time.*

> *It's very human to feel superior to one person or another. Has this ever happened to you? What was the result?*

Related Journey of Faith Lesson

E1, "Election: Saying Yes to Jesus"

Themes

Call
    E1, "Election: Saying Yes to Jesus"
Vigilance
    E7, "The Meaning of Holy Week"

Fourth Sunday of Lent, Year C

READING 1, JOSHUA 5:9A, 10–12

The LORD said to Joshua, "Today I have removed the reproach of Egypt from you." While the Israelites were encamped at Gilgal on the plains of Jericho, they celebrated the Passover on the evening of the fourteenth of the month. On the day after the Passover, they ate of the produce of the land in the form of unleavened cakes and parched grain. On that same day after the Passover, on which they ate of the produce of the land, the manna ceased. No longer was there manna for the Israelites, who that year ate of the yield of the land of Canaan.

PSALM 34:2–3, 4–5, 6–7

READING 2, 2 CORINTHIANS 5:17–21

Brothers and sisters: Whoever is in Christ is a new creation: the old things have passed away; behold, new things have come. And all this is from God, who has reconciled us to himself through Christ and given us the ministry of reconciliation, namely, God was reconciling the world to himself in Christ, not counting their trespasses against them and entrusting to us the message of reconciliation. So we are ambassadors for Christ, as if God were appealing through us. We implore you on behalf of Christ, be reconciled to God. For our sake he made him to be sin who did not know sin, so that we might become the righteousness of God in him.

GOSPEL, LUKE 15:1–3, 11–32

Tax collectors and sinners were all drawing near to listen to Jesus, but the Pharisees and scribes began to complain, saying, "This man welcomes sinners and eats with them." So to them Jesus addressed this parable: "A man had two sons, and the younger son said to his father, 'Father give me the share of your estate that should come to me.' So the father divided the property between them. After a few days, the younger son collected all his Belongings and set off to a distant country where he squandered his inheritance on a life of dissipation. When he had freely spent everything, a severe famine struck that country, and he found himself in dire need. So he hired himself out to one of the local citizens who sent him to his farm to tend the swine.

And he longed to eat his fill of the pods on which the swine fed, but nobody gave him any. Coming to his senses he thought, 'How many of my father's hired workers have more than enough food to eat, but here am I, dying from hunger. I shall get up and go to my father and I shall say to him, "Father, I have sinned against heaven and against you. I no longer deserve to be called your son; treat me as you would treat one of your hired workers."' So he got up and went back to his father. While he was still a long way off, his father caught sight of him, and was filled with compassion. He ran to his son, embraced him and kissed him. His son said to him, 'Father, I have sinned against heaven and against you; I no longer deserve to be called your son.' But his father ordered his servants, 'Quickly bring the finest robe and put it on him; put a ring on his finger and sandals on his feet. Take the fattened calf and slaughter it. Then let us celebrate with a feast, because this son of mine was dead, and has come to life again; he was lost and has been found.' Then the celebration began. Now the older son had been out in the field and, on his way back, as he neared the house, he heard the sound of music and dancing. He called one of the servants and asked what this might mean. The servant said to him, 'Your brother has returned, and your father has slaughtered the fattened calf because he has him back safe and sound.' He became angry, and when he refused to enter the house, his father came out and pleaded with him. He said to his father in reply, 'Look, all these years I served you and not once did I disobey your orders; yet you never gave me even a young goat to feast on with my friends. But when your son returns who swallowed up your property with prostitutes, for him you slaughter the fattened calf.' He said to him, 'My son, you are here with me always; everything I have is yours. But now we must celebrate and rejoice, because your brother was dead and has come to life again; he was lost and has been found.'"

Laetare—Rejoice

The entrance antiphon for the fourth Sunday of Lent is taken from Isaiah: "Rejoice, Jerusalem, and all who love her. Be joyful, all who were in mourning...." The Latin imperative for "rejoice" is *laetare*. For centuries this midpoint of Lent has offered a little break from the Lenten disciplines. In times past, those who were abstaining from meat could eat meat on this day; flowers could decorate the altar; and people celebrated that they were God's children and sent offerings to the mother church—the Cathedral in their diocese. Because of that, the feast is still known as Mothering Sunday in parts of England.

Here, Laetare Sunday seems like a fitting name because the readings reflect a freedom from bondage, a change of life, and the reconciliation with God. There is much about which we can rejoice.

The Celebration of Freedom

After Moses died, Joshua led the people into the Promised Land of Canaan. Even before they secured the land, the people kept the Passover on the plains of Jericho, as they had been commanded in the Book of Exodus. The day after, the Book of Joshua records that they ate the produce of the land and unleavened bread with grain. When it says the manna ceased that day, it means that they no longer had need for the miraculous intervention of God to feed them. He had done what he promised—he led them to a land in which they could prosper.

Ambassadors for Christ

What does it mean to be a new creation? For Paul it was a fulfillment of God's promise to do a new thing (See Isaiah 42:9 or 43:19) and help us throw off our old habits and ways of thinking. Our identity as a new creation hinges on our reconciliation with God which was accomplished through Christ. To reconcile is to bring people together again and restore the relationship they had before their separation. Paul talks about reconciliation as both a ministry and a message. As ambassadors for Christ, the apostles carried the message of a renewed relationship with God to which all people are invited. As those who have inherited that good news through baptism, so must we become ambassadors that others might be one with God.

Homecoming

The Prodigal Son is one of the best-loved parables in Luke's Gospel. We find ourselves mirrored in all three characters. We have been the youngest son who wants to strike out on his own and discovers that his father was smarter than he thought all along. We have been the eldest son who wonders why his brother keeps getting away with things that he would never do, and who thinks that his father's celebration means that his father doesn't love him as much. And we have been the father who rejoices when a child returns home even from college and, even more so, if they have been estranged. The story, though, is about God who continues to love us, even when we stray; even when we think we are not loved. It's about God who wants our relationship with him restored and who rejoices when it is. The Pharisees complained that Jesus ate with sinners and tax collectors. Of course, he did. God's love is so extravagant that he has more than enough to offer even to those who haven't lived their best lives. It's because of such a love that Christ died on the cross and gave us every reason to rejoice and follow him.

Fourth Sunday of Lent, Year C

Good News for All of Us

We are the recipients of extraordinary love. The love of God rolls away our shame, puts us in the right relationship with him so that we can radiate love and peace to others, and welcomes us home when we have been away. There is only one way to respond to such a gift. It is to offer the gift of reconciliation to others, to invite and then welcome everyone into the family of God, and finally to lift up those who have been oppressed either by others or by their own fears and doubts. The love we have been given compels us to pass it on.

Questions for Reflection and Discussion

> Describe a time when you have been like any one of the characters in the Prodigal Son story. Does the memory make you want to cringe, laugh, or just smile?

> How might you practice the ministry of reconciliation in your life today?

Related Journey of Faith Lesson

E2, "Living Lent"

Themes

Forgiveness
   E1, "Election: Saying Yes to Jesus"
Reconciliation
   E3, "Scrutinies: Looking Within"
Repentance
   E2, "Living Lent"

Fifth Sunday of Lent, Year C

READING 1, ISAIAH 43:16–21

Thus says the LORD, who opens a way in the sea and a path in the mighty waters, who leads out chariots and horsemen, a powerful army, till they lie prostrate together, never to rise, snuffed out and quenched like a wick. Remember not the events of the past, the things of long ago consider not; see, I am doing something new! Now it springs forth, do you not perceive it? In the desert I make a way, in the wasteland, rivers. Wild beasts honor me, jackals and ostriches, for I put water in the desert and rivers in the wasteland for my chosen people to drink, the people whom I formed for myself, that they might announce my praise.

PSALM 126:1–2, 2–3, 4–5, 6

READING 2, PHILIPPIANS 3:8–14

Brothers and sisters: I consider everything as a loss because of the supreme good of knowing Christ Jesus my Lord. For his sake I have accepted the loss of all things and I consider them so much rubbish, that I may gain Christ and be found in him, not having any righteousness of my own based on the law but that which comes through faith in Christ, the righteousness from God, depending on faith to know him and the power of his resurrection and the sharing of his sufferings by being conformed to his death, if somehow, I may attain the resurrection from the dead. It is not that I have already taken hold of it or have already attained perfect maturity, but I continue my pursuit in hope that I may possess it, since I have indeed been taken possession of by Christ Jesus. Brothers and sisters, I for my part do not consider myself to have taken possession. Just one thing: forgetting what lies behind but straining forward to what lies ahead, I continue my pursuit toward the goal, the prize of God's upward calling, in Christ Jesus.

GOSPEL, JOHN 8:1–11

Jesus went to the Mount of Olives. But early in the morning he arrived again in the temple area, and all the people started coming to him, and he sat down and taught them. Then the scribes and the Pharisees brought a woman who had been caught in adultery and made her stand in the middle. They said to him, "Teacher, this woman was caught in the very act of committing adultery. Now in the law, Moses commanded us to stone such women. So what do you say?" They said this to test him, so that they could have some charge to bring against him. Jesus bent down and began to write on the ground with his finger. But when they continued asking him, he straightened up and said to them, "Let the one among you who is without sin be the first to throw a stone at her." Again, he bent down and wrote on the ground. And in response, they went away one by one, beginning with the elders. So he was left alone with the woman before him. Then Jesus straightened up and said to her, "Woman, where are they? Has no one condemned you?" She replied, "No one, sir." Then Jesus said, "Neither do I condemn you. Go, and from now on do not sin anymore."

Behold, I Am Doing Something New

Many who heard Jesus preach were astounded at his wisdom. Many felt the first stirrings of hope in a long time. Some others were challenged and afraid. Our Gospel today suggests all three reactions. The crowds were astounded, the Pharisees were challenged, and the woman felt her first faint hope. When people talk about this passage, they often wonder what Jesus was writing on the ground. It doesn't really matter. The Pharisees hoped to trick him into speaking against the Law. Jesus refused to fall into their trap, preferring instead to get their attention and then to give them a single direction. The one without sin could cast the first stone. No one would have been so bold. Like us they were all sinners who made their judgment over other suspect. After they left, we still don't know what Jesus wrote, but he had the woman's attention now. Jesus' refusal to condemn the woman was an invitation to follow God more faithfully—to become a disciple of Christ.

In his actions with the woman caught in adultery, Jesus did something new. Rather than follow the letter of the law, Jesus chose to emphasize and embody God's mercy and compassion. It was an opportunity to remember that God wants our conversion, not our destruction. Isaiah envisions God's redemption as giving a drink of fresh water to his thirsty people and creating rivers in the desert such that even the animals praise him. The people of Isaiah's time had sinned and been taken into exile. God forgave their sin and brought them back to Israel, inviting their change of heart and a commitment to live faithful lives.

The Value of Knowing the Lord

"I want to know Christ," Paul says, "and the power of his resurrection." To that end it seems that Paul would do anything. Knowing Jesus has become the greatest value in his life. Sharing in Jesus' suffering and death in the hope of sharing his resurrection is worth more than any earthly think Paul has. Did Paul live as if that were true? He walked away from his former life for which he was, no doubt, well compensated. He became an itinerant preacher, helping establish Christian communities in the far-flung places of Asia Minor. He was imprisoned, beaten, and ridiculed. He got into fights with Peter, for both were strong-willed and stubborn. He considered himself a slave for Jesus and in that found his greatest freedom. He was ultimately martyred for his faith. He was willing to give up everything to follow Christ, but he also recognized that this was a lifelong process. That's why Paul talks about continuing his pursuit to the very end where he will obtain the heavenly call of God.

Good News for All of Us

There may be times when we feel we have so completely messed things up that we can never be forgiven. The natural impulse in such a time is to deny what happened or hide in shame. In the sacrament of reconciliation, we can name our sinfulness and our shame before God and the Church. We can talk to someone about what we've done and, in humility, ask forgiveness. Sometimes people make excuses about why they won't participate in the sacrament: "It's between me and God," they will say, or "I know God forgives me." What many people forget is that sin that breaks our relationship with God also breaks our relationship with other people. Where there is sin, a community suffers as well. The sacrament allows us to speak to the priest in his role as *persona Christi* (the person of Christ) and his role as the public face of the community. From him we will hear words similar to what the woman heard: "Neither do I condemn you. Go and sin no more." If our relationship with Christ is as valuable as Paul says it is, we can let go of our pride, our stubbornness, and our fear to obtain the goal of knowing Christ in every way possible, including reconciliation.

Questions for Reflection and Discussion

➤ *Is there any sin so heinous that God cannot forgive it? What would someone have to do to obtain forgiveness?*

➤ *Reflect on times in your life when you started something new—a new job, a new family situation, a new school. What were your feelings in that situation? What feeling dominated the others? Did the feelings change over time?*

Related Journey of Faith Lesson

E3, "Scrutinies: Looking Within"

Themes

Doubt
    E3, "Scrutinies: Looking Within"
Faith
    E4, "The Creed"
Perseverance
    E5, "The Way of the Cross"

Passion (Palm) Sunday, Year C

PROCESSION WITH PALMS, LUKE 19:28–40

Jesus proceeded on his journey up to Jerusalem. As he drew near to Bethphage and Bethany at the place called the Mount of Olives, he sent two of his disciples. He said, "Go into the village opposite you, and as you enter it you will find a colt tethered on which no one has ever sat. Untie it and bring it here. And if anyone should ask you, 'Why are you untying it?' you will answer, 'The Master has need of it.'" So those who had been sent went off and found everything just as he had told them. And as they were untying the colt, its owners said to them, "Why are you untying this colt?" They answered, "The Master has need of it." So they brought it to Jesus, threw their cloaks over the colt, and helped Jesus to mount. As he rode along, the people were spreading their cloaks on the road; and now as he was approaching the slope of the Mount of Olives, the whole multitude of his disciples began to praise God aloud with joy for all the mighty deeds they had seen. They proclaimed: "Blessed is the king who comes in the name of the Lord. Peace in heaven and glory in the highest." Some of the Pharisees in the crowd said to him, "Teacher, rebuke your disciples." He said in reply, "I tell you, if they keep silent, the stones will cry out!"

READING 1, ISAIAH 50:4–7

The Lord GOD has given me a well-trained tongue, that I might know how to speak to the weary a word that will rouse them. Morning after morning he opens my ear that I may hear; and I have not rebelled, have not turned back. I gave my back to those who beat me, my cheeks to those who plucked my beard; my face I did not shield from buffets and spitting. The Lord GOD is my help; therefore, I am not disgraced; I have set my face like flint, knowing that I shall not be put to shame.

PSALM 22:8–9, 17–18, 19–20, 23–24

READING 2, PHILIPPIANS 2:6–11

Christ Jesus, though he was in the form of God, did not regard equality with God something to be grasped. Rather, he emptied himself, taking the form of a slave, coming in human likeness; and found human in appearance, he humbled himself, becoming obedient to the point of death, even death on a cross. Because of this, God greatly exalted him and bestowed on him the name, which is above every name, that at the name of Jesus every knee should bend, of those in heaven and on earth and under the earth, and every tongue confess that Jesus Christ is Lord, to the glory of God the Father.

GOSPEL, LUKE 22:14—23:56

When the hour came, Jesus took his place at table with the apostles. He said to them, "I have eagerly desired to eat this Passover with you before I suffer, for, I tell you, I shall not eat it again until there is fulfillment in the kingdom of God." Then he took a cup, gave thanks, and said, "Take this and share it among yourselves; for I tell you that from this time on I shall not drink of the fruit of the vine until the kingdom of God comes." Then he took the bread, said the blessing, broke it, and gave it to them, saying, "This is my body, which will be given for you; do this in memory of me." And likewise, the cup after they had eaten, saying, "This cup is the new covenant in my blood, which will be shed for you.

"And yet behold, the hand of the one who is to betray me is with me on the table; for the Son of Man indeed goes as it has been determined; but woe to that man by whom he is betrayed." And they began to debate among themselves who among them would do such a deed.

Then an argument broke out among them about which of them should be regarded as the greatest. He said to them, "The kings of the Gentiles lord it over them and those in authority over them are addressed as 'Benefactors'; but among you it shall not be so. Rather, let the greatest among you be as the youngest, and the leader as the servant. For who is greater: the one seated at table or the one who serves? Is it not the one seated at table? I am among you as the one who serves. It is you who have stood by me in my trials; and I confer a kingdom on you, just as my Father has conferred one on me, that you may eat and drink at my table in my kingdom; and you will sit on thrones judging the twelve tribes of Israel.

"Simon, Simon, behold Satan has demanded to sift all of you like wheat, but I have prayed that your own faith may not fail; and once you have turned back, you must strengthen your brothers." He said to him, "Lord, I am prepared to go to prison and to die with you." But he replied, "I tell you, Peter, before the cock crows this day, you will deny three times that you know me."

He said to them, "When I sent you forth without a money bag or a sack or sandals, were you in need of anything?" "No, nothing, "they replied. He said to them, "But now one who has a money bag should take it, and likewise a sack, and one who does not have a sword should sell his cloak and buy one. For I tell you that this Scripture must be fulfilled in me, namely, He was counted among the wicked; and indeed, what is written about me is coming to fulfillment." Then they said, "Lord, look, there are two swords here." But he replied, "It is enough!"

Then going out, he went, as was his custom, to the Mount of Olives, and the disciples followed him. When he arrived at the place he said to them, "Pray that you may not undergo the test." After withdrawing about a stone's throw from them and kneeling, he prayed, saying, "Father, if you are willing, take this cup away from me; still, not my will but yours be done." And to strengthen him an angel from heaven appeared to him. He was in such agony and he prayed so fervently that his sweat became like drops of blood falling on the ground. When he rose from prayer and returned to his disciples, he found them sleeping from grief. He said to them, "Why are you sleeping? Get up and pray that you may not undergo the test."

While he was still speaking, a crowd approached and in front was one of the Twelve, a man named Judas. He went up to Jesus to kiss him. Jesus said to him, "Judas, are you betraying the Son of Man with a kiss?" His disciples realized what was about to happen, and they asked, "Lord, shall we strike with a sword?" And one of them struck the high priest's servant and cut off his right ear. But Jesus said in reply, "Stop, no more

of this!" Then he touched the servant's ear and healed him. And Jesus said to the chief priests and temple guards and elders who had come for him, "Have you come out as against a robber, with swords and clubs? Day after day I was with you in the temple area, and you did not seize me; but this is your hour, the time for the power of darkness."

After arresting him they led him away and took him into the house of the high priest; Peter was following at a distance. They lit a fire in the middle of the courtyard and sat around it, and Peter sat down with them. When a maid saw him seated in the light, she looked intently at him and said, "This man too was with him." But he denied it saying, "Woman, I do not know him." A short while later someone else saw him and said, "You too are one of them"; but Peter answered, "My friend, I am not." About an hour later, still another insisted, "Assuredly, this man too was with him, for he also is a Galilean." But Peter said, "My friend, I do not know what you are talking about." Just as he was saying this, the cock crowed, and the Lord turned and looked at Peter; and Peter remembered the word of the Lord, how he had said to him, "Before the cock crows today, you will deny me three times." He went out and began to weep bitterly. The men who held Jesus in custody were ridiculing and beating him. They blindfolded him and questioned him, saying, "Prophesy! Who is it that struck you?" And they reviled him in saying many other things against him.

When day came the council of elders of the people met, both chief priests and scribes, and they brought him before their Sanhedrin. They said, "If you are the Christ, tell us," but he replied to them, "If I tell you, you will not believe, and if I question, you will not respond. But from this time on the Son of Man will be seated at the right hand of the power of God." They all asked, "Are you then the Son of God?" He replied to them, "You say that I am." Then they said, "What further need have we for testimony? We have heard it from his own mouth."

Then the whole assembly of them arose and brought him before Pilate. They brought charges against him, saying, "We found this man misleading our people; he opposes the payment of taxes to Caesar and maintains that he is the Christ, a king." Pilate asked him, "Are you the king of the Jews?" He said to him in reply,

Passion (Palm) Sunday, Year C

"You say so." Pilate then addressed the chief priests and the crowds, "I find this man not guilty." But they were adamant and said, "He is inciting the people with his teaching throughout all Judea, from Galilee where he began even to here."

On hearing this Pilate asked if the man was a Galilean; and upon learning that he was under Herod's jurisdiction, he sent him to Herod who was in Jerusalem at that time. Herod was very glad to see Jesus; he had been wanting to see him for a long time, for he had heard about him and had been hoping to see him perform some sign. He questioned him at length, but he gave him no answer. The chief priests and scribes, meanwhile, stood by accusing him harshly. Herod and his soldiers treated him contemptuously and mocked him, and after clothing him in resplendent garb, he sent him back to Pilate. Herod and Pilate became friends that very day, even though they had been enemies formerly. Pilate then summoned the chief priests, the rulers, and the people and said to them, "You brought this man to me and accused him of inciting the people to revolt. I have conducted my investigation in your presence and have not found this man guilty of the charges you have brought against him, nor did Herod, for he sent him back to us. So no capital crime has been committed by him. Therefore, I shall have him flogged and then release him."

But all together they shouted out, "Away with this man! Release Barabbas to us."—Now Barabbas had been imprisoned for a rebellion that had taken place in the city and for murder. —Again, Pilate addressed them, still wishing to release Jesus, but they continued their shouting, "Crucify him! Crucify him!" Pilate addressed them a third time, "What evil has this man done? I found him guilty of no capital crime. Therefore, I shall have him flogged and then release him." With loud shouts, however, they persisted in calling for his crucifixion, and their voices prevailed. The verdict of Pilate was that their demand should be granted. So he released the man who had been imprisoned for rebellion and murder, for whom they asked, and he handed Jesus over to them to deal with as they wished.

As they led him away, they took hold of a certain Simon, a Cyrenian, who was coming in from the country; and after laying the cross on him, they made him carry it behind Jesus.

A large crowd of people followed Jesus, including many women who mourned and lamented him. Jesus turned to them and said, "Daughters of Jerusalem, do not weep for me; weep instead for yourselves and for your children for indeed, the days are coming when people will say, 'Blessed are the barren, the wombs that never bore and the breasts that never nursed.' At that time people will say to the mountains, 'Fall upon us!' and to the hills, 'Cover us!' for if these things are done when the wood is green what will happen when it is dry?"

Now two others, both criminals, were led away with him to be executed. When they came to the place called the Skull, they crucified him and the criminals there, one on his right, the other on his left. Then Jesus said, "Father, forgive them, they know not what they do." They divided his garments by casting lots. The people stood by and watched; the rulers, meanwhile, sneered at him and said, "He saved others, let him save himself if he is the chosen one, the Christ of God." Even the soldiers jeered at him. As they approached to offer him wine they called out, "If you are King of the Jews, save yourself." Above him there was an inscription that read, "This is the King of the Jews."

Now one of the criminals hanging there reviled Jesus, saying, "Are you not the Christ? Save yourself and us." The other, however, rebuking him, said in reply, "Have you no fear of God, for you are subject to the same condemnation? And indeed, we have been condemned justly, for the sentence we received corresponds to our crimes, but this man has done nothing criminal." Then he said, "Jesus, remember me when you come into your kingdom." He replied to him, "Amen, I say to you, today you will be with me in Paradise."

It was now about noon and darkness came over the whole land until three in the afternoon because of an eclipse of the sun. Then the veil of the temple was torn down the middle. Jesus cried out in a loud voice, "Father, into your hands I commend my spirit"; and when he had said this, he breathed his last.

Here all kneel and pause for a short time.

The centurion who witnessed what had happened glorified God and said, "This man was innocent beyond doubt." When all the people who had gathered for this spectacle saw what had happened, they returned home beating their breasts; but all his acquaintances stood at a distance, including the women who had followed him from Galilee and saw these events.

Now there was a virtuous and righteous man named Joseph who, though he was a member of the council, had not consented to their plan of action. He came from the Jewish town of Arimathea and was awaiting the kingdom of God. He went to Pilate and asked for the body of Jesus. After he had taken the body down, he wrapped it in a linen cloth and laid him in a rock-hewn tomb in which no one had yet been buried. It was the day of preparation, and the sabbath was about to begin. The women who had come from Galilee with him followed behind, and when they had seen the tomb and the way in which his body was laid in it, they returned and prepared spices and perfumed oils. Then they rested on the sabbath according to the commandment.

A Triumphant Entry
When Jesus enters Jerusalem, it is to the sound of triumphant shouts and loud praises of God. Everyone assembled had seen Jesus heal the sick, cast out demons, feed multitudes and preach the word of God. Surely this was the long-awaited king-messiah promised by God. The words of the crowd echo the words of the angels when Jesus was born: "Glory to God in the highest and peace to all on earth." Not even the Pharisees can stop the noise, and Jesus tells them the very earth would cry out if they tried. This begins Holy Week, and before the end of the Mass, triumph will turn to shock and disbelief. Jesus will be betrayed by one of those close to him and denied by the acknowledged head of the twelve apostles. He will be tempted to take things into his own hands again, as he was in the wilderness: "Let

him save himself, if he is the chosen one...If you are the King of the Jews, save yourself." And through it all, he will be the model of forgiveness, welcome, and humble obedience. What he won't be, for many people, is the fierce warrior they hoped would free them from Roman power. For the first time this week, we will come face to face with the paradox of the cross—someone who lays down his life for others and, by doing so, becomes more powerful than we can imagine. In dying, he conquers death and frees us from the bondage of sin.

A Face Like Flint
Every Gospel moves inexorably from the beginning of Jesus' ministry to his final days in Jerusalem. In Luke's version of the story, Jesus teaches in parables right up until the moment of his entry and displays humble silence during his trial and compassion to those he meets on the way to the cross. Isaiah's servant in the first reading is the precursor to this image of Jesus. He is a teacher. He sustains the weary. He listens to and obeys God. In the end, he does what he must do and turns toward his death not as an act of shame, but in obedience to his Father.

The Name Above All Names
Paul borrows the imagery for this beautiful hymn to Jesus from a different passage of Isaiah. In Isaiah 45:22–24, God says, "For I am God, and there is no other. By myself I have sworn, from my mouth has gone forth in righteousness a word that shall not return: 'To me every knee shall bow, every tongue shall swear.' Only in the Lord...are righteousness and strength." In his declaration that God has now spoken these words in reference to Jesus, Paul asserts that Jesus is Lord and that he shows forth the glory of God the Father.

Passion (Palm) Sunday, Year C

Good News for All of Us

Lent is a time set apart for reflection and conversion. Holy Week intensifies that journey as we hear the story of Jesus' passion and death not once, but twice. In our soul and imagination, we can walk these last few days with Jesus. We are at the Last Supper and at his betrayal. We witness Peter deny him. We walk with the women who accompanied him from Galilee, and we stand with them at the tomb, daring to look his death in the face and doing what needed to be done for him—preparing the spices for his burial. There is something that empties us out this week, and we ask ourselves questions in the depths of our hearts: "How far will I go with this Teacher? Who is he for me? Do I believe that God can take something as awful as death on a cross, and turn it into good? And what does that mean for me?

Questions for Reflection and Discussion

➤ *As you remember the story of the passion and death of Jesus, what parts stand out? What might God be inviting you to think about as you remember those parts?*

➤ *Paul says Jesus did not deem equality with God as something to be grasped at. We might also say that he did not deem equality with human beings as something to be despised. What does it mean for you that God, as Jesus, walked in our shoes for a little while and died for us?*

Related Journey of Faith Lesson

E5, "The Way of the Cross"

Themes

Death
    E5, "The Way of the Cross"
Life
    E7, "The Meaning of Holy Week"
Obedience
    E1, "Election: Saying Yes to Jesus"

Easter Sunday, Year C

READING 1, ACTS 10,34A, 37–43

Peter proceeded to speak and said: "You know what has happened all over Judea, beginning in Galilee after the baptism that John preached, how God anointed Jesus of Nazareth with the Holy Spirit and power. He went about doing good and healing all those oppressed by the devil, for God was with him.
We are witnesses of all that he did both in the country of the Jews and in Jerusalem. They put him to death by hanging him on a tree. This man God raised on the third day and granted that he be visible, not to all the people, but to us, the witnesses chosen by God in advance, who ate and drank with him after he rose from the dead. He commissioned us to preach to the people and testify that he is the one appointed by God as judge of the living and the dead. To him all the prophets bear witness, that everyone who believes in him will receive forgiveness of sins through his name."

PSALM 118:1–2,16–17,22–23

READING 2, COLOSSIANS 3:1–4

Brothers and sisters: If then you were raised with Christ, seek what is above, where Christ is seated at the right hand of God. Think of what of what is above, not is on earth. For you have died, and your life is hidden with Christ in God. When Christ your life appears, then you too will appear with him in glory.

GOSPEL, JOHN 20:1–9

On the first day of the week, Mary of Magdala came to the tomb early in the morning, while it was still dark, and saw the stone removed from the tomb. So she ran and went to Simon Peter and to the other disciple whom Jesus loved, and told them, "They have taken the Lord from the tomb, and we don't know where they put him." So Peter and the other disciple went out and came to the tomb. They both ran, but the other disciple ran faster than Peter and arrived at the tomb first; he bent down and saw the burial cloths there, but did not go in. When Simon Peter arrived after him, he went into the tomb and saw the burial cloths there, and the cloth that had covered his head, not with the burial cloths but rolled up in a separate place. Then the other disciple also went in, the one who had arrived at the tomb first, and he saw and believed. For they did not yet understand the Scripture that he had to rise from the dead.

Lord of All

The flowers have been returned to the altar; the banners are hung; glorious shouts of "Hallelujah" fill the air. The long season of Lent is over, and Christ has risen. If this Holy Week has done anything for us, it has given us the chance to witness once again Christ's last days, the betrayal of Judas, the denial of Peter, Jesus' crucifixion, and his burial. And now, we rejoice in the empty tomb and his rising from the dead. Indeed, if we think back to the baptism of Jesus which closed out the Christmas season and the many stories of healing we heard since then, we realize that we are privileged to have heard the message that God sent to the people and that Peter now preaches to those who are listening. Peter's story makes sense to us because we have been hearing it from Sunday to Sunday these last several weeks. Peter's assertion that Jesus is ordained to judge the living and the dead seems equally reasonable because his followers saw him and ate with him after the resurrection and believed him to be alive in their midst. Through him they receive forgiveness of sins. Jesus is indeed the Lord of all.

Hidden with Christ in God

For Paul, being raised with Christ meant being raised to new life. Christians were no longer enslaved to sin or the cares and passions of this world. Instead, they were free to seek the "things that are above," where Christ is. In his Letter to the Colossians, Paul describes this new life as being "hidden with Christ in God." When Christ appears (which Paul thought would happen relatively soon), all the baptized would live with him in the presence of God.

Believe the Women

The resurrection is a story about mystery. Everyone saw Jesus die; the women and Joseph of Arimathea saw him buried in the tomb. And the first thing the women saw when they came the next day was an empty tomb and then, suddenly, two men in dazzling clothes (the same word is used of Jesus' clothes at the transfiguration). The young men ask a profound question: "Why do you seek the living among the dead?" They go on to say: "He has been raised… remember how he told you…" In the Scriptures, to remember something is to act on it. When the women remember Jesus' teaching about the Son of Man, they return to the apostles and tell them everything that happened. The men did not believe the women—these first preachers of the resurrection. But Peter decided to check out their story, finds everything as they said, and goes home, amazed, which, when the word is used elsewhere in the Gospel, usually means that he wasn't sure what was going on. It's a lesson for all of us: believe the women.

Good News for All of Us

God always surprises us. We were looking for a warrior-Messiah; he came as a baby. We wanted someone who could conquer the Romans; he laid down his life on a cruel instrument of torture. We thought he had died; and he rose from the dead. From the very beginning, things that we thought were impossible, God has made possible, and in the process, he has shown us the possibilities for our lives. Many of us suffer doubts about our talents and our ability to make a difference in the world. If we have learned anything, it's that God can take us as we are and make something extraordinary of us. And he does it out of love for us. Along the way, God gives us spiritual guides and the grace of the sacraments to help us discern our path. Believe the Good News you have heard. Christ is risen for you and for all of us and we live in him.

Questions for Reflection and Discussion

➤ *Put yourself in the place of the women at the tomb. What would you have thought at seeing it empty? How would you have felt if you shared what you saw and heard, and no one believed you?*

➤ *Paul preached with others; the women came with one another to the tomb. Who walks with you on your faith journey?*

Related *Journey of Faith* Lesson

E7, "The Meaning of Holy Week"

Themes

Resurrection
    E7, "The Meaning of Holy Week"
Universality
    E4, "The Creed"
Wonder and Awe
    E8, "Easter Vigil Retreat"

READING 1, ACTS 5:12–16

Many signs and wonders were done among the people at the hands of the apostles. They were all together in Solomon's portico. None of the others dared to join them, but the people esteemed them. Yet more than ever, believers in the Lord, great numbers of men and women, were added to them. Thus they even carried the sick out into the streets and laid them on cots and mats so that when Peter came by, at least his shadow might fall on one or another of them. A large number of people from the towns in the vicinity of Jerusalem also gathered, bringing the sick and those disturbed by unclean spirits, and they were all cured.

PSALM 118:2–4, 13–15, 22–24

READING 2, REVELATION 1:9–11A, 12–13, 17–19

I, John, your brother, who share with you the distress, the kingdom, and the endurance we have in Jesus, found myself on the island called Patmos because I proclaimed God's word and gave testimony to Jesus.

I was caught up in spirit on the Lord's day and heard behind me a voice as loud as a trumpet, which said, "Write on a scroll what you see." Then I turned to see whose voice it was that spoke to me, and when I turned, I saw seven gold lampstands and in the midst of the lampstands one like a son of man, wearing an ankle-length robe, with a gold sash around his chest. When I caught sight of him, I fell down at his feet as though dead. He touched me with his right hand and said, "Do not be afraid. I am the first and the last, the one who lives. Once I was dead, but now I am alive forever and ever. I hold the keys to death and the netherworld. Write down, therefore, what you have seen, and what is happening, and what will happen afterwards."

GOSPEL, JOHN 20:19–31

On the evening of that first day of the week, when the doors were locked, where the disciples were, for fear of the Jews, Jesus came and stood in their midst and said to them, "Peace be with you." When he had said this, he showed them his hands and his side. The disciples rejoiced when they saw the Lord. Jesus said to them again, "Peace be with you. As the Father has sent me, so I send you." And when he had said this, he breathed on them and said to them, "Receive the Holy Spirit. Whose sins you forgive are forgiven them, and whose sins you retain are retained." Thomas, called Didymus, one of the Twelve, was not with them when Jesus came. So the other disciples said to him, "We have seen the Lord." But he said to them, "Unless I see the mark of the nails in his hands and put my finger into the nail marks and put my hand into his side, I will not believe." Now a week later his disciples were again inside, and Thomas was with them. Jesus came, although the doors were locked, and stood in their midst and said, "Peace be with you." Then he said to Thomas, "Put your finger here and see my hands, and bring your hand and put it into my side, and do not be unbelieving, but believe." Thomas answered and said to him, "My Lord and my God!" Jesus said to him, "Have you come to believe because you have seen me? Blessed are those who have not seen and have believed." Now Jesus did many other signs in the presence of his disciples that are not written in this book. But these are written that you may come to believe that Jesus is the Christ, the Son of God, and that through this belief you may have life in his name.

Signs and Wonders

Jesus says, "Amen, amen, I say to you, whoever believes in me will do the works that I do, and will do greater ones than these, because I am going to the Father" (John 14:12). In our first reading, we see that prophecy come true. Jesus cured the sick with a touch or a word. In our first reading, all the sick and possessed people had to do was allow Peter's shadow to fall on them. Does this mean that Peter was greater than Jesus? No. It was Peter's faith in Jesus that allowed him to do such things. If the disciples had asked Peter the source of his power, he would have been very quick to say that any power he had was from the Lord.

The Living One

Many people wonder what the Book of Revelation means. The descriptions of visions and beasts, and great wars between God and the dragon are, in turn, frightening and fascinating. That's typical of apocalyptic literature which uses visions and dreams and coded language to talk about good and evil and the ultimate battle between them. The last half of Daniel and the Book of Revelation are extended examples of this literature, which usually emerges in times of persecution and upheaval.

In our second reading, we join John, who is exiled on the island of Patmos. Out of his prayer on the Lord's day, he hears a voice and sees a vision of "one like a Son of Man" who is the first (Alpha) and the last (Omega) and the living one. The Book of Revelation is John's account of the rest of his vision, written at the command of the Lord. Spoiler alert: God wins the ultimate battle.

Receive the Holy Spirit

After the death of Jesus, the disciples were understandably afraid. Would the same fate happen to them? And what happened to the body of Jesus? John's description of their first encounter with the risen Christ shows that Jesus is changed. They are in a locked room; Jesus suddenly appears standing with them. Was it a vision? But, his first words are so like the man they knew, they became convinced that it was Jesus: "Peace be with you." He had said the same thing to them before the crucifixion (John 14:27). He showed them his hands and his side. They could see the scars. And finally, he breathed the Holy Spirit on them. Here, the image of God breathing life into the human being he made from the dust in Genesis comes to mind. *Breath* and *spirit* come from the same Greek root. The Holy Spirit Jesus breathes into them is a sign of new life and gives them authority to forgive sins. It is a foretaste of the Spirit that will fill the earth at Pentecost. For Thomas, the Spirit comes a little bit later, but when he utters, "My Lord and my God," which we don't hear from the other disciples, we know the Spirit is at work, even in someone who had his doubts.

Good News for All of Us

As the disciples did, we receive the Holy Spirit in the sacrament of confirmation. The grace of that sacrament makes possible our deepening relationship with Jesus. Confirmation also allows us both to understand what Christ did for us in the crucifixion, in other words, to see his wounds and know his suffering, and to cry out in joy at his resurrection, knowing that we are now reconciled to God and his adopted children. Like Thomas, we will also encounter Jesus and say, "My Lord and my God."

Questions for Reflection and Discussion

> *We hear a lot about forgiving sins in the sacrament of reconciliation, but we hear very little about retaining sins. Are there any sins which a priest would not forgive?*

> *Does doubt have any place in the life of faith? Can you have doubts and still be a "good" Catholic?*

Related Journey of Faith Lesson

M1, "Conversion: A Lifelong Process"

Themes

Belief
    M1, "Conversion: A Lifelong Process"
Fear
    M4, "Discernment"

READING 1, ACTS 5:27–32

When the captain and the court officers had brought the apostles in and made them stand before the Sanhedrin, the high priest questioned them, "We gave you strict orders, did we not, to stop teaching in that name? Yet you have filled Jerusalem with your teaching and want to bring this man's blood upon us." But Peter and the apostles said in reply, "We must obey God rather than men. The God of our ancestors raised Jesus, though you had him killed by hanging him on a tree. God exalted him at his right hand as leader and savior to grant Israel repentance and forgiveness of sins. We are witnesses of these things, as is the Holy Spirit whom God has given to those who obey him." The Sanhedrin ordered the apostles to stop speaking in the name of Jesus and dismissed them. So they left the presence of the Sanhedrin, rejoicing that they had been found worthy to suffer dishonor for the sake of the name.

PSALM 30:2, 4, 5–6, 11–12, 13

READING 2, REVELATION 5:11–14

I, John, looked and heard the voices of many angels who surrounded the throne and the living creatures and the elders. They were countless in number, and they cried out in a loud voice: "Worthy is the Lamb that was slain to receive power and riches, wisdom and strength, honor and glory and blessing." Then I heard every creature in heaven and on earth and under the earth and in the sea, everything in the universe, cry out: "To the one who sits on the throne and to the Lamb be blessing and honor, glory and might, forever and ever." The four living creatures answered, "Amen," and the elders fell down and worshiped.

GOSPEL, JOHN 21:1–19

At that time, Jesus revealed himself again to his disciples at the Sea of Tiberias. He revealed himself in this way. Together were Simon Peter, Thomas called Didymus, Nathanael from Cana in Galilee, Zebedee's sons, and two others of his disciples. Simon Peter said to them, "I am going fishing." They said to him, "We also will come with you." So they went out and got into the boat, but that night they caught nothing. When it was already dawn, Jesus was standing on the shore; but the disciples did not realize it was Jesus. Jesus said to them, "Children, have you caught anything to eat?" They answered him, "No." So he said to them, "Cast the net over the right side of the boat and you will find something." So they cast it, and were not able to pull it in because of the number of fish. So the disciple whom Jesus loved said to Peter, "It is the Lord." When Simon Peter heard that it was the Lord, he tucked in his garment, for he was lightly clad, and jumped into the sea. The other disciples came in the boat, for they were not far from shore, only about a hundred yards, dragging the net with the fish. When they climbed out on shore, they saw a charcoal fire with fish on it and bread. Jesus said to them, "Bring some of the fish you just caught." So Simon Peter went over and dragged the net ashore full of one hundred fifty-three large fish. Even though there were so many, the net was not torn. Jesus said to them, "Come, have breakfast." And none of the disciples dared to ask him, "Who are you?" because they realized it was the Lord. Jesus came over and took the bread and gave it to them, and in like manner the fish. This was now the third time Jesus was revealed to his disciples after being raised from the dead. When they had finished breakfast, Jesus said to Simon Peter, "Simon, son of John, do you love me more than these?" Simon Peter answered him, "Yes, Lord, you know that I love you." Jesus said to him, "Feed my lambs." He then said to Simon Peter a second time, "Simon, son of John, do you love me?" Simon Peter answered him, "Yes, Lord, you know that I love you." Jesus said to him, "Tend my sheep." Jesus said to him the third time, "Simon, son of John, do you love me?" Peter was distressed that Jesus had said to him a third time, "Do you love me?" and he said to him, "Lord, you know everything; you know that I love you." Jesus said to him, "Feed my sheep. Amen, amen, I say to you, when you were younger, you used to dress yourself and go where you wanted; but when you grow old, you will stretch out your hands, and someone else will dress you and lead you where you do not want to go." He said this signifying by what kind of death he would glorify God. And when he had said this, he said to him, "Follow me."

Feed My Sheep

In Luke's Gospel, the call of Peter, James, and John takes place toward the beginning of Jesus' ministry and follows a miraculous catch of fish. Today, at the end of John's Gospel, we have another catch of fish and a renewed call to Simon Peter: "Feed my sheep." Peter had encountered Jesus at the beginning when his brother Andrew came to him and said he had found the Messiah (John 2:41). Peter decided to follow Jesus even then. But in the beginning, he didn't know everything that entailed. He wasn't aware that Jesus' path would bring him to crucifixion. In this second call story Jesus asks his question of an older and wiser Peter, who knows exactly what being a disciple means. This renewed call comes in three parts. The questions come first. Jesus asks, "Do you love me," not once but three times. Peter seemed to be frustrated by the end. "You know I love you!" Each time Jesus responded with a command—the second part of the call: "Feed my sheep." Jesus won't turn over the flock of the Lord to anyone who doesn't love them. Finally, Jesus lays everything out for Peter. When Peter was young, he could go where he wanted, but now "someone else will dress you and lead you where you do not want to go." Being a disciple means giving over your life to God. The invitation, and the last part of the call is immediate: "Follow me."

The Name of Jesus

After the resurrection and the coming of the Holy Spirit, the disciples preached to anyone who would listen and quite a few who would not. They could do no less for the Good News of forgiveness through Christ who filled them. The religious leaders worried about being blamed for Jesus' death and had their doubts about the teaching on the resurrection—it was not a widely held belief, and these men claimed to witness just such a thing. The leaders felt they had to stop what the disciples were doing. Our reading today doesn't record the argument in the Sanhedrin (the court of the high priest). But one rabbi, Gamaliel, urged the others not to kill the disciples but to let them go. He knew that if their preaching came from God, they wouldn't stop, and the Sanhedrin would find itself fighting against God. The other rabbis and the chief priest decided to have the disciples flogged and ordered not to preach in the name of Jesus. Gamaliel was right. The disciples didn't stop teaching and felt proud to have been dishonored for Jesus' sake.

The disciples couldn't wait to tell the story of Jesus' exaltation and his place in heaven as leader and Savior of Israel. Their proclamation is echoed in the heavenly vision of John in Revelation. John sees the angels, the elders, the four living creatures and every creature in heaven and on earth united in glorious praise to Jesus, the Lamb on the throne. There they fell and worshiped him. (See Ezekiel 1:2–13 for a description of the creatures, who ultimately became associated with the four evangelists.)

Third Sunday of Easter, Year C

Good News for All of Us

We are loved by God and called to be his people. Our response to that call begins with baptism. In our first imaginations about what we will be when we are children, God is forming us to be his instruments in the world. But there are many paths to discipleship, and we don't walk in the same one as anyone else. Andrew's invitation to discipleship was simply, "Come and...see (John 1:39)." Peter was called at the beginning of Jesus' ministry in Matthew's Gospel: "Come, I will make you fishers of men (Matthew 4:19)." He's called again at the end of John's story: "Follow me." The truth is, God calls us every day, because every day we change. We don't always know the specifics of God's call, but Jesus once said not to worry that we didn't know our way, because Jesus, himself, is the way (John 14:6). If we keep our eyes on him, we cannot go wrong.

Questions for Reflection and Discussion

> ➤ If someone told you that you will stretch out your hands, and someone else will dress you and lead you where you do not want to go, and then told you to follow him, would you do it?

> ➤ Has someone ever told you to stop doing something that you felt you had to do? Were there consequences for your actions?

Related Journey of Faith Lesson

M5, "Our Call to Holiness"

Themes

End Times, Glory
    M5, "Our Call to Holiness"

READING 1, ACTS 13:14, 43–52

Paul and Barnabas continued on from Perga and reached Antioch in Pisidia. On the sabbath they entered the synagogue and took their seats. Many Jews and worshipers who were converts to Judaism followed Paul and Barnabas, who spoke to them and urged them to remain faithful to the grace of God. On the following sabbath almost the whole city gathered to hear the word of the Lord. When the Jews saw the crowds, they were filled with jealousy and with violent abuse contradicted what Paul said. Both Paul and Barnabas spoke out boldly and said, "It was necessary that the word of God be spoken to you first, but since you reject it and condemn yourselves as unworthy of eternal life, we now turn to the Gentiles. For so the Lord has commanded us, 'I have made you a light to the Gentiles, that you may be an instrument of salvation to the ends of the earth.'" The Gentiles were delighted when they heard this and glorified the word of the Lord. All who were destined for eternal life came to believe, and the word of the Lord continued to spread through the whole region. The Jews, however, incited the women of prominence who were worshipers and the leading men of the city, stirred up a persecution against Paul and Barnabas, and expelled them from their territory. So they shook the dust from their feet in protest against them, and went to Iconium. The disciples were filled with joy and the Holy Spirit.

PSALM 100:1–2, 3, 5

READING 2, REVELATION 7:9, 14B–17

I, John, had a vision of a great multitude, which no one could count, from every nation, race, people, and tongue. They stood before the throne and before the Lamb, wearing white robes and holding palm branches in their hands. Then one of the elders said to me, "These are the ones who have survived the time of great distress; they have washed their robes and made them white in the blood of the Lamb. "For this reason, they stand before God's throne and worship him day and night in his temple. The one who sits on the throne will shelter them. They will not hunger or thirst anymore, nor will the sun or any heat strike them. For the Lamb who is in the center of the throne will shepherd them and lead them to springs of life-giving water, and God will wipe away every tear from their eyes."

GOSPEL, JOHN 10:27–30

Jesus said: "My sheep hear my voice; I know them, and they follow me. I give them eternal life, and they shall never perish. No one can take them out of my hand. My Father, who has given them to me, is greater than all, and no one can take them out of the Father's hand. The Father and I are one."

A Light to the Nations

Paul and Barnabas took their call as apostles seriously. *Apostle* means "messenger," or "one sent forth." They understood Jesus to have sent them out to preach to every person. This wasn't always easy, as we see from today's reading. While many people came to believe in Jesus Christ because of their preaching, many others rejected their message. Those who were in power might have been afraid of losing it. Others were not convinced of what they were saying. Whenever people are threatened, they usually react by running away or turning to fight. In today's reading, the Jewish authorities and other influential people decided to persecute the apostles for their message.

Why didn't Paul and Barnabas simply stop preaching where they weren't wanted? The answer was easy, for they remembered one of Isaiah's prophecies about the servant of the Lord: "I will make you a light to the nations, that my salvation may reach to the ends of the earth" (Isaiah 49:6b). This was their call, and it came from Jesus.

Springs of Living Water

One of the purposes of apocalyptic literature is to encourage a persecuted people to stay strong in faith because God will win the battle. John's description of heaven in the second reading envisions more people than we can count from every nation, tribe, and tongue. In a world that is often rocked by division, it is sometimes hard to imagine a place where everyone can come together in mutual love and respect. In John's vision, every person stands before the Lamb of God (Jesus) wearing and carrying the symbols of victory and joy (white robes and palm branches). John learns these are the persecuted Christians who will now experience joy forever in the heavenly temple because the Lamb will be their shepherd and lead them to springs of living water. John's language in the last few lines can be found in another prophecy of Isaiah which details what the day of the Lord will be like for those who are faithful (25:6–8).

The Flock of the Lord

Two shepherding images grace our Scriptures today. In the short Psalm 100, we remember that we belong to the Lord. "We are his people, the flock he shepherds." There is no more appropriate response than to offer praise and thanksgiving in the temple. The second image comes from the Gospel at the very end of Jesus' lesson on the good Shepherd. Three important phrases stand out. "My Sheep hear my voice…and they follow me," "No one will snatch them out of my hand," and "The Father and I are one." In one of the shortest passages in our *Lectionary*, Jesus manages to convey his love and connection with his flock, his connection with the Father who has entrusted the flock to him, and the protection the flock enjoys because of his connection to the Father. John was written about twenty-five years after the other Gospels. Early Church leaders were beginning to articulate their belief that Christ is God more and more, so there are a few places where our Lord says clearly: I and the Father are one. That's good news for those of us who are sheep.

Good News for All of Us

At the end of Matthew's Gospel, Jesus says: "I am with you always, until the end of the age" (Matthew 28:20). Jesus has promised he will be with us in our joy and sorrow, in times of trouble, in war and in peace. We find that hope expressed in the decision of the apostles to keep preaching, even if they have to move on; in John's vision of a glorious end for those who suffer, and in Jesus' assurance that his flock is safe. When we look at the long history of the Catholic Church, and we wonder how the Church continues to exist in spite of crusades, inquisitions, the time there were three popes, schisms, the abuse crisis, and more, we have only to remember that Christ is alive now in this body of the Church. We see the evidence in the lives of saints, in those who work for justice, and in those who treat others with dignity and respect every day.

Questions for Reflection and Discussion

➤ *Have you ever felt the need to speak up for someone or something, knowing that someone would object?*

➤ *Is it OK to tell people they shouldn't mind suffering because they will get their reward in heaven?*

Related Journey of Faith Lesson

M2, "The Role of the Laity"

Themes

Discipleship
    M2, "The Role of the Laity"
Scripture
    Q7, "Your Prayer Life"

READING 1, ACTS 14:21–27

After Paul and Barnabas had proclaimed the good news to that city and made a considerable number of disciples, they returned to Lystra and to Iconium and to Antioch. They strengthened the spirits of the disciples and exhorted them to persevere in the faith, saying, "It is necessary for us to undergo many hardships to enter the kingdom of God." They appointed elders for them in each church and, with prayer and fasting, commended them to the Lord in whom they had put their faith. Then they traveled through Pisidia and reached Pamphylia. After proclaiming the word at Perga they went down to Attalia. From there they sailed to Antioch, where they had been commended to the grace of God for the work they had now accomplished. And when they arrived, they called the church together and reported what God had done with them and how he had opened the door of faith to the Gentiles.

PSALM 145:8–9, 10–11, 12–13

READING 2, REVELATION 21:1–5A

Then I, John, saw a new heaven and a new earth. The former heaven and the former earth had passed away, and the sea was no more. I also saw the holy city, a new Jerusalem, coming down out of heaven from God, prepared as a bride adorned for her husband. I heard a loud voice from the throne saying,
"Behold, God's dwelling is with the human race. He will dwell with them and they will be his people and God himself will always be with them as their God. He will wipe every tear from their eyes, and there shall be no more death or mourning, wailing or pain, for the old order has passed away." The One who sat on the throne said, "Behold, I make all things new."

GOSPEL, JOHN 13:31–33A, 34–35

When Judas had left them, Jesus said, "Now is the Son of Man glorified, and God is glorified in him. If God is glorified in him, God will also glorify him in himself, and God will glorify him at once. My children, I will be with you only a little while longer. I give you a new commandment: love one another. As I have loved you, so you also should love one another. This is how all will know that you are my disciples, if you have love for one another."

A New Life

In the heady days following the resurrection and the coming of the Holy Spirit, the apostles could not contain their excitement. They preached their message of Jesus everywhere they could. Those they told, told others. The Book of Acts is filled with phrases like, "They added 4,000 to their number in a single day." The work wasn't always easy. Not everyone accepted what they said and more than a few would have them persecuted, jailed, and even killed for their words. But these men and women considered persecution an honor for the privilege of telling Jesus' story. The new life they felt so deeply could not be quenched. The gospel was a gift that "opened the door to faith for the Gentiles," and, in each place, from among the disciples who were baptized, they appointed elders who would carry on their work in the local house church.

Making All Things New

In a time of persecution and grief, hope comes from a deep confidence that this will not last forever and God will reign. John's vision at the end of Revelation is one of the most popular readings for funerals when the families and friends gather, both rejoicing and crying, as they recall God's promise that death and mourning shall cease, and all will gather as one with God. The vision itself is an echo of Isaiah 25, which pictures a great banquet at the end of all things. John adds his own touch. This is the heavenly city ready to live with God as a bride, and God himself promises to dwell with them as their God, continuing to make all things new. We celebrate that message in our psalm response—a glorious praise of God.

A New Commandment

Just before he goes to Jerusalem, Jesus gives an extended teaching to his disciples. John tends to repeat words and phrases, particularly when he talks about Jesus and the Father. This reading is no exception as John talks about the glorification of the Father in the Son. In this way, John emphasizes the intimacy between Jesus and the Father. Even in John's language, the Father and Jesus are one. But the movement here helps us focus on Jesus' new commandment: "Love one another." And here Jesus repeats the word as he talks about the intimacy between the disciples and Jesus. "Just as I have loved you, you also should love one another." Jesus and the Father are one in a way we cannot be. But Jesus wants everyone to know that we are his disciples. He encourages us to find that bond in our love for Jesus and for others.

Good News for All of Us

In baptism, we become a new creation. What does that mean for us? Do we live every day rejoicing in the new life God gives us? Truthfully, many of us probably don't think about our baptisms every day or the grace we are given to choose God in every moment. But it is exciting when adults get baptized at the Easter vigil. We recognize that they made a personal commitment because they desired to worship God through the Catholic community. Families rejoice when they welcome their children to the Church in baptism as well. At Easter and at infant baptisms, we recite the Creed together. We pray that God will renew the grace of baptism in each of us. And if we are filled with joy, it might just break out, into love for one another, into invitation for others to come, into a fight for justice on behalf of the marginalized. They'll know we are Christians then—walking together with Jesus.

Questions for Reflection and Discussion

> ➤ When was the last time you shared something about your faith with someone else? What did you share and why?

> ➤ From the cartoon strip Peanuts, Linus said, "I love mankind, it's people I can't stand." Is Jesus' command to love one another realistic? Are there limits to love?

Related Journey of Faith Lesson

M1, "Conversion: A Lifelong Process"

Themes

Faith
    M1, "Conversion: A Lifelong Process"
Love
    M5, "Our Call to Holiness"

Sixth Sunday of Easter, Year C

READING 1, ACTS 15:1–2, 22–29

Some who had come down from Judea were instructing the brothers, "Unless you are circumcised according to the Mosaic practice, you cannot be saved." Because there arose no little dissension and debate by Paul and Barnabas with them, it was decided that Paul, Barnabas, and some of the others should go up to Jerusalem to the apostles and elders about this question. The apostles and elders, in agreement with the whole church, decided to choose representatives and to send them to Antioch with Paul and Barnabas. The ones chosen were Judas, who was called Barsabbas, and Silas, leaders among the brothers. This is the letter delivered by them: "The apostles and the elders, your brothers, to the brothers in Antioch, Syria, and Cilicia of Gentile origin: greetings. Since we have heard that some of our number who went out without any mandate from us have upset you with their teachings and disturbed your peace of mind, we have with one accord decided to choose representatives and to send them to you along with our beloved Barnabas and Paul, who have dedicated their lives to the name of our Lord Jesus Christ. So we are sending Judas and Silas who will also convey this same message by word of mouth: 'It is the decision of the Holy Spirit and of us not to place on you any burden beyond these necessities, namely, to abstain from meat sacrificed to idols, from blood, from meats of strangled animals, and from unlawful marriage. If you keep free of these, you will be doing what is right. Farewell.'"

PSALM 67:2–3, 5, 6, 8

READING 2, REVELATION 21:10–14, 22–23

The angel took me in spirit to a great, high mountain and showed me the holy city Jerusalem coming down out of heaven from God. It gleamed with the splendor of God. Its radiance was like that of a precious stone, like jasper, clear as crystal. It had a massive, high wall, with twelve gates where twelve angels were stationed and on which names were inscribed, the names of the twelve tribes of the Israelites.

There were three gates facing east, three north, three south, and three west. The wall of the city had twelve courses of stones as its foundation, on which were inscribed the twelve names of the twelve apostles of the Lamb. I saw no temple in the city for its temple is the Lord God almighty and the Lamb. The city had no need of sun or moon to shine on it, for the glory of God gave it light, and its lamp was the Lamb.

GOSPEL, JOHN 14:23–29

Jesus said to his disciples: "Whoever loves me will keep my word, and my Father will love him, and we will come to him and make our dwelling with him. Whoever does not love me does not keep my words; yet the word you hear is not mine but that of the Father who sent me. "I have told you this while I am with you. The Advocate, the Holy Spirit, whom the Father will send in my name, will teach you everything and remind you of all that I told you. Peace I leave with you; my peace I give to you. Not as the world gives do I give it to you. Do not let your hearts be troubled or afraid. You heard me tell you, 'I am going away and I will come back to you.' If you loved me, you would rejoice that I am going to the Father; for the Father is greater than I. And now I have told you this before it happens, so that when it happens you may believe."

Twelve Gates into the City

Throughout the Old Testament, Jerusalem, the city of David, is the center of religious life because the temple was located there. After Solomon built the temple, God said: "I have heard the prayer of petition which you offered in my presence. I have consecrated this house which you have built and I set my name there forever; my eyes and my heart shall be there always" (1 Kings 9:3). It should come as no surprise, then, that John's vision of heaven in Revelation is the holy city more beautiful and life-filled than it had ever been. At the time Revelation was written, the temple had been destroyed for the second time. John incorporated that into his vision, telling the people there was no need for a temple because the temple is the Lord and the Lamb.

The question of who gets into the heavenly city concerns everyone. John's vision of the twelve gates represents the twelve tribes of Israel. The Messiah was to unite the twelve tribes so that there would be one flock, but by the time John wrote his vision, that unification had already expanded to include the Gentiles. The heavenly city has room for all people who follow the way of the Lord, no matter which direction they come from.

Who Can Be Saved?

The great debate at the first Council of Jerusalem was whether Gentiles had to be circumcised in order to be baptized. After prayer and discussion (and there were good people on both sides), the apostles and elders (and the Holy Spirit) reached a consensus that circumcision was not required of Gentiles. You can read about the council in the section of Acts 15 we miss here. But it's important to know that in Acts 2:11, Peter says "we are saved through the grace of the Lord Jesus." The letter that they send to the Gentiles calms their fears and presents a united front. Circumcision is not necessary, but the Gentiles must abstain from certain practices. In the Church today, you may encounter people who insist that you can only pray a certain way, say certain words, or use certain gestures, or you are "doing it wrong." While the Church does have rules to follow and works hard to help us form conscience, there is far more leeway when it comes to prayer and gestures of reverence than you might imagine. If you have a question, don't hesitate to ask your priest or another pastoral minister for advice.

We encounter the same issues in the world. When people form extreme opinions on topics, they tend to demonize those who don't agree, preferring to listen only to their own points of view and refusing to be persuaded to anything else. Many of us remember the fight about wearing masks during the pandemic. An invitation to dialogue and accompaniment, which Pope Francis advocates, is one solution to the problem. We might find that many more can be saved than we think, because it was never us who was doing the saving.

Good News for All of Us

The Gospel returns us to the last discourse of Jesus and his promise to send the Holy Spirit. Here we get another look at the mission of the Holy Spirit—to be an advocate—one who speaks on behalf of another, and a teacher, who will teach us everything and remind us of what Jesus said. The Holy Spirit even now enlivens the Church for its mission and brings peace to the most troubled heart. Because of the Holy Spirit, the Church has endured for more than 2,000 years and continues to bear witness to Christ today. We are blessed indeed. Come, Holy Spirit, fill the hearts of your people.

Questions for Reflection and Discussion

➤ *One of the joys of the internet is that we can find almost anything we want to know. One of the challenges of the internet is we can find a lot of misinformation. Have you ever read a report or article that claimed to be true, but really wasn't? How do you determine what's truthful or factual, and is thus worthy of your time?*

➤ *People have a stereotype of the street preacher coming up and asking, "Are you saved?" What would be your answer to that question?*

Related Journey of Faith Lesson

M8, "Evangelization"

Themes

Hope
    M1, "Conversion: A Lifelong Process"
Perseverance
    Q7, "Your Prayer Life"
Tolerance
    M8, "Evangelization"

Seventh Sunday of Easter, Year C

READING 1, ACTS 7:55–60

Stephen, filled with the Holy Spirit, looked up intently to heaven and saw the glory of God and Jesus standing at the right hand of God, and Stephen said, "Behold, I see the heavens opened and the Son of Man standing at the right hand of God." But they cried out in a loud voice, covered their ears, and rushed upon him together. They threw him out of the city and began to stone him. The witnesses laid down their cloaks at the feet of a young man named Saul. As they were stoning Stephen, he called out, "Lord Jesus, receive my spirit." Then he fell to his knees and cried out in a loud voice, "Lord, do not hold this sin against them;" and when he said this, he fell asleep.

PSALM 97:1–2, 6–7, 9

READING 2, REVELATION 22:12–14, 16–17, 20

I, John, heard a voice saying to me: "Behold, I am coming soon. I bring with me the recompense I will give to each according to his deeds. I am the Alpha and the Omega, the first and the last, the beginning and the end." Blessed are they who wash their robes so as to have the right to the tree of life and enter the city through its gates. "I, Jesus, sent my angel to give you this testimony for the churches. I am the root and offspring of David, the bright morning star." The Spirit and the bride say, "Come." Let the hearer say, "Come." Let the one who thirsts come forward, and the one who wants it receive the gift of life-giving water. The one who gives this testimony says, "Yes, I am coming soon." Amen! Come, Lord Jesus!

GOSPEL, JOHN 17:20–26

Lifting up his eyes to heaven, Jesus prayed saying: "Holy Father, I pray not only for them, but also for those who will believe in me through their word, so that they may all be one, as you, Father, are in me and I in you, that they also may be in us, that the world may believe that you sent me. And I have given them the glory you gave me, so that they may be one, as we are one, I in them and you in me, that they may be brought to perfection as one, that the world may know that you sent me, and that you loved them even as you loved me. Father, they are your gift to me. I wish that where I am they also may be with me, that they may see my glory that you gave me, because you loved me before the foundation of the world.

Righteous Father, the world also does not know you, but I know you, and they know that you sent me. I made known to them your name and I will make it known that the love with which you loved me may be in them and I in them."

Come, Lord Jesus

The end of the Revelation to John uses words and images we find at the beginning. Jesus identifies himself as the Alpha and Omega, the beginning and the end. He blesses those "who have washed their robes," by which he means the martyrs and those who have suffered persecution for the sake of Jesus, and we hear about the tree of life and the city with the gates. As Jesus speaks there is no doubt that he is the long-awaited Messiah descended from the house of David and the one whom the prophets foretold.

The early Church continued to think that Jesus was coming again very soon to usher in the reign of God. Two invitations are issued at the end of the second reading. The first is to all who thirst to come and take the water of life. The world was invited to be baptized. The second is a plea as much as an invitation and is addressed to Jesus himself. "Amen! Come, Lord Jesus."

A Witness for Faith

In the great persecutions of the Jews in the second century before Christ, those who chose to die, rather than violate the Law came to be held in high esteem. We hear some of their stories in 2 Maccabees, and they are included in our *Lectionary*. The early Christians felt the same way about their persecuted brothers and sisters. The ones who died were called martyrs, from the Greek word for witness. Stephen, whose death is recorded in our first reading, reports seeing Jesus (the Son of Man) standing in judgment at God's right hand. When Stephen gives up his spirit to Jesus and forgives his tormentors, he reminds us of Jesus in Luke's story of the crucifixion. That wasn't an accident. All the disciples worked hard to be like the master they served.

That We May All Be One

Once again, using repeated words and phrases, John's Gospel describes the unity of relationship between Jesus, the Father, and Jesus' disciples. The passage is part of a prayer Jesus speaks to God. We want to notice that Jesus prays not only for his disciples, but for all those who will follow Jesus because of the disciple's witness and teaching. Fervently Jesus prays that they may be one in Christ and in the Father. How else will the world know the truth of the Incarnation, death, and resurrection? Jesus has the answer. The world will know by the love that is in them.

Good News for All of Us

Jesus indicates that the unity of the Christian Church makes it a witness of God's love to the world. That's a challenge for us today. We have many Christian denominations, each claiming to tell the truth about Jesus and yet practicing different things and espousing different principles for living. But there is hope. Christian churches share a common creed. The Apostles' Creed (and its close relative, the Nicene Creed) lay out the shared beliefs of the followers of Jesus. It's a starting point for unity. Most of our disagreements come in the way we organize our churches and the best way to practice our faith—the things about which the Creed is silent. For decades now, Catholics have gathered with their Anglican and Lutheran brothers and sisters to dialogue about our differences and see if we might find more places of agreement that will perhaps lead to greater unity. And every year, we dedicate a week to pray for Christian unity (usually January 18–25). It's a small but important gesture. In the meantime, the law of love should guide us and bring us ever closer to God.

Questions for Reflection and Discussion

➤ *Why do some Christian churches welcome anyone to share holy Communion while the Catholic Church does not?*

➤ *What would you be willing to die for?*

Related *Journey of Faith* Lesson

M8, "Evangelization"

Themes

Church
    M2, "The Role of the Laity"
Ecumenism
    M8, "Evangelization"

READING 1, ACTS 2:1–11

When the time for Pentecost was fulfilled, they were all in one place together. And suddenly there came from the sky a noise like a strong driving wind, and it filled the entire house in which they were. Then there appeared to them tongues as of fire, which parted and came to rest on each one of them. And they were all filled with the Holy Spirit and began to speak in different tongues, as the Spirit enabled them to proclaim. Now there were devout Jews from every nation under heaven staying in Jerusalem. At this sound, they gathered in a large crowd, but they were confused because each one heard them speaking in his own language. They were astounded, and in amazement they asked, "Are not all these people who are speaking Galileans? Then how does each of us hear them in his native language? We are Parthians, Medes, and Elamites, inhabitants of Mesopotamia, Judea and Cappadocia, Pontus and Asia, Phrygia and Pamphylia, Egypt and the districts of Libya near Cyrene, as well as travelers from Rome, both Jews and converts to Judaism, Cretans and Arabs, yet we hear them speaking in our own tongues of the mighty acts of God."

PSALM 104:1, 24, 29–30, 31, 34

READING 2, 1 CORINTHIANS 12:3B–7, 12–13

Brothers and sisters: No one can say, "Jesus is Lord," except by the Holy Spirit. There are different kinds of spiritual gifts but the same Spirit; there are different forms of service but the same Lord; there are different workings but the same God who produces all of them in everyone. To each individual the manifestation of the Spirit is given for some benefit. As a body is one though it has many parts, and all the parts of the body, though many, are one body, so also Christ. For in one Spirit, we were all baptized into one body, whether Jews or Greeks, slaves or free persons, and we were all given to drink of one Spirit.

GOSPEL, JOHN 20:19–23

On the evening of that first day of the week, when the doors were locked, where the disciples were, for fear of the Jews, Jesus came and stood in their midst and said to them, "Peace be with you."

When he had said this, he showed them his hands and his side. The disciples rejoiced when they saw the Lord. Jesus said to them again, "Peace be with you. As the Father has sent me, so I send you." And when he had said this, he breathed on them and said to them, "Receive the Holy Spirit. Whose sins you forgive are forgiven them, and whose sins you retain are retained."

The Gift of the Holy Spirit

Fifty days after Easter Sunday, the Church celebrates the fulfillment of Jesus' promise to send the Holy Spirit, the ongoing living presence of Christ in the Church. We often call it the birthday of the Church, when, in wind and fire, the Spirit transforms a small group of disciples into missionaries who carried the message of the Good News. It's often assumed that only the twelve were in the upper room, but Luke is vague on this. Just before the passage we read today, he clearly states that those praying together included the twelve as well as Mary, the mother of Jesus along with some of the women and his brothers (Acts 1:14). The story is interrupted to talk about the selection of Judas' replacement and, when Luke picks up the narrative, Luke simply says they were all together in one place. We don't know exactly where it was and exactly who was there. But it is clear that, filled with the Spirit, the apostles immediately began to preach the gospel and, in such a way, that all who heard it could understand. What they heard that day was the proclamation of God's mighty power.

When the apostles began to preach about Jesus, Luke records that each person heard them in their own language. This is either because the apostles spoke in different tongues, or because the Spirit gave the gift of interpretation of tongues to the crowds who heard the first preaching. When the prophet Joel prophesied about the Day of the Lord, God spoke to him saying: "I will pour out my spirit upon all flesh" (Joel 3:1). Whether the Spirit was given only to the Twelve Apostles or to the whole world on Pentecost, the effects were immediate. Paul would go on to say that the Spirit gives even the gift of faith to say, "Jesus is Lord." And from Paul's letters, we are aware that the gifts of preaching, teaching, prophecy, healing, administration, speaking in tongues, and interpreting tongues, among others are given to the members of the community as the Spirit wills and for the common good. Paul's organic analogy for the early Church, the body of Christ, suggests that all of us have something to give to the whole.

The Breath of the Holy Spirit

In a striking contrast to the wind and fire of the first reading, the Gospel reading repeats a passage we have heard before. John does not have a Pentecost story like Luke. Here Jesus comes on the evening of the first day to stand quietly among them, wish them peace, and breathe the Holy Spirit into them. For John, the Holy Spirit enables the disciples to pass on the gifts of peace and the forgiveness of sins, as Christ did during his ministry. Not every manifestation of the Spirit is a fiery showstopper. The gifts of the Spirit can be as quiet as a peaceful heart, and as loving as forgiveness offered to the sinner. We cannot lift up one as more important than another. Rather, we must remember that each is given so that we might be drawn closer to God.

Good News for All of Us

The Holy Spirit is still active in the Church today, guiding us, keeping us safe, and helping to provide any course correction we might need. The gifts of the Spirit are active too in every member of the Church, lay and ordained members. Many have heard the call to serve the people of God in a variety of ministries. Still others understand their mission to witness to the love of God in the workplace, in school, or in the home. In each case, the Spirit gives the graces necessary to live a life in such a way that it is evident that God is in the world. By using the gifts, we have been given, we can show others and tell them of the power of God's love for all of us.

Questions for Reflection and Discussion

> *What gifts do you think the Holy Spirit has given you? You can find some lists in Romans 12:1-11, 1 Corinthians 12:7–10, 27–31, and Ephesians 4:11–13. Recognize that there may be other gifts that are not named here.*

> *How do you embrace and use those gifts?*

Related Journey of Faith Lesson

M4, "Discernment"

Themes

Body of Christ
    M7, "Family Life"
Holy Spirit
    M4, "Discernment"
Witness
    M8, "Evangelization"

READING 1, PROVERBS 8:22-31

Thus says the wisdom of God: "The LORD possessed me, the beginning of his ways, the forerunner of his prodigies of long ago; from of old I was poured forth, at the first, before the earth. When there were no depths I was brought forth, when there were no fountains or springs of water; before the mountains were settled into place, before the hills, I was brought forth; while as yet the earth and fields were not made, nor the first clods of the world. When the Lord established the heavens, I was there, when he marked out the vault over the face of the deep; when he made firm the skies above, when he fixed fast the foundations of the earth; when he set for the sea its limit, so that the waters should not transgress his command; then was I beside him as his craftsman, and I was his delight day by day, playing before him all the while, playing on the surface of his earth; and I found delight in the human race."

PSALM 8:4–5, 6–7, 8–9

READING 2, ROMANS 5:1–5

Brothers and sisters: Therefore, since we have been justified by faith, we have peace with God through our Lord Jesus Christ, through whom we have gained access by faith to this grace in which we stand, and we boast in hope of the glory of God. Not only that, but we even boast of our afflictions, knowing that affliction produces endurance, and endurance, proven character, and proven character, hope, and hope does not disappoint, because the love of God has been poured out into our hearts through the Holy Spirit that has been given to us.

GOSPEL, JOHN 16:12–15

Jesus said to his disciples: "I have much more to tell you, but you cannot bear it now. But when he comes, the Spirit of truth, he will guide you to all truth. He will not speak on his own, but he will speak what he hears, and will declare to you the things that are coming. He will glorify me, because he will take from what is mine and declare it to you. Everything that the Father has is mine; for this reason I told you that he will take from what is mine and declare it to you."

God's Love Poured into Our Hearts

Most of the priests I know have a healthy respect of Trinitarian doctrine and a little bit of concern that they will not do justice to the mystery when they preach on Trinity Sunday. It's a challenging task, but over the years, a couple of things have stood out in the best homilies I've heard. The first is the idea of relationship—God is a relationship in and of himself. We grasp pieces of the relationship when we think about the Father, Son, and Holy Spirit, but we understand God to be all of these "persons," loving and giving love for all eternity. We go out of our way to think of analogies that express the intimacy and efficacy of the Trinity. For some the Father is Love who pours out the Beloved (Son) and the love between them is the Holy Spirit. (See Bishop Robert Barron's video on the Holy Spirit.) Still others talk about the source, the river that flows from it, and the wellspring which bubbles up and flows out. Both images try to capture both the oneness and the "threeness" of persons in God. The truth is, though, our language is still somewhat impoverished when it comes to talking about this mystery. We have to remember that a mystery is that about which there is always more to know. Our readings today get us started by talking about the loving relationship that is God and about the way that love spills out into our own hearts.

The Artisan

Our reading from Proverbs presents a delightful picture of *Wisdom* (in Greek, *Sophia*, and in Hebrew, *Hokhmah*). As we hear the reading, we catch phrases that sound like they might describe Jesus: "When he established the heavens, there was I...When he fixed the foundations of the earth, then was I beside him as an artisan...having my delight with human beings." Recall the beginning of John's Gospel: In the beginning was the Word...He was in the beginning with God. All things came to be through him, and without him nothing came to be (John 1:2–3). John borrowed the language about Wisdom to talk about Jesus. For John, Jesus was the artisan (or, in another translation, the master builder). For the early Church, Jesus was always in the picture. Saint Paul, in his Letter to the Romans describes that gift slightly differently. For Paul, Jesus gives access to the grace and peace of God, which allows Paul to describe even suffering as an opportunity to enter more deeply into faith. Jesus suffered and was raised from the dead, showing us that physical death is not the end of all things but an entrance fully into the new life begun in us at baptism. This is our hope, born in God's love that is poured through the Holy Spirit.

Good News for All of Us

We are not alone. Just before his death, Jesus told his disciples that there was much more he wanted to say. But he recognized that they would not be able to fully understand it at the time. That too is the nature of mystery. We grasp it in pieces, and over the whole of our lives. To that end Jesus promised to send the Spirit of truth who will guide us into the truth and teach us everything God (who is Father, Son and Holy Spirit) wants us to know. We are not alone. The Spirit is with us even now in this community we call Church. And we walk together into the mystery that is God.

Questions for Reflection and Discussion

> ➤ *If someone asked you about the Trinity, what images would you use?*

> ➤ *God lives the divine life in relationship. If we are made in the image of God, what does that tell us about our lives?*

Related *Journey of Faith* Lesson

Q3, "The Holy Trinity"

Themes

Trinity
    Q2, "What Is Faith?"
    Q3, "The Holy Trinity"
    M4, "Discernment"
Truth
    M1, "Conversion: A Lifelong Process"
    Q13, "The Church as Community"
Wisdom
    M5, "Our Call to Holiness"

READING 1, GENESIS 14:18–20

In those days, Melchizedek, king of Salem, brought out bread and wine, and being a priest of God Most High, he blessed Abram with these words: "Blessed be Abram by God Most High, the creator of heaven and earth; and blessed be God Most High, who delivered your foes into your hand." Then Abram gave him a tenth of everything.

PSALM 110:1, 2, 3, 4

READING 2, CORINTHIANS 11:23-26

Brothers and sisters: I received from the Lord what I also handed on to you, that the Lord Jesus, on the night he was handed over, took bread, and, after he had given thanks, broke it and said, "This is my body that is for you. Do this in remembrance of me." In the same way also the cup, after supper, saying, "This cup is the new covenant in my blood. Do this, as often as you drink it, in remembrance of me." For as often as you eat this bread and drink the cup, you proclaim the death of the Lord until he comes.

GOSPEL, LUKE 9:11B–17

Jesus spoke to the crowds about the kingdom of God, and he healed those who needed to be cured. As the day was drawing to a close, the Twelve approached him and said, "Dismiss the crowd so that they can go to the surrounding villages and farms and find lodging and provisions; for we are in a deserted place here." He said to them, "Give them some food yourselves." They replied, "Five loaves and two fish are all we have, unless we ourselves go and buy food for all these people." Now the men there numbered about five thousand. Then he said to his disciples, "Have them sit down in groups of about fifty." They did so and made them all sit down. Then taking the five loaves and the two fish, and looking up to heaven, he said the blessing over them, broke them, and gave them to the disciples to set before the crowd. They all ate and were satisfied. And when the leftover fragments were picked up, they filled twelve wicker baskets.

Taken, Blessed, Broken, Given

There aren't many stories of Jesus that are common to all the Gospels. One of the few is the feeding of the 5,000. Each Gospel tells the story in its own way. The emphasis is often on the little amount of bread available in contrast to the large crowd who must be fed. It was a miracle that stood out for everyone who experienced it. But if we look closer, every one of the Gospels describes Jesus' actions in the same way. He takes bread, blesses it, breaks it, and gives it to the disciples to hand out. Those actions are at the heart of the Eucharist and at the heart of our spiritual life. In the Eucharist, the bread that is taken up becomes the Body and Blood, soul and divinity of Jesus Christ. The wine becomes his Blood. We eat and drink what we will become—the body of Christ. In our spiritual lives, it is we who are taken up into God's love, blessed into existence, broken open by our suffering and the suffering of others, and given to the world to be a sign of God's presence and an instrument of God's justice. What God has given to us is enough to share with everyone and all will be satisfied.

In Remembrance of Me

We hear the passage from Corinthians on Holy Thursday, as well as today. Paul recalls the Last Supper, and the actions are the same as in the feeding of the 5,000. Jesus takes bread, blesses it, breaks it, and gives it to those gathered. Paul hands on the faith by telling the story again and adding the command to "do this in remembrance of me." Memory is one of the most important concepts in the Bible. When God remembers, God acts. When we remember, we can choose our course of action again. To participate in the Eucharist in memory of Jesus is to place ourselves at the Last Supper again, to eat the Body and Blood of Christ, and to choose to follow him to the cross and beyond. In the famous Da Vinci painting of the Last Supper, Jesus and all the disciples are on one side of the table. At Mass, we are on the other side of the table, watching and praying as Christ prepares the feast. That's why we must gather, at least once a week, to hear the story again, to remember, and to do what Jesus commanded so that we can go out and hand the story on to others.

Bread and Wine—An Ancient Symbol

In ancient Israel, bread, wine, and oil were the dietary staples for the people and considered a gift of God. Their significance made it natural for the Israelites to incorporate them into religious ritual and celebratory feasts. The priest, Melchizedek is one of the earliest examples. He comes from Salem (likely Jerusalem) to give thanks when Abraham defeats the four kings (Genesis 14:1–17). Melchizedek shows up in Psalm 110 and in the Letter to the Hebrews where Jesus is referred to as a "priest forever in the order of Melchizedek." The Church uses that phrase during the ordination rite.

Good News for All of Us

It's hard to imagine there was a time when few people received the Eucharist. The Church even made it a rule that Catholics must receive at least once a year during the Easter season. In many churches now, it would be unusual not to receive such a gift every week or even every day. Vatican II called the Eucharist the "source and summit of Christian life." Without it we cannot find the grace and strength to carry on the mission of Jesus. At the Eucharistic table, we become one with Christ and one another. Because of that, we do well to prepare ourselves to receive what Christ freely gives. Prayer, frequent reception of the sacrament of reconciliation, and an open heart are good ways for us to bring our whole self to the Mass, where the grace of what we receive will help us fill the whole world with Good News.

Questions for Reflection and Discussion

➤ *What are some of the reasons you might not receive the Eucharist when you come to Mass?*

➤ *Some Christian Churches have an open communion table where anyone can receive. Why does the Catholic Church insist (with rare exceptions) that people must be baptized Catholic to receive the Eucharist?*

Related Journey of Faith Lesson

Q9, "The Mass"

Themes

Blessing
    Q8, "Catholic Prayers and Practices"
    M3, "Your Spiritual Gifts"
Eucharist
    Q9, "The Mass"
    Q7, "Your Prayer Life"
Food
    M7, "Family Life"

READING 1, 1 KINGS 8:41–43

In those days, Solomon prayed in the temple, saying, "To the foreigner, who is not of your people Israel, but comes from a distant land to honor you—since they will learn of your great name and your mighty hand and your outstretched arm —, when he comes and prays toward this temple, listen from your heavenly dwelling. Do all that foreigner asks of you, that all the peoples of the earth may know your name, may fear you as do your people Israel, and may acknowledge that this temple which I have built is dedicated to your honor."

PSALM 117:1, 2

READING 2, GALATIANS 1:1–2, 6–10

Paul, an apostle not from human beings nor through a human being but through Jesus Christ and God the Father who raised him from the dead, and all the brothers who are with me, to the churches of Galatia. I am amazed that you are so quickly forsaking the one who called you by the grace of Christ for a different gospel—not that there is another. But there are some who are disturbing you and wish to pervert the gospel of Christ. But even if we or an angel from heaven should preach to you a gospel other than the one that we preached to you, let that one be accursed! As we have said before, and now I say again, if anyone preaches to you a gospel other than what you have received, let that one be accursed! Am I now currying favor with humans or with God? Or am I seeking to please people? If I were still trying to please people, I would not be a slave of Christ.

GOSPEL, LUKE 7:1–10

When Jesus had finished all his words to the people, he entered Capernaum. A centurion there had a slave who was ill and about to die, and he was valuable to him. When he heard about Jesus, he sent elders of the Jews to him, asking him to come and save the life of his slave. They approached Jesus and strongly urged him to come, saying, "He deserves to have you do this for him, for he loves our nation and built the synagogue for us." And Jesus went with them, but when he was only a short distance from the house, the centurion sent friends to tell him, "Lord, do not trouble yourself, for I am not worthy to have you enter under my roof. Therefore, I did not consider myself worthy to come to you; but say the word and let my servant be healed. For I too am a person subject to authority, with soldiers subject to me. And I say to one, 'Go,' and he goes; and to another, 'Come here,' and he comes; and to my slave, 'Do this,' and he does it." When Jesus heard this he was amazed at him and, turning, said to the crowd following him, "I tell you, not even in Israel have I found such faith." When the messengers returned to the house, they found the slave in good health.

All Will Know Your Name

We often talk about the things we must do to welcome people in church, invite them to know more about Jesus, and make the faith so attractive they will want to get involved. This is good and right. Solomon, in today's first reading, also wants to make sure God is doing his part. His prayer, as he stands in the newly built temple, is charming. He reminds God that people will hear about the miracles God has done on behalf of Israel and that they might want to come and pray before such a God. His advice? Listen to their prayer and do what they ask so that "all the peoples of the earth may know your name." God probably didn't need that reminder, but Solomon's request also suggests that he is aware that God is God of the whole creation and not just of Israel; that God can show mercy and hear the prayers of foreigners, as well as sinners. The followers of Christ experienced that firsthand as Jesus reached out to foreigners, lepers, and all who were marginalized.

A Different Gospel?

It's easy to get distracted by the many things that claim our attention. Political candidates hope to influence us to vote for them. Advertising campaigns try to convince us that our lives are not worthwhile unless we purchase a particular product. One company promised "More stuff, faster," as if quantity was the key to happiness. And we often fall for a cheap price, the degree from a famous university—even if it's not the best choice for us. We make false gods out of wealth, degrees, the approval of everyone else, and more stuff because someone has told us that's the way to get ahead or to make something of ourselves. In the case of the Galatians, there was a dispute about the correct way to be a Christian. Some were still claiming that converts to Christianity had to follow Mosaic Law regarding circumcision and other things. They cast doubt on Paul's preaching and turned Christians away from apostolic teaching. They placed themselves first and the teachings of Jesus second. They made a false God. In his letter, Paul calls out all who make themselves the center of attention and the sole judge of what's right. There is no other gospel, but what Paul has preached. And there is no Good News unless Jesus is the center of it.

A Faith Such as This

As if to underscore the first reading and its acknowledgment that God is Lord of all, Luke recounts the story of a Centurion—a Roman soldier who understands who Jesus is even more so than the Israelites. His request is simple: "heal my servant." In the mythology of the surrounding nations, one nation's gods did not do favors for another nation. In first-century Capernaum, Jews did not do favors for Romans, but this centurion was different—he had tried to help the Jews. The centurion, hearing what was happening, put his faith in Jesus' power and said the words we repeat at every Mass: "I am not worthy to have you enter under my roof…but say the word and let my servant be healed." The centurion knew Jesus and trusted in his power. Jesus listened to this foreigner and did as he asked. The centurion is an example of faith for all time.

Good News for All of Us

One of the enduring truths of the Gospel is that Jesus Christ came to redeem the world, not just our little part of it. The Gospel of Christ includes everyone who earnestly seeks admission. And God hears the prayers of all who call on him, regardless of who they are. But Jesus sent his disciples out to preach his message to everyone so that all might have a chance to participate fully in his grace. He sends us, too, to carry on his mission in a world sorely in need of it.

Questions for Reflection and Discussion

➤ *There are many people who don't believe in God and yet lead good lives. What do you think guides them? Could God be working through them, anyway? And, if so, why should they become Catholic?*

➤ *What are the false gods that tempt you away from the gospel? How do you resist them?*

Related Journey of Faith Lesson

Q2, "What Is Faith?"

Themes

Discipleship
    Q15, "The Saints"
    M2, "The Role of the Laity"
Faith
    Q2, "What Is Faith?"
    M1, "Conversion: A Lifelong Process"
Universality
    Q13, "The Church as Community"
    M8, "Evangelization"

READING 1, 1 KINGS 17:17–24

Elijah went to Zarephath of Sidon to the house of a widow. The son of the mistress of the house fell sick, and his sickness grew more severe until he stopped breathing. So she said to Elijah, "Why have you done this to me, O man of God? Have you come to me to call attention to my guilt and to kill my son?" Elijah said to her, "Give me your son." Taking him from her lap, he carried the son to the upper room where he was staying, and put him on his bed. Elijah called out to the LORD: "O LORD, my God, will you afflict even the widow with whom I am staying by killing her son?" Then he stretched himself out upon the child three times and called out to the LORD: "O LORD, my God, let the life breath return to the body of this child." The LORD heard the prayer of Elijah; the life breath returned to the child's body and he revived. Taking the child, Elijah brought him down into the house from the upper room and gave him to his mother. Elijah said to her, "See! Your son is alive." The woman replied to Elijah, "Now indeed I know that you are a man of God. The word of the LORD comes truly from your mouth."

PSALM 30:2, 4, 5–6, 11, 12, 13

READING 2, GALATIANS 1:11–19

I want you to know, brothers and sisters, that the gospel preached by me is not of human origin. For I did not receive it from a human being, nor was I taught it, but it came through a revelation of Jesus Christ. For you heard of my former way of life in Judaism, how I persecuted the church of God beyond measure and tried to destroy it, and progressed in Judaism beyond many of my contemporaries among my race, since I was even more a zealot for my ancestral traditions. But when God, who from my mother's womb had set me apart and called me through his grace, was pleased to reveal his Son to me, so that I might proclaim him to the Gentiles, I did not immediately consult flesh and blood, nor did I go up to Jerusalem to those who were apostles before me; rather, I went into Arabia and then returned to Damascus. Then after three years I went up to Jerusalem to confer with Cephas and remained with him for fifteen days. But I did not see any other of the apostles, ONLY James the brother of the Lord.

GOSPEL, LUKE 7:11–17

Jesus journeyed to a city called Nain, and his disciples and a large crowd accompanied him. As he drew near to the gate of the city, a man who had died was being carried out, the only son of his mother, and she was a widow. A large crowd from the city was with her. When the Lord saw her, he was moved with pity for her and said to her, "Do not weep." He stepped forward and touched the coffin; at this the bearers halted, and he said, "Young man, I tell you, arise!" The dead man sat up and began to speak, and Jesus gave him to his mother. Fear seized them all, and they glorified God, exclaiming, "A great prophet has arisen in our midst," and "God has visited his people." This report about him spread through the whole of Judea and in all the surrounding region.

That You May Have Life

The stories of two widows dominate our readings today. In ancient Israel, the loss of a husband and sons was a calamity for the wife left behind. Women traditionally could not own property or support themselves. They lived on the generosity of others. The widow in Elijah's story thinks he has caused the death of her son by bringing her sins to God. It wasn't unusual to think God punished sin in this way. But Elijah prays to God and the child is brought to life. In Luke's Gospel, the mother doesn't know Jesus; he comes on the scene in Nain and simply has compassion on the woman. There is no lying down on the corpse or a great cry to God. Jesus only has to touch the bier and call out to the young man, who rises from the dead. In both stories, the crowd reacts by praising God and acknowledging that Elijah and Jesus are prophets (men of God) who speak the truth of God's power. But it is clear to the reader that Jesus holds even greater power than Elijah.

If either widow or their sons could have written a psalm on the spot, it would have sounded much like Psalm 30. This great response to the first reading gives voice to the gratitude for God's healing power who "brought my soul up from Sheol…and let me live." The psalm praises the Lord, who can turn mourning into dancing and who wants what's best for all his people. The psalmist makes a promise to be forever thankful. The two widows assuredly were.

A Gospel Not of Human Origin

Last week Paul expressed his disappointment that the Galatians were so easily persuaded to follow preaching that was contrary to Jesus' message through Paul. Here, he continues his Letter to the Galatians with a defense of his preaching and his authority. He did not make up the Gospel or decide for himself what it should contain or what part of the Law people must follow to obtain the grace of God. Indeed, for Paul, it is not specific actions that make someone worthy, only faith can do that. Paul proves it by talking about his early life and the persecution of Christians that he undertook so eagerly. The only thing that could counter that was a revelation from Jesus and the recognition that God had called him "before he was born" to a different work—that of preaching to the Gentiles. Those who have read the beginning of Jeremiah's prophecy will recognize a similarity between Paul's words and the words the Lord speaks to Jeremiah (1:4–5). Paul is clear that no human being put words in his mouth. What he does, he does as a servant of God.

Good News for All of Us

When we hear stories about people being raised from the dead, it seems almost too good to be true. We might think, *that was then, and maybe they weren't really dead.* We might wonder where God was when our parents, children, or other loved ones died. We would surely be among those rejoicing if such a miracle did occur. But the point of these stories is to highlight the compassion and power of God in life and in death. In the Creed, we express our hope in that power when we say, "I look forward to the resurrection of the dead and the life of the world to come." What Jesus has shown us is that eternal life through him is the truth and that death is a lie. It isn't that our bodies live forever. Rather, our souls are in the hands of God, where we hope to live for all eternity. That's why we hear so many stories of Catholics who die in peace because they aren't afraid. Instead, they look forward to seeing Jesus in the end.

Questions for Reflection and Discussion

➤ *When loved ones die, we are naturally sad and will miss them. While everyone grieves differently, there are also moments of laughter and joy. What turns our mourning into dancing?*

➤ *What gives you hope in this world and in your life?*

Related Journey of Faith Lesson

Q2, "What Is Faith?"

Themes

Death
    Q2, "What Is Faith?"
    M1, "Conversion: A Lifelong Process"
Healing
    Q8, "Catholic Prayers and Practices"
    M4, "Discernment"
Life
    Q15, "The Saints"
    M5, "Our Call to Holiness"

READING 1, 2 SAMUEL 12:7–10, 13

Nathan said to David: "Thus says the LORD God of Israel: 'I anointed you king of Israel. I rescued you from the hand of Saul. I gave you your lord's house and your lord's wives for your own. I gave you the house of Israel and of Judah. And if this were not enough, I could count up for you still more. Why have you spurned the Lord and done evil in his sight? You have cut down Uriah the Hittite with the sword; you took his wife as your own, and him you killed with the sword of the Ammonites. Now, therefore, the sword shall never depart from your house, because you have despised me and have taken the wife of Uriah to be your wife.' Then David said to Nathan, "I have sinned against the LORD." Nathan answered David: "The LORD on his part has forgiven your sin: you shall not die."

PSALM 32:1–2, 5, 7, 11

READING 2, GALATIANS 2:16, 19–21

Brothers and sisters: We who know that a person is not justified by works of the law but through faith in Jesus Christ, even we have believed in Christ Jesus that we may be justified by faith in Christ and not by works of the law, because by works of the law no one will be justified. For through the law I died to the law, that I might live for God. I have been crucified with Christ; yet I live, no longer I, but Christ lives in me; insofar as I now live in the flesh, I live by faith in the Son of God who has loved me and given himself up for me. I do not nullify the grace of God; for if justification comes through the law, then Christ died for nothing.

GOSPEL, LUKE 7:36—8:3

A Pharisee invited Jesus to dine with him, and he entered the Pharisee's house and reclined at table. Now there was a sinful woman in the city who learned that he was at table in the house of the Pharisee. Bringing an alabaster flask of ointment, she stood behind him at his feet weeping and began to bathe his feet with her tears. Then she wiped them with her hair, kissed them, and anointed them with the ointment.

When the Pharisee who had invited him saw this he said to himself, "If this man were a prophet, he would know who and what sort of woman this is who is touching him, that she is a sinner." Jesus said to him in reply, "Simon, I have something to say to you." "Tell me, teacher, " he said."Two people were in debt to a certain creditor; one owed five hundred days' wages and the other owed fifty. Since they were unable to repay the debt, he forgave it for both. Which of them will love him more?" Simon said in reply, "The one, I suppose, whose larger debt was forgiven." He said to him, "You have judged rightly." Then he turned to the woman and said to Simon, "Do you see this woman? When I entered your house, you did not give me water for my feet, but she has bathed them with her tears and wiped them with her hair. You did not give me a kiss, but she has not ceased kissing my feet since the time I entered. You did not anoint my head with oil, but she anointed my feet with ointment. So I tell you, her many sins have been forgiven because she has shown great love. But the one to whom little is forgiven, loves little." He said to her, "Your sins are forgiven." The others at table said to themselves, "Who is this who even forgives sins?" But he said to the woman, "Your faith has saved you; go in peace." Afterward he journeyed from one town and village to another, preaching and proclaiming the good news of the kingdom of God. Accompanying him were the Twelve and some women who had been cured of evil spirits and infirmities, Mary, called Magdalene, from whom seven demons had gone out, Joanna, the wife of Herod's steward Chuza, Susanna, and many others who provided for them out of their resources.

Surrounded by Forgiveness

In Jewish and Christian history and imagination, King David looms large as the shepherd king from whose line the Messiah would be born. It's often disconcerting to find out that our heroes were also flawed human beings. Our first reading begins in the middle of the story of David and Bathsheba. The young king was taken with the married Bathsheba. The text reads that he "took her" and she became pregnant as a result. To cover up his sin, David orders her husband, Uriah, to the front line of battle where he was killed. When the prophet, Nathan, finds out, he tells David a parable of a powerful man who takes a poor man's sheep. Rightly incensed, David immediately declares the man should be put to death for his deed. Our story picks up with Nathan's reply and God's account of the evil David has done. We would probably agree that David needs to be punished for his sin, and God does so. You can read more about the details in the extended passage from 2 Samuel. But what's remarkable is that David immediately realizes his sin and confesses it. And the Lord does not respond as David did and demand the death of this king. Even though God punishes David harshly, God doesn't kill him. Instead, the Lord "removes" the sin and gives David another chance.

Loved and Forgiven

The Pharisee in Luke's Gospel was concerned about interacting with sinners. He seemed to think the best course of action was to avoid them altogether, partly so as not to be influenced by them and partly to shame them for their sin. We know nothing of the woman who came to Jesus other than what the narrator tells us—she is a sinner. Some would have you believe it was Mary Magdalene, but there is no evidence for that in the Scripture itself. Two things are important to see. The woman bathes Jesus' feet, dries them, and kisses them

in reverence—a loving gesture the Pharisee could not bring himself to do. The second is that Jesus holds the woman up as an example of someone who knows she was a sinner and has been forgiven (which is why she could love Jesus as she did) in contrast to the Pharisee, who probably didn't think he had any sins that needed forgiving and therefore had no experience of the love that God gives that he could pass on. The words Jesus speaks to the woman are for the benefit of those at the table who wonder who he is who can forgive sin.

No Longer I Alone, but Christ in Me

Saint Paul writes one of his most famous lines in his Letter to the Galatians. When he was baptized, Paul experienced himself as an utterly new person who was bound to and justified by Jesus Christ, whom Paul identifies as one who "has loved me and given himself up for me." That free gift of love allows Paul and every Christian to live in this world but not be subject to it. The only law to follow is the law of Christ.

Good News for All of Us

Forgiveness is an expression of God's love and care. It is not a license to do whatever we want because God will take care of it. We must strive to live according to Christ's law of love, which includes passing that love and forgiveness on to others. But we know that we are subject to human weakness, and temptation can get the better of us. When it does, we can be like David and immediately confess our sin to God through the Church's sacrament of reconciliation. There, God removes our sin and gives us the chance to start our journey with him again.

Questions for Reflection and Discussion

> *Who is it harder to ask forgiveness from: God, yourself, or someone else?*

> *How often do you think people should participate in the sacrament of reconciliation (confession)? What guides your answer?*

Related Journey of Faith Lesson

C6, "The Sacrament of Penance and Reconciliation"

Themes

Forgiveness, Love, Reconciliation
    C6, "Sacrament of Penance and Reconciliation"
Faith
    Q2, "What Is Faith?"
    M1, "Conversion: A Lifelong Process"

Twelfth Sunday in Ordinary Time, Year C

READING 1, ZECHARIAH 12:10–11; 13:1

Thus says the LORD: I will pour out on the house of David and on the inhabitants of Jerusalem a spirit of grace and petition; and they shall look on him whom they have pierced, and they shall mourn for him as one mourns for an only son, and they shall grieve over him as one grieves over a firstborn. On that day the mourning in Jerusalem shall be as great as the mourning of Hadadrimmon in the plain of Megiddo. On that day there shall be open to the house of David and to the inhabitants of Jerusalem, a fountain to purify from sin and uncleanness.

PSALM 63:2, 3–4, 5–6, 8–9

READING 2, GALATIANS 3:26-29

Brothers and sisters: Through faith you are all children of God in Christ Jesus. For all of you who were baptized into Christ have clothed yourselves with Christ. There is neither Jew nor Greek, there is neither slave nor free person, there is not male and female; for you are all one in Christ Jesus. And if you belong to Christ, then you are Abraham's descendant, heirs according to the promise.

GOSPEL, LUKE 9:18–24

Once when Jesus was praying in solitude, and the disciples were with him, he asked them, "Who do the crowds say that I am?" They said in reply, "John the Baptist; others, Elijah; still others, 'One of the ancient prophets has arisen.'" Then he said to them, "But who do you say that I am?" Peter said in reply, "The Christ of God." He rebuked them and directed them not to tell this to anyone. He said, "The Son of Man must suffer greatly and be rejected by the elders, the chief priests, and the scribes, and be killed and on the third day be raised." Then he said to all, "If anyone wishes to come after me, he must deny himself and take up his cross daily and follow me. For whoever wishes to save his life will lose it, but whoever loses his life for my sake will save it."

Who Do You Say That I Am?

When Jesus asked the disciples, "Who do you say that I am," I wonder if they were tempted to answer as the crowds did, naming John the Baptist, Elijah, or one of the other prophets. After all, it's only natural to compare great people we know now to the heroes of the past. The past gives us language to talk about the present. In this case, the crowds thought of Jesus as a great preacher like John or a great prophet like Elijah. In this way they could get a handle on Jesus and know what he was like. The truth is, they had never experienced anyone like Jesus before. And Peter tells us why: "[You are] the Messiah of God." Everybody had an idea about the kind of person the Messiah was, but no one had met him. What happens next tells Peter, the disciples, and all of us just how much our lives will change when we acknowledge Jesus for who he is. We learn of his passion and death; he hints at the resurrection to come. Then Jesus issues an uncomfortable invitation: "If anyone wishes to come after me, he must deny himself, take up his cross daily, and follow me." Being a disciple means hard work, not just once but every day. It means loving when love doesn't seem possible, suffering for the sake of others. It might even mean laying down one's life for friends. Discipleship means choosing every day to follow Christ and to demonstrate that choice wherever we find ourselves.

A Spirit of Mercy

The brief passage that forms our first reading from Zechariah, seems familiar because the Gospel of John quotes it in the passion narrative (John 19:37). In this case, the "one whom they pierced," is an unknown figure who might have been a king or a great prophet. The mourning probably refers to the mourning over the death of the King Josiah in 609 BC. Josiah uncovered the book of the Law (likely Deuteronomy) and was the last great king of Judah before the Babylonian Exile.

One in Christ Jesus

We are all children of God through faith, says St. Paul as we continue reading the Letter to the Galatians. Baptism makes us brothers and sisters in Christ and one in him. Read against the backdrop of the body of Christ, we also infer that no one is better than any other. When we belong to Christ, our equality bridges racial, social, economic, and sexual differences, the very thing we often see as barriers between people.

Good News for All of Us

We humans may face many troubles in which we yearn to feel the presence of God. In his prayer, the psalmist reveals a way to find that presence: "I remember you through the watches of the night…" When the psalmist remembers God, he is immediately comforted for he knows God has been with him throughout his life. We hear that echo in the refrain: "Your love is better than life." In times of trouble, remember God and the ways God has blessed you. Know that he walks with you, even (and maybe especially) in times of trouble.

Questions for Reflection and Discussion

➤ *A lot of people didn't understand who Jesus was. When he asks his question of the disciples, only Peter has the courage to say, "The Messiah of God." Who are the people who know you the best? What do you think Jesus would say if you asked him, "Who do you say that I am?"*

➤ *The Catholic Church in the United States sometimes seems as polarized as the rest of the country, but Paul says all the baptized are one in Christ and equal at the table of the Lord. Where does division in our Catholic community come from? Do you think we will be able to move closer to Paul's vision of communion?*

Related Journey of Faith Lesson

Q13, "The Church as Community"

Themes

Equality
    Q13, "The Church as Community"
    M2, "The Role of the Laity"
Fulfillment
    Q7, "Your Prayer Life"
    E1, "Election: Saying Yes to Jesus"
Identity
    M4, "Discernment"

Thirteenth Sunday in Ordinary Time, Year C

READING 1, 1 KINGS 19:16B, 19–21

The LORD said to Elijah: "You shall anoint Elisha, son of Shaphat of Abelmeholah, as prophet to succeed you." Elijah set out and came upon Elisha, son of Shaphat, as he was plowing with twelve yoke Of oxen; he was following the twelfth. Elijah went over to him and threw his cloak over him. Elisha left the oxen, ran after Elijah, and said, "Please, let me kiss my father and mother goodbye, and I will follow you." Elijah answered, "Go back! Have I done anything to you?" Elisha left him, and taking the yoke of oxen, slaughtered them; he used the plowing equipment for fuel to boil their flesh, and gave it to his people to eat. Then Elisha left and followed Elijah as his attendant.

PSALM 16:1–2, 5, 7–11

READING 2, GALATIANS 5:1, 13–18

Brothers and sisters: For freedom Christ set us free; so stand firm and do not submit again to the yoke of slavery. For you were called for freedom, brothers and sisters. But do not use this freedom as an opportunity for the flesh; rather, serve one another through love. For the whole law is fulfilled in one statement, namely, You shall love your neighbor as yourself. But if you go on biting and devouring one another, beware that you are not consumed by one another. I say, then: live by the Spirit and you will certainly not gratify the desire of the flesh. For the flesh has desires against the Spirit, and the Spirit against the flesh; these are opposed to each other, so that you may not do what you want. But if you are guided by the Spirit, you are not under the law.

GOSPEL, LUKE 9:51–62

When the days for Jesus' being taken up were fulfilled, he resolutely determined to journey to Jerusalem, and he sent messengers ahead of him. On the way they entered a Samaritan village to prepare for his reception there, but they would not welcome him because the destination of his journey was Jerusalem. When the disciples James and John saw this they asked, "Lord, do you want us to call down fire from heaven to consume them?" Jesus turned and rebuked them, and they journeyed to another village. As they were proceeding on their journey someone said to him, "I will follow you wherever you go." Jesus answered him, "Foxes have dens and birds of the sky have nests, but the Son of Man has nowhere to rest his head." And to another he said, "Follow me." But he replied, "Lord, let me go first and bury my father." But he answered him, "Let the dead bury their dead. But you, go and proclaim the kingdom of God." And another said, "I will follow you, Lord, but first let me say farewell to my family at home." To him Jesus said, "No one who sets a hand to the plow and looks to what was left behind is fit for the kingdom of God."

The Path of Life

The Lord is my "portion and cup," who has "made my destiny secure." These words in today's responsorial psalm display a confidence in God that is an example to us, particularly in times of trouble. In the last verses, the psalmist asserts that God will show him the path of life and joy in the presence of God forever. "Show me the path of life" could be our prayer every day as we navigate through work, family, and community.

All three readings today talk about the path of life—and our response to God's call to follow in it. The story from 1 Kings records the anointing of Elijah as the successor of the prophet Elijah. Our colloquial phrase about "passing on the mantle" in a change of leadership comes from this story. It's important to note that passing the mantle in this story indicates a period of apprenticeship or servanthood before Elisha will formally assume the authority of Elijah. Elisha likely was surprised at Elijah's unexpected action, and that may have accounted for his initial hesitation to follow. His request seems reasonable: "Let me kiss my parents goodbye." Elijah challenges Elisha to think about what the mantle means, and in response, Elisha slaughters the oxen, boils the flesh, and feeds the people. In this way he signals that he is leaving his old life to follow a different path. Remember, the disciples in the New Testament also had to abruptly leave their old lives behind.

Following Jesus

In the Gospel, multiple people are given a chance to follow Jesus, who is the path of life. Luke says that Jesus' face is set toward Jerusalem. His journey will take him to his death. For that reason, that Samaritans did not follow him, for Jews considered Samaritans to be inferior. When James and John want to call down punishment from heaven, Jesus rebukes them. The choice to follow Jesus must be made freely. God invites, he doesn't force. The three people Jesus encounters on the way to Jerusalem are each tested. The first is told the road will be hard. "The Son of Man has nowhere to lay his head." The second wants to bury his father first, but Jesus reminds him that the job to proclaim the kingdom is already waiting for him. The third is like Elisha, who wants to say goodbye to his family. Neither of these two requests is unimportant, and Jesus doesn't deny either of them. Rather, he expresses the urgency of his message to follow and give the whole self to the task. The reference to putting a hand on the plow is one that farmers will understand. To plow a straight furrow with oxen, you have to walk in a straight line with eyes looking ahead. If you turn your head to look back, the oxen will also turn, and the furrow will be crooked. When we decide to follow Jesus, he wants us to make a full commitment.

A Path of Freedom

God's path of life is a path of freedom. But it isn't freedom to do whatever we want, or as St. Paul says, "an opportunity for the flesh." Rather, God's path is the freedom to serve one another in love and be led by the Holy Spirit. Only by doing this will we truly be free.

Good News for All of Us

Discerning God's call isn't a matter of making a decision one time forever. Rather, we make the decision every day: "I want to follow Jesus." That may take us to places and situations we never expected to be, cause us to change jobs, choose majors in college, or pursue more education. We may volunteer with different groups or leave everything to work with the poor or serve the Church. God never forces us to do any of those things; he simply invites over and over again until we are ready to find our path of life.

Questions for Reflection and Discussion

➤ *Can you say with certainty that what you are doing now is part of God's call for you? Do you think there is something more God wants you to do?*

➤ *Jesus wants us to respond freely to his call. What are some of the things that might prevent us from doing so? How do we ask God for help in those times?*

Related Journey of Faith Lesson

M4, "Discernment"

Themes

Call, Journey
    Q1, "Welcome to the OCIA!"
    Q13, "The Church as Community"
    M1, "Conversion: A Lifelong Process"
Decision-making
    M4, "Discernment"

Fourteenth Sunday in Ordinary Time, Year C

READING 1, ISAIAH 66:10–14C

Thus says the LORD: Rejoice with Jerusalem and be glad because of her, all you who love her; exult, exult with her, all you who were mourning over her! Oh, that you may suck fully of the milk of her comfort, that you may nurse with delight at her abundant breasts! For thus says the LORD: Lo, I will spread prosperity over Jerusalem like a river, and the wealth of the nations like an overflowing torrent. As nurslings, you shall be carried in her arms, and fondled in her lap; as a mother comforts her child, so will I comfort you; in Jerusalem you shall find your comfort. When you see this, your heart shall rejoice and your bodies flourish like the grass; the LORD's power shall be known to his servants.

PSALM 66:1–3, 4–5, 6–7, 16, 20

READING 2, GALATIANS 6:14–18

Brothers and sisters: May I never boast except in the cross of our Lord Jesus Christ, through which the world has been crucified to me, and I to the world. For neither does circumcision mean anything, nor does uncircumcision, but only a new creation. Peace and mercy be to all who follow this rule and to the Israel of God. From now on, let no one make troubles for me; for I bear the marks of Jesus on my body. The grace of our Lord Jesus Christ be with your spirit, brothers and sisters. Amen.

GOSPEL, LUKE 10:1–12, 17–20

At that time the Lord appointed seventy-two others whom he sent ahead of him in pairs to every town and place he intended to visit. He said to them, "The harvest is abundant but the laborers are few; so ask the master of the harvest to send out laborers for his harvest. Go on your way; behold, I am sending you like lambs among wolves. Carry no money bag, no sack, no sandals; and greet no one along the way. Into whatever house you enter, first say, 'Peace to this household.' If a peaceful person lives there, your peace will rest on him; but if not, it will return to you. Stay in the same house and eat and drink what is offered to you, for the laborer deserves his payment. Do not move about from one house to another. Whatever town you enter and they welcome you, eat what is set before you, cure the sick in it and say to them, 'The kingdom of God is at hand for you.' Whatever town you enter and they do not receive you, go out into the streets and say, 'The dust of your town that clings to our feet, even that we shake off against you.'

Yet know this: the kingdom of God is at hand. I tell you, it will be more tolerable for Sodom on that day than for that town." The seventy-two returned rejoicing, and said, "Lord, even the demons are subject to us because of your name." Jesus said, "I have observed Satan fall like lightning from the sky. Behold, I have given you the power to 'tread upon serpents' and scorpions and upon the full force of the enemy and nothing will harm you. Nevertheless, do not rejoice because the spirits are subject to you, but rejoice because your names are written in heaven."

Mother Love

When Cyrus of Persia conquered Babylon, he allowed the exiles from Judah to return to their homeland and to Jerusalem, the city of David. There wasn't much to return to since the temple had been destroyed and the country they knew remained under foreign power. But the Israelites rejoiced in the providence of God, and Isaiah's vision gives voice to their hope that God will fully restore them as a people. Not only is Jerusalem envisioned as a mother from whom prosperity will come like mother's milk to a hungry infant, but God is pictured as a mother who comforts her children and helps them flourish. This isn't the only female image of God in the Bible. Isaiah (42:24 and 49:15), Hosea (11:1–4), the Book of Deuteronomy (32:11–12, 18), and Matthew (23:37) among others all use female imagery to speak of God. God's "mother" love conveys the infinite compassion God has on the people God calls his own.

New Creation

At the end of his letters, Paul reminds the Galatians not to follow the teachings of those who insist that they must be circumcised in order to become Christian. Specific rituals do not make someone Christian; rather, the conversion of heart and the recognition of Christ as the Savior are the only things necessary to become a new creation. That's why Paul talks about boasting in the cross and not in anything he himself has done. The peace Paul wishes on those who follow Christ is the peace of God himself. Finally, Paul refers to the marks of Jesus branded on his body. A brand on a slave often indicates who the owner was. Paul isn't referring to stigmata here, but probably the scars from persecution for preaching the gospel. They indicate that he belongs to Christ.

Eat What's Put in Front of You

In order to preach the Good News, the disciples were sent out two by two to every town where Jesus would go. Their mission was to wish peace on the town, cure the sick, and tell them the kingdom of God is at hand. Jesus gives what may well be one of the most difficult commands for his followers. "Eat what's put in front of you." In order to preach well, the disciples must come to know the people, sit at the kitchen table, learn about their lives, and make the connection between what they need and what Jesus offers them. They have to help them know who Jesus is and why that's important for them. What people offer to eat is an invitation to share in their lives. Every disciple has to be prepared even to eat something they may not like in order to become the friend that invites someone to come to Jesus. Jesus also tells them one other thing. If they are not welcomed, the disciples are to shake the dust from their feet. They aren't to take the disappointment with them or think they are failures. Their peace comes from the knowledge that the kingdom is coming and that they are doing the work of God.

Good News for All of Us

Preaching the gospel is about establishing a relationship first with Jesus and then with one another. Just as children learn love first from their parents who love them, those who don't know Christ learn about him from those who care enough to share their faith with them. All of us can do this with family members and friends in ways as simple as answering a question about why we believe, why we go to Church, inviting others to come to a Bible study, or join us for prayer and liturgy. We do it by sitting at their kitchen table and eating what they have to offer so we might share the food that gives us life as well.

Questions for Reflection and Discussion

> *Have you visited someone who served something you didn't like? What did you do and why?*

> *We pray most frequently to God as Father, following Jesus' invitation to do so. Is it OK to think about God as mother—that is to say, embodying a mother's qualities?*

Related Journey of Faith Lesson

M8, "Evangelization"

Themes

Kingdom (of God)
    Q7, "Your Prayer Life"
    M5, "Our Call to Holiness"
Ministry
    Q1, "Welcome to the OCIA!"
    M2, "The Role of the Laity"
Mission
    M8, "Evangelization"

READING 1, DEUTERONOMY 30:10–14

Moses said to the people: "If only you would heed the voice of the LORD, your God, and keep his commandments and statutes that are written in this book of the law, when you return to the LORD, your God, with all your heart and all your soul. "For this command that I enjoin on you today is not too mysterious and remote for you. It is not up in the sky, that you should say, 'Who will go up in the sky to get it for us and tell us of it, that we may carry it out?' Nor is it across the sea, that you should say, 'Who will cross the sea to get it for us and tell us of it, that we may carry it out?' No, it is something very near to you, already in your mouths and in your hearts; you have only to carry it out."

PSALM 69:14, 17, 30–31, 33–34, 36, 37

READING 2, COLOSSIANS 1:15–20

Christ Jesus is the image of the invisible God, the firstborn of all creation. For in him were created all things in heaven and on earth, the visible and the invisible, whether thrones or dominions or principalities or powers; all things were created through him and for him. He is before all things, and in him all things hold together. He is the head of the body, the church. He is the beginning, the firstborn from the dead, that in all things he himself might be preeminent. For in him all the fullness was pleased to dwell, and through him to reconcile all things for him, making peace by the blood of his cross through him, whether those on earth or those in heaven.

GOSPEL, LUKE 10:25–37

There was a scholar of the law who stood up to test him and said, "Teacher, what must I do to inherit eternal life?" Jesus said to him, "What is written in the law? How do you read it?" He said in reply, You shall love the Lord, your God, with all your heart, with all your being, with all your strength, and with all your mind, and your neighbor as yourself." He replied to him, "You have answered correctly; do this and you will live." But because he wished to justify himself, he said to Jesus, "And who is my neighbor?" Jesus replied, "A man fell victim to robbers as he went down from Jerusalem to Jericho. They stripped and beat him and went off leaving him half-dead. A priest happened to be going down that road, but when he saw him, he passed by on the opposite side. Likewise a Levite came to the place, and when he saw him, he passed by on the opposite side. But a Samaritan traveler who came upon him was moved with compassion at the sight. He approached the victim, poured oil and wine over his wounds and bandaged them. Then he lifted him up on his own animal, took him to an inn, and cared for him. The next day he took out two silver coins and gave them to the innkeeper with the instruction, 'Take care of him. If you spend more than what I have given you, I shall repay you on my way back.' Which of these three, in your opinion, was neighbor to the robbers' victim?" He answered, "The one who treated him with mercy." Jesus said to him, "Go and do likewise."

The Word Is Very Near You

From the beginning, God's word has the power to create. In the first chapter of Genesis, God simply spoke a word like "light," and there was light. Rabbinical tradition tells us that the mere echo of God's word, continues to create light to this very day. In his Gospel, John says Jesus is God's Word (logos) and is God himself. Jesus is the one through whom all things are made. The readings today talk about God's word and God's Word, both of which are very near us and closely connected to the commandment to love God and love our neighbor. In the first reading, Moses gives some final instructions to the Israelites before they cross over into the promised land. Moses cannot go with them. He exhorts them to keep the commandments, not out of obligation, but because they love the Lord and want to do what God requests. He points out that God's word isn't far away. Rather, it is already on their lips. And with the ears of the heart, they can hear and obey it.

The psalm response (our words to God) comes from a lament. The psalmist fears death but prays to God. In the very act of praying, he becomes convinced that God will rescue all the Israelites and bring them safely to a restored country.

The Word of Eternal Life

The Good Samaritan is one of the parables that most people can recall by heart, probably because the story is both simple in its telling and powerful in its message. How do we inherit eternal life? Jesus, like Moses, stands at a threshold point with the young scholar who wants to inherit eternal life—his "promised land." Jesus asks him to recite the heart of the Law and it is, indeed, on his lips and in his heart: Love God and love your neighbor as yourself. The scholar wants to get it right. "Who's my neighbor?" he asks. The parable that follows reveals a deeper and more challenging definition than the scholar may have expected. The neighbor is the one who cares for others even when they do not wish him well. The Jews looked down on the Samaritans as inferior and yet this Samaritan did what he could to care for the Jew who had been robbed and beaten. The neighbor is the one who shows another mercy. Jesus' command is clear—"Go and do likewise." Like Moses Jesus exhorted obedience to the heart of the Law and a deeper understanding of what it meant.

The Word of the New Creation

We may recognize some of the phrases of our second reading because they are similar to those we use in the Creed. Paul's Letter to the Colossians contains this ancient Christian hymn regarding Jesus. Here Jesus is described as the "firstborn of all creation… through whom all things were created, both visible and invisible." The true importance of Jesus, though, is in the phrase, "in him all the fullness was pleased to dwell." Paul refers to the fullness of God. When we know Jesus, we know the Father for Christ is one with the Father. We are a new creation because the Word that is God made us so.

Good News for All of Us

It's relatively easy to be vulnerable and open with someone when we love the person; it's much harder to do with a stranger. It's especially hard to do if we consider the other to be someone who doesn't like us or whom we think is inferior to us. While we admire the Samaritan who took a chance to help a stranger who didn't like him, we might also imagine what it was like for the man who was robbed and had to accept help from the Samaritan. Suddenly he (and everyone listening) had to question his assumptions about what Samaritans were like. The command to be like the Samaritan was a challenge not only to be a neighbor to anyone in need, but to allow those in need to be neighbors to us.

Questions for Reflection and Discussion

➤ *Who needs you to be a neighbor to them today? Who have you allowed to be a neighbor to you?*

➤ *Name a time when you knew the right thing to do in a situation without anyone telling you. Could that have been the word of God in your heart?*

Related Journey of Faith Lesson

M5, "Our Call to Holiness"

Themes

Compassion
> Q13, "The Church as Community"
> M4, "Discernment"

Forgiveness
> Q15, "The Saints"
> Q7, "Your Prayer Life"

Love
> M5, "Our Call to Holiness"

Sixteenth Sunday in Ordinary Time, Year C

READING 1, GENESIS 18:1–10A

The LORD appeared to Abraham by the terebinth of Mamre, as he sat in the entrance of his tent, while the day was growing hot. Looking up, Abraham saw three men standing nearby. When he saw them, he ran from the entrance of the tent to greet them; and bowing to the ground, he said: "Sir, if I may ask you this favor, please do not go on past your servant. Let some water be brought, that you may bathe your feet, and then rest yourselves under the tree. Now that you have come this close to your servant, let me bring you a little food, that you may refresh yourselves; and afterward you may go on your way." The men replied, "Very well, do as you have said." Abraham hastened into the tent and told Sarah, "Quick, three measures of fine flour! Knead it and make rolls." He ran to the herd, picked out a tender, choice steer, and gave it to a servant, who quickly prepared it. Then Abraham got some curds and milk, as well as the steer that had been prepared, and set these before the three men; and he waited on them under the tree while they ate. They asked Abraham, "Where is your wife Sarah?" He replied, "There in the tent." One of them said, "I will surely return to you about this time next year, and Sarah will then have a son."

PSALM 15:2–3, 3–4, 5

READING 2, COLOSSIANS 1:24–28

Brothers and sisters: Now I rejoice in my sufferings for your sake, and in my flesh I am filling up what is lacking in the afflictions of Christ on behalf of his body, which is the church, of which I am a minister in accordance with God's stewardship given to me to bring to completion for you the word of God, the mystery hidden from ages and from generations past. But now it has been manifested to his holy ones, to whom God chose to make known the riches of the glory of this mystery among the Gentiles; it is Christ in you, the hope for glory. It is he whom we proclaim, admonishing everyone and teaching everyone with all wisdom, that we may present everyone perfect in Christ.

GOSPEL, LUKE 10:38–42

Jesus entered a village where a woman whose name was Martha welcomed him. She had a sister named Mary who sat beside the Lord at his feet listening to him speak. Martha, burdened with much serving, came to him and said, "Lord, do you not care that my sister has left me by myself to do the serving? Tell her to help me." The Lord said to her in reply, "Martha, Martha, you are anxious and worried about many things. There is need of only one thing. Mary has chosen the better part and it will not be taken from her."

To Whom Does God Speak?

We are sometimes so sure about where and to whom God's word and promise will be given. The first reading and Gospel for today should shatter that illusion and give us a healthy dose of humility where God is concerned. The visit of the three strangers in Genesis throws Abraham into a frenzy. Guests were welcomed in the Middle East and often given the best the house had to offer. The little food and water that Abraham offers turns into loaves of bread, a fatted calf, and curds and milk, all prepared by Sarah in the kitchen and the servant in the house. Abraham remains attentive to the strangers, wondering what they will say. Their first words were, "Where is Sarah, your wife?" She was in the kitchen. Where else would she be? The message was not for Abraham, but for Sarah in the kitchen. Sarah will have a son. God's promise fell on Sarah this time.

In the Gospel, Martha has learned the lesson of Sarah well. Where was Sarah when God spoke? She was in the kitchen. Where is Martha going to stay? In the kitchen taking care of Jesus the guest. There was a lot to do for guests and I wonder if Martha feared that Mary was going to miss the thanks and the word of Jesus by sitting at his feet. It was a sure thing that Martha was going to miss Mary's help. But when Martha asks Jesus to tell her sister to help, Jesus surprises her by inviting Mary to stay. She has chosen the "better part." The message here was not for Martha, but for Mary who was sitting at the feet of Jesus just like a disciple.

We are all a little bit like Abraham and a little bit like Martha, and we think that we know exactly what we should be doing when God comes calling. But just when we think we have it all figured out, along comes Sarah and Mary, who point out that the word and promise of God falls on whomever it will and wherever God chooses. It's a good lesson.

Making the Word of God Known

The Colossians did not know Paul very well. In this first chapter of Colossians, Paul presents his understanding of his authority as a "minister in accordance with God's stewardship." He understands God to have commissioned him to bring the word of God to completion for them—in other words, to make the word of God fully known. Paul, of course, felt this most keenly for the Gentiles in whom he sees the mystery of God unfolding every day. Paul's goal is to present everyone as perfected in Christ when Christ finally appears on Judgment Day.

Good News for All of Us

Genesis and Luke both tell us that God's call and promise is not limited only to those who hold a certain role or inhabit a certain place. Both men and women are called by God as disciples, as bearers of the promise, and as preachers of the Good News. Both serve the guests at the house and sit at the feet of the Master. To maintain a narrow understanding of who is called to do what is to stifle the Spirit whose gifts fall on whomever the Spirit chooses to give them. Is there no role for tradition in theology? Of course, there is. But we must be on guard that the human tendency to want to control everything and dictate to God what God may do does not turn our theology and tradition into relics of the past. What gifts are being given to what people today? And how do they benefit the entire community?

Questions for Reflection and Discussion

➤ *How do you see God most active in the Church today? Are we making room for God to work in unexpected places?*

➤ *Have you ever been surprised by someone's sudden insight and/or really good idea? Why were you surprised?*

Related Journey of Faith Lesson

Q12, "Who Shepherds the Church?"

Themes

Hospitality
    Q13, "The Church as Community"
    M2, "The Role of the Laity"
Roles, Sexism
    Q12, "Who Shepherds the Church?"
    M3, "Your Spiritual Gifts"

READING 1, GENESIS 18:20–32

In those days, the LORD said: "The outcry against Sodom and Gomorrah is so great, and their sin so grave, that I must go down and see whether or not their actions fully correspond to the cry against them that comes to me. I mean to find out." While Abraham's visitors walked on farther toward Sodom, the LORD remained standing before Abraham. Then Abraham drew nearer and said: "Will you sweep away the innocent with the guilty? Suppose there were fifty innocent people in the city; would you wipe out the place, rather than spare it for the sake of the fifty innocent people within it? Far be it from you to do such a thing, to make the innocent die with the guilty so that the innocent and the guilty would be treated alike! Should not the judge of all the world act with justice?" The LORD replied, "If I find fifty innocent people in the city of Sodom, I will spare the whole place for their sake." Abraham spoke up again: "See how I am presuming to speak to my Lord, though I am but dust and ashes! What if there are five less than fifty innocent people? Will you destroy the whole city because of those five?" He answered, "I will not destroy it, if I find forty-five there." But Abraham persisted, saying "What if only forty are found there?" He replied, "I will forbear doing it for the sake of the forty." Then Abraham said, "Let not my Lord grow impatient if I go on. What if only thirty are found there?" He replied, "I will forbear doing it if I can find but thirty there." Still Abraham went on, "Since I have thus dared to speak to my Lord, what if there are no more than twenty?" The LORD answered, "I will not destroy it, for the sake of the twenty." But he still persisted: "Please, let not my Lord grow angry if I speak up this last time. What if there are at least ten there?" He replied, "For the sake of those ten, I will not destroy it."

PSALM 138:1–3, 6–8

READING 2, COLOSSIANS 2:12–14

Brothers and sisters: You were buried with him in baptism, in which you were also raised with him through faith in the power of God, who raised him from the dead. And even when you were dead in transgressions and the uncircumcision of your flesh, he brought you to life along with him, having forgiven us all our transgressions; obliterating the bond against us, with its legal claims, which was opposed to us, he also removed it from our midst, nailing it to the cross.

GOSPEL, LUKE 11:1–13

Jesus was praying in a certain place, and when he had finished, one of his disciples said to him, "Lord, teach us to pray just as John taught his disciples." He said to them, "When you pray, say: Father, hallowed be your name, your kingdom come. Give us each day our daily bread and forgive us our sins for we ourselves forgive everyone in debt to us, and do not subject us to the final test." And he said to them, "Suppose one of you has a friend to whom he goes at midnight and says, 'Friend, lend me three loaves of bread, for a friend of mine has arrived at my house from a journey and I have nothing to offer him,' and he says in reply from within, 'Do not bother me; the door has already been locked and my children and I are already in bed. I cannot get up to give you anything.' I tell you, if he does not get up to give the visitor the loaves because of their friendship, he will get up to give him whatever he needs because of his persistence. "And I tell you, ask and you will receive; seek and you will find; knock and the door will be opened to you. For everyone who asks, receives; and the one who seeks, finds; and to the one who knocks, the door will be opened. What father among you would hand his son a snake when he asks for a fish? Or hand him a scorpion when he asks for an egg? If you then, who are wicked, know how to give good gifts to your children, how much more will the Father in heaven give the Holy Spirit to those who ask him?"

Lord, Teach Us to Pray

The Lord's Prayer we are taught as children and pray each Sunday at Mass is taken from Matthew's Gospel (6:9–15). We hear Luke's simpler version today, and while we recognize all the elements, the flow is very different. The address is direct, "Father," followed by an element of praise and an openness to God's coming kingdom. Three petitions in quick succession end the prayer. "Give us our daily bread," "forgive our sins," and "do not subject us to the final test." But Jesus, who was at prayer when the disciples asked how to pray, goes on to talk about being persistent in prayer. The story of the friend asking for bread late at night suggests that we also should be persistent in our prayer with God. When Jesus talks about the answer to prayer, we might be tempted to think that the specific thing we ask for will be granted. But Jesus never says that. Instead, Jesus says if we ask, we will receive. He doesn't say what we will receive, but we are assured that whatever God gives us will be something good. And indeed, it is. In the last line, Jesus reveals that the Father will give us the Holy Spirit whenever we come to him in prayer. And the Holy Spirit may be what we need most of all.

Face to Face with God

A former campus ministry director talked frequently about the need to be "brutally honest" with God in prayer. "Tell God what you're feeling, no matter how wrong you think the feelings may be." He reasoned (and with good sense) that the more open we are with God, the more intimate our relationship with God can be, and the more God can enter our hearts. Abraham is a good illustration. Troubled by God's decision to destroy Sodom and Gomorrah, Abraham stands before God to have a frank conversation. We might think that's bold. But Abraham is persistent, appealing to God's justice. Is it right to punish the righteous in the same way as the wicked? Is there a threshold for righteousness? Abraham is certainly respectful as he talks with God, and he keeps lowering the number. Each time, the Lord responds with mercy—for the sake of "ten, I will not destroy it." Abraham was honest with God in his questions and God answered him honestly. If we continued the story, we would find out that righteousness was in short supply in Sodom and Gomorrah. But God remembers Abraham's words and saves the one righteous man in the cities. Lot and his family are able to flee from the destruction that comes.

Dead in Sin, Alive in Christ

Throughout his letters, Paul consistently makes reference to the paschal mystery: what was once dead is now alive. The crucifixion and resurrection of Christ signaled a new beginning for a world that had lost its way. For the individual believer, baptism was an initiation both into the death of Christ and into his resurrection, accomplished by the power and grace of God. That's why Paul returns over and over to the idea that we are a new creation, reconciled to God, and able to live in the hope of the world to come when God reigns forever. The short passage from Colossians for today is a reminder of what we died to and what we live for.

Seventeenth Sunday in Ordinary Time, Year C

Good News for All of Us

Prayer is a powerful instrument. The psalmists knew it. The Hebrew word for psalm is *tehillim*, meaning "praise." In order to praise God properly, we have to trust God with the deepest secrets of our hearts—joyful praise, heartfelt thanks, abject sadness, violent anger, and profound need. We may think God wants to hear only nice emotions and that there is something wrong with anger, fear, or darkness. Sometimes all we can do is lay those emotions at the feet of God, hoping he will lead us through them and channel them into something positive. Prayer is also where we listen to what God has to say to us, whether it's a word of comfort, challenge, or call. Praying every day tunes our hearts to God's presence and our ear to his voice.

Questions for Reflection and Discussion

➤ *What kind of prayer are you comfortable with? What kinds of prayer would you like to know more about?*

➤ *Do you think you could approach God as Abraham did and be brutally honest?*

Related *Journey of Faith* Lesson

Q8, "Catholic Prayers and Practices"

Themes

Persistence, Praise, Prayer
    Q8, "Catholic Prayers and Practices"
    Q7, "Your Prayer Life"
    E6, "The Lord's Prayer"

Eighteenth Sunday in Ordinary Time, Year C

READING 1, ECCLESIASTES 1:2; 2:21–23

Vanity of vanities, says Qoheleth, vanity of vanities! All things are vanity! Here is one who has labored with wisdom and knowledge and skill, and yet to another who has not labored over it, he must leave property. This also is vanity and a great misfortune. For what profit comes to man from all the toil and anxiety of heart with which he has labored under the sun? All his days sorrow and grief are his occupation; even at night his mind is not at rest. This also is vanity.

PSALM 90:3–4, 5–6, 12–13, 14, 17

READING 2, COLOSSIANS 3:1–5, 9–11

Brothers and sisters: If you were raised with Christ, seek what is above, where Christ is seated at the right hand of God. Think of what is above, not of what is on earth. For you have died, and your life is hidden with Christ in God. When Christ your life appears, then you too will appear with him in glory. Put to death, then, the parts of you that are earthly: immorality, impurity, passion, evil desire, and the greed that is idolatry. Stop lying to one another, since you have taken off the old self with its practices and have put on the new self, which is being renewed, for knowledge, in the image of its creator. Here there is not Greek and Jew, circumcision and uncircumcision, barbarian, Scythian, slave, free; but Christ is all and in all.

GOSPEL, LUKE 12:13–21

Someone in the crowd said to Jesus, "Teacher, tell my brother to share the inheritance with me." He replied to him, "Friend, who appointed me as your judge and arbitrator?" Then he said to the crowd, "Take care to guard against all greed, for though one may be rich, one's life does not consist of possessions." Then he told them a parable. "There was a rich man whose land produced a bountiful harvest. He asked himself, 'What shall I do, for I do not have space to store my harvest?' And he said, 'This is what I shall do: I shall tear down my barns and build larger ones. There I shall store all my grain and other goods and I shall say to myself, "Now as for you, you have so many good things stored up for many years, rest, eat, drink, be merry!"' But God said to him, 'You fool, this night your life will be demanded of you; and the things you have prepared, to whom will they belong?' Thus will it be for all who store up treasure for themselves but are not rich in what matters to God."

Seek What Is Above

The world is filled with many delights and temptations! We revel in the love of family, the awe of a beautiful sunset, and the simple pleasure of cool water on a hot day. We are also tempted by what the world can offer—wealth, possessions, the satisfaction of desire without the responsibility of commitment, and the lure of power. When St. Paul asks us to put earthly things to death, he names greed as the last and calls it idolatry. We sometimes worship other things besides God. Baptism is an entry into the life of Christ and into his mission. Most of us are taught that after the fact, but those who come into the Church as adults learn well what Paul meant when he said, "think of what is above and not is on earth." In other words, he wanted us to turn our minds and hearts to God and become the new people we were meant to be—one in Christ. Paul realizes we can't see all of this now, but is confident that when Jesus returns, we will appear with him in glory.

The Gospel takes up the warning against greed as Jesus describes the man who has so many crops they can't fit into his barn. Whenever I read this story, I start dreaming about having a place to store all my stuff. And I often reflect that if this parable were told today, the man would have thought, "I don't need a bigger barn. I just need to get more organized." The problem with bigger barns or more bins is this: the more stuff we have, the more we need to spend time with it, protecting it, keeping it safe, making sure it's not stolen. Our stuff becomes more important than anything else. It becomes an idol. We end up locked in the barn with it and become the opposite of the generous God who lavishes love on all and who loves his children equally.

Vanity of Vanities

The Book of Ecclesiastes was among the last to be approved for the Hebrew canon. It is not like most of the other books of the Old Testament. There is no theology of God's Chosen People, no praise of Jerusalem as the city of God. There is just a rather dark reflection on the human condition. "Vanity of Vanities," says the Teacher. *Hebel* is Hebrew for "vanity." Its meaning includes words like futility, absurdity, and nothingness. As with the rest of the Wisdom books, the author of Ecclesiastes (the teacher Qoheleth) draws on life itself for his inspiration. Many scholars place the writing around the third century during a time of great tribulation for the Jews, who were under foreign rule. In this small passage as well as in much of the book, Qoheleth comments on the human condition, noting that all will die, that life often seems unfair, and—as he says here—others will enjoy what you have worked so hard for. What's the point, he wonders, it all seems futile vanity. Qoheleth actually has a strong faith and understands that we cannot know the mind of God or God's plans. But he knows they will be revealed in the end.

Good News for All of Us

What can be better news than that we have been raised with Christ? We were freed from the power of sin by Jesus' death on the cross. In baptism we received the grace to resist temptation and live as children of God. While the world is full of temptations, we can't help but know it is also "charged with the grandeur of God" (G. M. Hopkins). In our practice of faith, in our delight in creation, and in our love for one another, we find evidence of God's presence. We may not always know where we are going or what the plan is, but if our focus is on God and not on what the world offers, we will surely find heaven at the end.

Questions for Reflection and Discussion

> *Have you ever regretted buying something and wondered why you did it in the first place?*

> *What do you find yourself collecting and storing these days? Why is it important to have those things?*

Related Journey of Faith Lesson

M1, "Conversion: A Lifelong Process"

Themes

Greed
    M1, "Conversion: A Lifelong Process"
Preparedness
    Q2, "What Is Faith?"
    M5, "Our Call to Holiness"
Vanity
    Q15, "The Saints"
    Q14, "Mary"
    M3, "Your Spiritual Gifts"

Nineteenth Sunday in Ordinary Time, Year C

READING 1, WISDOM 18:6–9

The night of the passover was known beforehand to our fathers, that, with sure knowledge of the oaths In which they put their faith, they might have courage. Your people awaited the salvation of the just and the destruction of their foes. For when you punished our adversaries, in this you glorified us whom you had summoned. For in secret the holy children of the good were offering sacrifice and putting into effect with one accord the divine institution.

PSALM 33:1, 12, 18–19, 20–22

READING 2, HEBREWS 11:1–2, 8–19

Brothers and sisters: Faith is the realization of what is hoped for and evidence of things not seen. Because of it the ancients were well attested. By faith Abraham obeyed when he was called to go out to a place that he was to receive as an inheritance; he went out, not knowing where he was to go. By faith he sojourned in the promised land as in a foreign country, dwelling in tents with Isaac and Jacob, heirs of the same promise; for he was looking forward to the city with foundations, whose architect and maker is God. By faith he received power to generate, even though he was past the normal age—and Sarah herself was sterile—for he thought that the one who had made the promise was trustworthy. So it was that there came forth from one man, himself as good as dead, descendants as numerous as the stars in the sky and as countless as the sands on the seashore. All these died in faith. They did not receive what had been promised but saw it and greeted it from afar and acknowledged themselves to be strangers and aliens on earth, for those who speak thus show that they are seeking a homeland. If they had been thinking of the land from which they had come, they would have had opportunity to return. But now they desire a better homeland, a heavenly one. Therefore, God is not ashamed to be called their God, for he has prepared a city for them. By faith Abraham, when put to the test, offered up Isaac, and he who had received the promises was ready to offer his only son, of whom it was said, "Through Isaac descendants shall bear your name." He reasoned that God was able to raise even from the dead, and he received Isaac back as a symbol.

GOSPEL, LUKE 12:32–48

Jesus said to his disciples: "Do not be afraid any longer, little flock, for your Father is pleased to give you the kingdom. Sell your belongings and give alms. Provide money bags for yourselves that do not wear out, an inexhaustible treasure in heaven that no thief can reach nor moth destroy. For where your treasure is, there also will your heart be. "Gird your loins and light your lamps and be like servants who await their master's return from a wedding, ready to open immediately when he comes and knocks. Blessed are those servants whom the master finds vigilant on his arrival. Amen, I say to you, he will gird himself, have them recline at table, and proceed to wait on them. And should he come in the second or third watch and find them prepared in this way, blessed are those servants. Be sure of this: if the master of the house had known the hour when the thief was coming, he would not have let his house be broken into. You also must be prepared, for at an hour you do not expect, the Son of Man will come."

Then Peter said, "Lord, is this parable meant for us or for everyone?" And the Lord replied, "Who, then, is the faithful and prudent steward whom the master will put in charge of his servants to distribute the food allowance at the proper time? Blessed is that servant whom his master on arrival finds doing so. Truly, I say to you, the master will put the servant in charge of all his property. But if that servant says to himself, 'My master is delayed in coming,' and begins to beat the menservants and the maidservants, to eat and drink and get drunk, then that servant's master will come on an unexpected day and at an unknown hour and will punish the servant severely and assign him a place with the unfaithful. That servant who knew his master's will but did not make preparations nor act in accord with his will shall be beaten severely; and the servant who was ignorant of his master's will but acted in a way deserving of a severe beating shall be beaten only lightly. Much will be required of the person entrusted with much, and still more will be demanded of the person entrusted with more."

The Assurance of Things Hoped for

"I hope I get the job." "I hope I pass this exam." When we talk about hope, it is always in reference to something that hasn't happened yet. And we are rarely sure of the outcome. But hope is what a Christian lives in. Hope tells us that beyond this mortal life there is something even better. Hope reminds us that, however weak and sinful we are, God loves us and sees what we can become if we open our heart to him.

The Letter to the Hebrews tells us that Christian hope is not an exercise in futility. Rather, faith assures us that what we hope for and what we can't yet see is a better home, a heavenly country where we will dwell with God forever. God has made this promise to us and faith tells us it is true. The author uses Abraham as his example. Abraham obeyed God even when he was told to seek out a land he didn't know and to expect a son when he was old. Through faith, Abraham even trusted God when he was told to offer up his son, believing that God had ultimate power, even over death.

When we feel like strangers in a strange land, remembering Abraham, Sarah, and all our ancestors in faith can help us to recover the hope and trust in God that faith brings. The psalmist prays so beautifully, "May your mercy, LORD, be upon us as we put our hope in you." When our journeys take us through dark days, it may be the only thing to cling to.

Where Is Your Treasure?

The very end of Luke's Gospel is a little challenging no matter how much faith we have. In no uncertain terms, Jesus tells us that if we have been given a lot, a lot will be required and if God has trusted us with much, even more will be demanded. Luke combines two parables that caution his hearers to be alert for the coming day of the Lord. The first recounts the reward for those who stay awake—a banquet in which they are served by the Master himself. The second is a little darker as it reports what happens if the slave who is put in charge of others shirks his responsibility. The one who knew what his master wanted and that he would return was to be beaten; the other slaves who didn't know what the master wanted and didn't stay alert and do their job were to be given a lighter beating. Just because they weren't in charge didn't mean they didn't have a job to do. Jesus is quick to point out that the more responsibility we are given, the greater the fall if we do not follow it.

What does this have to do with the treasure Luke speaks about in the beginning of the passage? That little passage is the end of Luke's version of the "flowers of the field," whose message is do not worry about what you are to eat. The bridge between the two passages is Luke's comment about the treasure. In the passage just before this one, the treasure in heaven is one we don't have to worry about because no one can take it from us. In the passage just after the phrase, the treasure is doing the will of the master. We have nothing to worry about if our focus is on what the Master (God) wants.

Nineteenth Sunday in Ordinary Time, Year C

Good News for All of Us

Faith and hope (along with their partner, love) are guiding graces in the Christian life. The Book of Wisdom could look at the past deeds of God at the exodus (the night the passage refers to) and rejoice that the people's trust in God had not failed them. Rather, in destroying the Egyptians at the Red Sea, God summoned the Israelites to himself and glorified them because of their continued faith. In our lives, faith in God and hope in what God promises can help us in times of uncertainty when we don't know where we are going. That's a treasure worth keeping.

Questions for Reflection and Discussion

➤ *What do you hope for in your life right now? What does God have to do with that?*

➤ *Where in your life do you need to trust God more. How might your faith help you do that?*

Related Journey of Faith Lesson

Q13, Conversion: "The Church as Community"

Themes

Faithfulness
  Q13, "The Church as Community"
  M1, "Conversion: A Lifelong Process"
Lifestyle
  Q12, "Who Shepherds the Church?"
  M4, "Discernment"
Promise
  E1, "Election: Saying Yes to Jesus"
  M5, "Our Call to Holiness"

READING 1, JEREMIAH 38:4–6, 8–10

In those days, the princes said to the king: "Jeremiah ought to be put to death; he is demoralizing the soldiers who are left in this city, and all the people, by speaking such things to them; he is not interested in the welfare of our people, but in their ruin." King Zedekiah answered: "He is in your power"; for the king could do nothing with them. And so they took Jeremiah and threw him into the cistern of Prince Malchiah, which was in the quarters of the guard, letting him down with ropes. There was no water in the cistern, only mud, and Jeremiah sank into the mud. Ebed-melech, a court official, went there from the palace and said to him: "My lord king, these men have been at fault in all they have done to the prophet Jeremiah, casting him into the cistern. He will die of famine on the spot, for there is no more food in the city." Then the king ordered Ebed-melech the Cushite to take three men along with him, and draw the prophet Jeremiah out of the cistern before he should die.

PSALM 40:2, 3, 4, 18

READING 2, HEBREWS 12:1-4

Brothers and sisters: Since we are surrounded by so great a cloud of witnesses, let us rid ourselves of every burden and sin that clings to us and persevere in running the race that lies before us while keeping our eyes fixed on Jesus, the leader and perfecter of faith. For the sake of the joy that lay before him he endured the cross, despising its shame, and has taken his seat at the right of the throne of God. Consider how he endured such opposition from sinners, in order that you may not grow weary and lose heart. In your struggle against sin you have not yet resisted to the point of shedding blood.

GOSPEL, LUKE 12:49–53

Jesus said to his disciples: "I have come to set the earth on fire, and how I wish it were already blazing! There is a baptism with which I must be baptized, and how great is my anguish until it is accomplished! Do you think that I have come to establish peace on the earth? No, I tell you, but rather division. From now on a household of five will be divided, three against two and two against three; a father will be divided against his son and a son against his father, a mother against her daughter and a daughter against her mother, a mother-in-law against her daughter-in-law and a daughter-in-law against her mother-in-law."

Prophetic Witness

The prophet of sacred Scripture did not see into the future or tell somebody's fortune. Rather, the prophet had two gifts: An openness to God that allowed him or her to hear or see God's messages and the unique ability to perceive where God was at work and read the signs of the times in the light of faith. This allowed the prophet to challenge the people in times of sinfulness and comfort them in times of trial. But in every instance, the prophet called the people to faithfulness to God's law.

But the life of a prophet was not easy. Many people refused to listen to the message the prophet offered, particularly if it challenged what they wanted to believe or required a change of behavior or thought. Jeremiah preached against the people of Israel, he accused them of turning their backs on the true God, "the source of living water," and instead building broken cisterns (wells) that could not hold water. Because of this, Jerusalem would be destroyed. Unhappy with Jeremiah's preaching, those in power threw him into a cistern. They would have let him die there, rather than believe what he had to say. The king finally relented and had Jeremiah pulled out. Psalm 40 celebrates God who "draws me up from the pit of destruction, out of the muddy clay."

Fire-Bringer

Jesus, the Son of God, was also known as a prophet. There are only a few places where we see the prophetic side of Christ calling people to faithfulness and challenging their practice of faith. Today's reading is one of them. Jesus comes as a disturber of the peace, to set the earth on fire. The image is ominous and seems at odds with the comforting images of the Good Shepherd or the Healing Master. But Jesus is aware that following him may well divide families and neighbors. Jesus advocated a different understanding of the Law, one that put a person at odds with some of the synagogue officials and certainly with the Romans. In our own families, we know how politics and religion can divide us. It wasn't different in Jesus' time. Trying to live in a radically different way is not a peaceful process. Trying to change long entrenched systems of behavior in a nation has led to war.

Good News for All of Us

We are still surrounded by a great cloud of witnesses who have survived the fire of transformation and the persecution of those who think differently. Christianity has lasted over 2,000 years and continues to draw people into a new way of life, daring them to become a radically new creation in Christ. The Hebrew Letter urges us to look to Jesus so that we "may not grow weary of losing heart." In our baptism, we were anointed into the mission of Christ, priest, prophet, and king. The prophetic part of that mission means that, like Jesus, we are always and everywhere to listen for the voice of God and call one another to faithfulness to God's Law. It isn't always easy. Sometimes it's like starting a fire and it may make some people mad. But the prophet steadfastly focuses on God, takes courage in the witnesses who have gone before, and does what is hard that God's will may be done on earth as it is in heaven.

Questions for Reflection and Discussion

➤ *Have you ever had to tell someone a truth that might make them mad? How did you work up the courage to do that?*

➤ *Who have been/are the prophets in our world today? What truth are they telling and how is it being received (they do not necessarily have to be Catholic)?*

Related Journey of Faith Lesson

Q15, "The Saints"

Themes

Conversion
    Q2, "What Is Faith?"
    M1, "Conversion: A Lifelong Process"
Mission
    Q13, "The Church as Community"
    M3, "Your Spiritual Gifts"
Prophet
    Q15, "The Saints"
    M4, "Discernment"

READING 1, ISAIAH 66:18–21

Thus says the LORD: I know their works and their thoughts, and I come to gather nations of every language; they shall come and see my glory. I will set a sign among them; from them I will send fugitives to the nations: to Tarshish, Put and Lud, Mosoch, Tubal and Javan, to the distant coastlands that have never heard of my fame, or seen my glory; and they shall proclaim my glory among the nations. They shall bring all your brothers and sisters from all the nations as an offering to the LORD, on horses and in chariots, in carts, upon mules and dromedaries, to Jerusalem, my holy mountain, says the LORD, just as the Israelites bring their offering to the house of the LORD in clean vessels. Some of these I will take as priests and Levites, says the LORD.

PSALM 117:1, 2

READING 2, HEBREWS 12:5–7, 11–13

Brothers and sisters, You have forgotten the exhortation addressed to you as children: "My son, do not disdain the discipline of the Lord or lose heart when reproved by him; for whom the Lord loves, he disciplines; he scourges every son he acknowledges." Endure your trials as "discipline"; God treats you as sons. For what "son" is there whom his father does not discipline? At the time, all discipline seems a cause not for joy but for pain, yet later it brings the peaceful fruit of righteousness to those who are trained by it. So strengthen your drooping hands and your weak knees. Make straight paths for your feet, that what is lame may not be disjointed but healed.

GOSPEL, LUKE 13:22–30

Jesus passed through towns and villages, teaching as he went and making his way to Jerusalem. Someone asked him, "Lord, will only a few people be saved?" He answered them, "Strive to enter through the narrow gate, for many, I tell you, will attempt to enter but will not be strong enough. After the master of the house has arisen and locked the door, then will you stand outside knocking and saying, 'Lord, open the door for us.' He will say to you in reply, 'I do not know where you are from. And you will say, 'We ate and drank in your company and you taught in our streets.' Then he will say to you, 'I do not know where you are from. Depart from me, all you evildoers!' And there will be wailing and grinding of teeth when you see Abraham, Isaac, and Jacob and all the prophets in the kingdom of God and you yourselves cast out. And people will come from the east and the west and from the north and the south and will recline at table in the kingdom of God. For behold, some are last who will be first, and some are first who will be last."

The Last Will Be First

There is a tendency in nations and peoples to give privilege to particular groups often at the expense of others. We see it at work in the sins of racism and sexism and in any way people try to cling to power "over" others rather than power "with" others. One of the radical notions of Christianity is that we are all on the same footing: "neither Jew nor Greek, slave nor free, male nor female," said St. Paul (Galatians 3:28). Even in the Old Testament, Isaiah envisioned a coming "Day of the Lord" when God will welcome the nations to the Holy City. Both the first and the third readings today suggest that, in some cases, God will welcome in the outcast and the "pagan" nations before those who claim to be the most religious of people. For those who are thinking that God will want them above all others, that has to sting a little bit.

The Preaching of the Nations

The last chapter of Isaiah's prophecy was written after the exile, probably around 500 BC. The homecoming for the exiles, while joyful, has had some rocky moments. How the people defined themselves as Jews without a temple or a country to call their own continued to be a question to which many felt they had the right answer. They disagreed. Into that situation, Isaiah preached his vision of God's word, which didn't focus exclusively on the Chosen People, but on the surrounding nations that had always occupied a kind of second place as far as Israel was concerned. Isaiah's prophecy is remarkable. God will put a sign in the nations; God will send the nations out to other nations to preach about the glory of God. God will use them to bring back all the Israelites from the different lands to which they had been scattered. And finally, in what may be the most disconcerting act of all, God will take some of them as priests and Levites. In Israel, the priests and Levites were hereditary roles from the original twelve tribes. They were the ones who would ultimately oversee the faithfulness of the people and carry out the law when necessary. Including the nations in Israel's vision of its future with God required an incredible shift in what it meant to be God's people.

The Narrow Gate

As Jesus moves to Jerusalem in Luke's Gospel, questions about the end times begin to occupy people's minds. In today's passage, the question is, "Will only a few be saved?" Jesus doesn't hold back. The narrow gate won't be open forever. He warns his listeners that merely eating or drinking with him or listening to him teach does not guarantee their place in heaven. And he also tells them that nations from the four corners of the earth will eat in the presence of God, while those that thought they were more privileged will be locked out. Where the invitation of God is concerned, all are welcome. We may be surprised at who takes Jesus up on it.

Good News for All of Us

Psalm 117, the shortest psalm, praises God whose mercy endures forever. This is a response to the love of God for all his people regardless of knowledge, wealth, power, possessions, or ancestry. It's also a praise of God who lovingly disciplines us when we go astray so that we can learn the right path to follow. The end of our second reading from Hebrews is a joyful shout that recognizes that even times of trial and suffering can reveal the path to God. "Make straight paths for your feet," says the author of Hebrews, "[so] that what is lame may not be dislocated but healed." Sometimes what needs to be healed is not a body part, but a wound of the spirit that suggests we are better than others or that we know more. In Proverbs 16:18 we read that pride goes before a fall. If we think we are better than anyone else, we will soon find out that is not the case, and it will be a painful lesson. The narrow gate tells us that we can't let our egos get too large, lest we be locked outside.

Questions for Reflection and Discussion

> *Have you ever felt like you were better than someone else or more deserving of reward? What would Jesus say to you?*

> *What kind of discipline is good for us?*

Related Journey of Faith Lesson

M1, "Conversion: A Lifelong Process"

Themes

Discipline
    Q2, "What Is Faith?"
    M1, "Conversion: A Lifelong Process"
Praise
    Q9, "The Mass"
    Q7, "Your Prayer Life"
Universality
    Q13, "The Church as Community"
    M8, "Evangelization"

READING 1, SIRACH 3:17–18, 20, 28–29

My child, conduct your affairs with humility, and you will be loved more than a giver of gifts. Humble yourself the more, the greater you are, and you will find favor with God. What is too sublime for you, seek not, into things beyond your strength search not. The mind of a sage appreciates proverbs, and an attentive ear is the joy of the wise. Water quenches a flaming fire, and alms atone for sins.

PSALM 68:4–5, 6–7, 10–11

READING 2, HEBREWS 12:18–19, 22–24A

Brothers and sisters: You have not approached that which could be touched and a blazing fire and gloomy darkness and storm and a trumpet blast and a voice speaking words such that those who heard begged that no message be further addressed to them. No, you have approached Mount Zion and the city of the living God, the heavenly Jerusalem, and countless angels in festal gathering, and the assembly of the firstborn enrolled in heaven, and God the judge of all, and the spirits of the just made perfect, and Jesus, the mediator of a new covenant, and the sprinkled blood that speaks more eloquently than that of Abel.

GOSPEL, LUKE 14:1, 7–14

On a sabbath Jesus went to dine at the home of one of the leading Pharisees, and the people there were observing him carefully. He told a parable to those who had been invited, noticing how they were choosing the places of honor at the table. "When you are invited by someone to a wedding banquet, do not recline at table in the place of honor. A more distinguished guest than you may have been invited by him, and the host who invited both of you may approach you and say, 'Give your place to this man,' and then you would proceed with embarrassment to take the lowest place. Rather, when you are invited, go and take the lowest place so that when the host comes to you he may say, 'My friend, move up to a higher position.' Then you will enjoy the esteem of your companions at the table. For every one who exalts himself will be humbled, but the one who humbles himself will be exalted." Then he said to the host who invited him, "When you hold a lunch or a dinner, do not invite your friends or your brothers or your relatives or your wealthy neighbors, in case they may invite you back and you have repayment. Rather, when you hold a banquet, invite the poor, the crippled, the lame, the blind; blessed indeed will you be because of their inability to repay you. For you will be repaid at the resurrection of the righteous."

Finding Our Place

In our church, people tend to sit in the same pews week after week. Once, when my children arrived a little later than usual, they automatically went to the third pew on the far-left side and were completely baffled to find another family sitting there. They just stood looking until I motioned them to another pew. We like our routines. Maybe it's harder to pray when you're not in your pew.

In the Gospel today, Jesus has a great deal to say about our place. It is not ours to automatically sit in the place of highest honor. Rather, it is ours to move to the lowest place so that others may sit. If the host wants to seat us elsewhere, he will do so. Just as the first were last in last week's reading, so now those who exalt themselves will be humbled. Our God is a God of reversals.

Jesus' lesson in humility comes to us at a time when getting ahead seems to be a priority for most people. There is nothing wrong with ambition, but if we have to step on others to get where we're going or tell people to move so that we can have "our place," then we have lost what Christ tried so hard to teach us—that love and service to one another is the only proper response to God's love for us. Jesus has another message for us this week. If we are to be in true solidarity with the poor and outcasts, we must be willing to invite them to our table and eat with them. It is easy to invite our friends who can repay us in kind; to invite those who cannot repay us is to open our hearts in generosity and gratitude for what we have been given. It is to eat at the table of the humble.

An Attentive Ear

The Wisdom literature always draws from the experiences of life for its profound lessons. Today is no exception. Sirach lifts up humility as a desired character trait, befitting the one whom the Lord accepts. The emphasis is on learning what we can and listening both to the one who is wise and to God in prayer. The advice is helpful for us today. When we are attentive to God, we will find our way to him.

The psalm that follows is another song of praise for God who defends the orphan and widow and leads prisoners out to prosperity. In other words, God exalts the ones who have been humbled.

A Place in Heaven

Our passage from Hebrews paints a picture of eternal life for us. It isn't like the foot of Mount Sinai where the Israelites heard the voice of God sounding like thunder coming out of a dark cloud. They were afraid of that voice and the gloom. They thought they would die if they touched the mountain. By contrast, the baptized come to the heavenly city where there is feasting and rejoicing. They come to Jesus who is the mediator of the new covenant, fulfilling all the promises God had made.

Good News for All of Us

What is our place? Where do we belong? We ask those questions all our lives because feeling like we belong is important to our well-being. God, who created us in love, holds out life with him forever as the place where we can belong and be our truest and best selves no matter what happens. The entrance fee is faith, disposition is the humility necessary to be a disciple of Christ for the rest of our lives. The reward is eternal life and joy forever.

Questions for Reflection and Discussion

> ➤ *Name some wise people in your life. Is there one piece of their advice that has stuck with you?*

> ➤ *Have you ever done something for someone anonymously? Why did you do that?*

Related Journey of Faith Lesson

M3, "Your Spiritual Gifts"

Themes

Charity
    Q15, "The Saints"
    M3, "Your Spiritual Gifts"
Motivation
    Q5, "The Bible"
    M2, "The Role of the Laity"
Reward
    M1, "Conversion: A Lifelong Process"

READING 1, WISDOM 9:13–18B

Who can know God's counsel, or who can conceive what the LORD intends? For the deliberations of mortals are timid, and unsure are our plans. For the corruptible body burdens the soul, and the earthen shelter weighs down the mind that has many concerns. And scarce do we guess the things on earth, and what is within our grasp we find with difficulty; but when things are in heaven, who can search them out? Or who ever knew your counsel, except you had given wisdom and sent your holy spirit from on high? And thus were the paths of those on earth made straight.

PSALM 90:3–4, 5–6, 12–13, 14–17

READING 2, PHILEMON 9–10, 12–17

I, Paul, an old man, and now also a prisoner for Christ Jesus, urge you on behalf of my child Onesimus, whose father I have become in my imprisonment; I am sending him, that is, my own heart, back to you. I should have liked to retain him for myself, so that he might serve me on your behalf in my imprisonment for the gospel, but I did not want to do anything without your consent, so that the good you do might not be forced but voluntary. Perhaps this is why he was away from you for a while, that you might have him back forever, no longer as a slave but more than a slave, a brother, beloved especially to me, but even more so to you, as a man and in the Lord. So if you regard me as a partner, welcome him as you would me.

GOSPEL, LUKE 14:25–33

Great crowds were traveling with Jesus, and he turned and addressed them, "If anyone comes to me without hating his father and mother, wife and children, brothers and sisters, and even his own life, he cannot be my disciple. Whoever does not carry his own cross and come after me cannot be my disciple.

Which of you wishing to construct a tower does not first sit down and calculate the cost to see if there is enough for its completion? Otherwise, after laying the foundation and finding himself unable to finish the work the onlookers should laugh at him and say, 'This one began to build but did not have the resources to finish.' Or what king marching into battle would not first sit down and decide whether with ten thousand troops he can successfully oppose another king advancing upon him with twenty thousand troops? But if not, while he is still far away, he will send a delegation to ask for peace terms. In the same way, anyone of you who does not renounce all his possessions cannot be my disciple."

The Gift of Wisdom

In the movie *October Sky*, high-schooler Homer Hickam, the son of a coal miner, dreams of building rockets and meeting Wernher von Braun, the great aerospace engineer. Several scenes in the film contrast the coal mine under the earth with the vastness of the sky and the stars. Homer's ambition succeeds with the help of friends and a teacher, and he later becomes a NASA engineer himself.

Homer's desire for knowledge beyond the small-town experience and his gift for mathematics enabled him to imagine that there were other paths to follow besides being a coal miner. That spark of wisdom comes from somewhere and our first reading today would argue that it comes from God. Who can discern what God wills? Only the person who has wisdom and who seeks the knowledge that God gives. With our focus on what God has given us, we will find the right path for ourselves. And we'll know that the path leads to God, even if we can't see all the steps.

In the psalm response, the psalmist drills home the belief that human plans are uncertain and emphasizes our smallness compared to God's greatness. The psalmist laments, asking God to have mercy and "teach us to count our days right that we may gain wisdom of heart."

From Slave to Brother

At twenty-five verses long, the Philemon Letter is the shortest of Paul's epistles and concerns the return of a slave named Onesimus who has been traveling with Paul. What is remarkable is Paul's request that Onesimus be accepted not just as a servant, but as a brother in Christ. To ask that Philemon welcome Onesimus as he would welcome Paul was breaking cultural barriers at least within the Christian community. Many people ask why Paul was not more forceful in speaking out against slavery. Because Paul and the early Christians expected that Christ would come again soon, and they were not in a position to change the social structure. But there are other letters in which Paul pointedly states that in the Christian community, there is no slave or free (see Galatians 3:28).

Who Is a Disciple?

The Book of Wisdom tells us that discerning what God wills is only possible with wisdom; Jesus, in Luke's Gospel, makes us see that following Jesus is not always going to be easy or carefree. When we decide to follow Jesus, he wants us to commit our lives. Does Jesus really want us to hate our families? The use of the word is a hard one. Jesus wants us to love him more and be willing to let go of our families if that's what it takes. In many religious orders, young men and women entering the novitiate rarely see their parents and families so they may concentrate on dedicating their lives to the Lord. Jesus also wants disciples to be willing to suffer persecution for his sake. Finally, every disciple must let go of possessions. Does that mean we can own nothing? If there is anything we have that gets in the way of following Jesus, we should get rid of it. Being a disciple is a full-time job.

Good News for All of Us

Jesus wants all of us to be disciples wherever we live and whatever we do. It is amazing to think that with all our flaws and imperfections, Jesus loves us and wants nothing more than for us to follow him until we stand face to face with the Lord at the end of our lives. We might hesitate. It sounds like a big commitment, and it might be a little scary. The path we take to follow Jesus will be different for each one of us. Homer Hickam chose not to be a coal miner, a path his father was not too happy about. But we are given grace, wisdom, access to God through prayer and sacraments, and wonderful role models in the saints and in those we see living a godly life every day to help us follow the Lord who calls us.

Questions for Reflection and Discussion

➤ *How closely are you following Jesus now? Would you consider yourself a disciple?*

➤ *Is there anything in your life that is getting in the way of listening to the voice of the Lord?*

Related Journey of Faith Lesson

M5, "Our Call to Holiness"

Themes

Life
    M1, "Conversion: A Lifelong Process"
    Q5, "The Bible"
    M4, "Discernment"
Wisdom
    Q15, "The Saints"
    M5, "Our Call to Holiness"

READING 1, EXODUS 32:7–11, 13–14

The LORD said to Moses, "Go down at once to your people, whom you brought out of the land of Egypt, for they have become depraved. They have soon turned aside from the way I pointed out to them, making for themselves a molten calf and worshiping it, sacrificing to it and crying out, 'This is your God, O Israel, who brought you out of the land of Egypt!' "I see how stiff-necked this people is, " continued the LORD to Moses. Let me alone, then, that my wrath may blaze up against them to consume them. Then I will make of you a great nation." But Moses implored the LORD, his God, saying, "Why, O Lord, should your wrath blaze up against your own people, whom you brought out of the land of Egypt with such great power and with so strong a hand? Remember your servants Abraham, Isaac, and Israel, and how you swore to them by your own self, saying, 'I will make your descendants as numerous as the stars in the sky; and all this land that I promised, I will give your descendants as their perpetual heritage.'" So the LORD relented in the punishment he had threatened to inflict on his people.

PSALM 51:3–4, 12–13, 17, 19

READING 2, 1 TIMOTHY 1:12–17

Beloved: I am grateful to him who has strengthened me, Christ Jesus our Lord, because he considered me trustworthy in appointing me to the ministry. I was once a blasphemer and a persecutor and arrogant, but I have been mercifully treated because I acted out of ignorance in my unbelief. Indeed, the grace of our Lord has been abundant, long with the faith and love that are in Christ Jesus. This saying is trustworthy and deserves full acceptance: Christ Jesus came into the world to save sinners. Of these I am the foremost. But for that reason I was mercifully treated, so that in me, as the foremost, Christ Jesus might display all his patience as an example for those who would come to believe in him for everlasting life.

To the king of ages, incorruptible, invisible, the only God, honor and glory forever and ever. Amen.

GOSPEL, LUKE 15:1–32 [OR 15:1–10]

Tax collectors and sinners were all drawing near to listen to Jesus, but the Pharisees and scribes began to complain, saying, "This man welcomes sinners and eats with them." So to them he addressed this parable. "What man among you having a hundred sheep and losing one of them would not leave the ninety-nine in the desert and go after the lost one until he finds it? And when he does find it, he sets it on his shoulders with great joy and, upon his arrival home, he calls together his friends and neighbors and says to them, 'Rejoice with me because I have found my lost sheep.' I tell you, in just the same way there will be more joy in heaven over one sinner who repents than over ninety-nine righteous people who have no need of repentance. "Or what woman having ten coins and losing one would not light a lamp and sweep the house, searching carefully until she finds it? And when she does find it, she calls together her friends and neighbors and says to them, 'Rejoice with me because I have found the coin that I lost.' In just the same way, I tell you, there will be rejoicing among the angels of God over one sinner who repents." Then he said, "A man had two sons, and the younger son said to his father, 'Father give me the share of your estate that should come to me.' So the father divided the property between them. After a few days, the younger son collected all his belongings and set off to a distant country where he squandered his inheritance on a life of dissipation. When he had freely spent everything, a severe famine struck that country, and he found himself in dire need. So he hired himself out to one of the local citizens who sent him to his farm to tend the swine. And he longed to eat his fill of the pods on which the swine fed, but nobody gave him any. Coming to his senses he thought, 'How many of my father's hired workers have more than enough food to eat, but here am I, dying from hunger. I shall get up and go to my father and I shall say to him, "Father, I have sinned against heaven and against you. I no longer deserve to be called your son; treat me as you would treat one of your hired workers."' So he got up and went back to his father. While he was still a long way off, his father caught sight of him, and was filled with compassion. He ran to his son, embraced him and kissed him. His son said to him, 'Father, I have sinned against heaven and against you; I no longer deserve to be called your son.' But his father ordered his servants, 'Quickly bring the finest robe and put it on him; put a ring on his finger and sandals on his feet. Take the fattened calf and slaughter it. Then let us celebrate with a feast, because this son of mine was dead, and has come to life again; he was lost, and has been found.' Then the celebration began. Now the older son had been out in the field and, on his way back, as he neared the house, he heard the sound of music and dancing. He called one of the servants and asked what this might mean. The servant said to him, 'Your brother has returned and your father has slaughtered the fattened calf because he has him back safe and sound.' He became angry, and when he refused to enter the house, his father came out and pleaded with him. He said to his father in reply, 'Look, all these years I served you and not once did I disobey your orders; yet you never gave me even a young goat to feast on with my friends. But when your son returns, who swallowed up your property with prostitutes, for him you slaughter the fattened calf.' He said to him, 'My son, you are here with me always; everything I have is yours. But now we must celebrate and rejoice, because your brother was dead and has come to life again; he was lost and has been found.'"

An Example for the World

No one knew better than Paul what his life had been—violent, ignorant, a persecutor of Christians consumed by his own self-righteousness. For Paul, the mercy that Jesus extended to him was a turning point. The worst of sinners (in his words), felt loved, accepted, and forgiven. Christ came into the world to save sinners. Paul's gratitude made him realize that he is the example of Christ's utmost patience with all of us who sin.

A Prodigal Love

Jesus' three examples of God's delight in having us return after wandering away are beloved. In the parable of the lost sheep, when a predator threatens a predator, it bands together to provide protection. The shepherd put himself in danger to retrieve the lost sheep. First-century women were not allowed to work, relying on family or community. The loss of a coin hurt, so she rejoices when she finds it. In the parables, God is both shepherd and the woman who diligently seeks out the lost and brings them home. In the Prodigal Son, pay attention to the father who wants his son home. The part to look at lies in the beginning of the long Gospel when the Pharisees and scribes observe that Jesus welcomes and eats with sinners and tax collectors. In their mind, God's love and mercy are wasted on sinners; the Pharisees are far more deserving. We are blessed that God "wastes" his love on us.

Love that Overcomes Anger

The reading from Exodus commands our attention because God is angry like a parent whose children misbehave. God decides to destroy the Israelites and tempts Moses by saying, "I'll make you a great nation." Moses doesn't give in. Instead, he reminds God that these are his chosen people and he made promises to the patriarchs. God's love overcomes his anger. God changes his mind. Such is the power of taking a deep breath and really thinking about what you want to do.

Good News for All of Us

When we've lost our way and gotten into trouble we didn't expect, God searches for us and extends his mercy. That's why Jesus gave the Church the sacrament of reconciliation.

Questions for Reflection and Discussion

➤ *Have you ever felt like your parents loved one of your siblings more than you? Why did you think that and what did you do about it?*

➤ *Where have you felt God's mercy?*

Related Journey of Faith Lesson

C6, "Sacrament of Penance and Reconciliation"

Themes

Mercy
 Q9, "The Mass"
 M5, "Our Call to Holiness"
Repentance, Sin
 C6, "Sacrament of Penance and Reconciliation"

READING 1, AMOS 8:4–7

Hear this, you who trample upon the needy and destroy the poor of the land! "When will the new moon be over," you ask, "that we may sell our grain, and the sabbath, that we may display the wheat? We will diminish the ephah, add to the shekel, and fix our scales for cheating! We will buy the lowly for silver, and the poor for a pair of sandals; even the refuse of the wheat we will sell!" The LORD has sworn by the pride of Jacob: Never will I forget a thing they have done!

PSALM 113:1–2, 4–6, 7–8

READING 2, 1 TIMOTHY 2:1–8

Beloved: First of all, I ask that supplications, prayers, petitions, and thanksgivings be offered for everyone, for kings and for all in authority, that we may lead a quiet and tranquil life in all devotion and dignity. This is good and pleasing to God our savior, who wills everyone to be saved and to come to knowledge of the truth. For there is one God. There is also one mediator between God and men, the man Christ Jesus, who gave himself as ransom for all. This was the testimony at the proper time. For this I was appointed preacher and apostle—I am speaking the truth, I am not lying—, teacher of the Gentiles in faith and truth. It is my wish, then, that in every place the men should pray, lifting up holy hands, without anger or argument.

GOSPEL, LUKE 16:1–13

Jesus said to his disciples, "A rich man had a steward who was reported to him for squandering his property. He summoned him and said, 'What is this I hear about you? Prepare a full account of your stewardship, because you can no longer be my steward.' The steward said to himself, 'What shall I do, now that my master is taking the position of steward away from me? I am not strong enough to dig and I am ashamed to beg. I know what I shall do so that, when I am removed from the stewardship, they may welcome me into their homes.' He called in his master's debtors one by one. To the

first he said, 'How much do you owe my master?' He replied, 'One hundred measures of olive oil.' He said to him, 'Here is your promissory note. Sit down and quickly write one for fifty.' Then to another the steward said, 'And you, how much do you owe?' He replied, 'One hundred kors of wheat.' The steward said to him, 'Here is your promissory note; write one for eighty.' And the master commended that dishonest steward for acting prudently. "For the children of this world are more prudent in dealing with their own generation than are the children of light. I tell you, make friends for yourselves with dishonest wealth, so that when it fails, you will be welcomed into eternal dwellings. The person who is trustworthy in very small matters is also trustworthy in great ones; and the person who is dishonest in very small matters is also dishonest in great ones. If, therefore, you are not trustworthy with dishonest wealth, who will trust you with true wealth? If you are not trustworthy with what belongs to another, who will give you what is yours? No servant can serve two masters. He will either hate one and love the other, or be devoted to one and despise the other. You cannot serve both God and mammon."

Whom Do We Serve?

Some stories in the Bible don't make a lot of sense at first. Luke's parable today seems to be commending dishonesty. Is Jesus suddenly saying it's OK to cheat? To understand, we need to know the place of the steward/manager in first-century Judea. The steward of a wealthy household took care of the property and managed his master's wealth. It was a lucrative position because the manager often added a hefty surcharge to any debt that was owed to the master. The steward is dishonest in squandering his master's property. When the master finds out and fires him, the steward goes to those who owe both the debt and the surcharge and removes the surcharge. He lets go of his own profit to make friends among the debtors, so they look kindly on him after he is dismissed. The master compliments his cleverness as a child of this age, but it doesn't make the steward less dishonest.

Dishonest wealth (the literal translation is "the mammon of iniquity"), is wealth that leads to greed and even power. In Greek, mammon is that in which you trust. Jesus' message is that we cannot trust and serve two masters. Either we trust completely in God and serve him, or we trust in the false God of mammon and try to make our way in the world by any means necessary, even if it turns out to be dishonest.

The Lord Will Remember

While the steward in the Gospel may have been shrewd in dealing with his predicament, the people that Amos addresses have allowed greed to overpower their humanity. They treat the poor and needy simply as tools to gain more wealth. Amos' prophecy is pointed: "I will never forget a thing they have done." The psalm that follows makes it clear that God himself will "raise up the needy and lift the poor from the ashes." We can only imagine what will happen to those who put them down in the first place.

A Prayer for All People

In the intercessory prayers of the faithful at every Mass, we pray for the Church and the world, the sick and the dead, and for any particular needs of the community. Often, in prayers for the world, special mention is made of those who lead and make decisions for others that the decisions might be just and bring peace. Paul's First Letter to Timothy praises this action as acceptable to God who wants all people to come to him. When we lay our needs before God, God inevitably answers in one way or another.

Good News for All of Us

How much wealth is too much? When does the love of money lead us to forget the needs of others and stop sharing what we have been given? We might have different answers to those questions, but Jesus is clear. When wealth becomes an obstacle to love, we have a problem. If all our attention is focused on getting more by whatever means necessary and spending for our own pleasure, then we are serving something other than God. "Love your neighbor as yourself" requires us to address the injustices caused by too much concentrated in the hands of too few. With God's help, we can find the grace necessary to change our little part of it.

Questions for Reflection and Discussion

➤ Jesus said, "The poor you will always have with you." Where do we start to address the enormous economic inequity in our country today?

➤ How often do you pray? What/whom do you pray for?

Related Journey of Faith Lesson

C13, "Christian Moral Living"

Themes

Money
    C13, "Christian Moral Living"
Poverty
    Q15, "The Saints"
    M5, "Our Call to Holiness"
Stewardship
    M2, "The Role of the Laity"
    M8, "Evangelization"

READING 1, AMOS 6:1A, 4–7

Thus says the LORD the God of hosts: Woe to the complacent in Zion! Lying upon beds of ivory, stretched comfortably on their couches, they eat lambs taken from the flock, and calves from the stall! Improvising to the music of the harp, like David, they devise their own accompaniment. They drink wine from bowls and anoint themselves with the best oils; yet they are not made ill by the collapse of Joseph! Therefore, now they shall be the first to go into exile, and their wanton revelry shall be done away with.

PSALM 146:7, 8–9, 9–10

READING 2, 1 TIMOTHY 6:11–16

But you, man of God, pursue righteousness, devotion, faith, love, patience, and gentleness. Compete well for the faith. Lay hold of eternal life, to which you were called when you made the noble confession in the presence of many witnesses. I charge you before God, who gives life to all things, and before Christ Jesus, who gave testimony under Pontius Pilate for the noble confession, to keep the commandment without stain or reproach until the appearance of our Lord Jesus Christ that the blessed and only ruler will make manifest at the proper time, the King of kings and Lord of lords, who alone has immortality, who dwells in unapproachable light, and whom no human being has seen or can see. To him be honor and eternal power. Amen.

GOSPEL, LUKE 16:19–31

Jesus said to the Pharisees: "There was a rich man who dressed in purple garments and fine linen and dined sumptuously each day. And lying at his door was a poor man named Lazarus, covered with sores, who would gladly have eaten his fill of the scraps that fell from the rich man's table. Dogs even used to come and lick his sores. When the poor man died, he was carried away by angels to the bosom of Abraham. The rich man also died and was buried, and from the netherworld, where he was in torment, he raised his eyes and saw Abraham far off and Lazarus at his side. And he cried out, 'Father Abraham, have pity on me. Send Lazarus to dip the tip of his finger in water and cool my tongue, for I am suffering torment in these flames.' Abraham replied, 'My child, remember that you received what was good during your lifetime while Lazarus likewise received what was bad; but now he is comforted here, whereas you are tormented. Moreover, between us and you a great chasm is established to prevent anyone from crossing who might wish to go from our side to yours or from your side to ours.' He said, 'Then I beg you, father, send him to my father's house, for I have five brothers, so that he may warn them, lest they too come to this place of torment.' But Abraham replied, 'They have Moses and the prophets. Let them listen to them.' He said, 'Oh no, father Abraham, but if someone from the dead goes to them, they will repent.' Then Abraham said, 'If they will not listen to Moses and the prophets, neither will they be persuaded if someone should rise from the dead.'"

How Does God Speak to Us?

In a wonderful folk tale called "The Preacher and the Flood," as a flood threatens his life, the preacher refuses the help of a rowboat, a motorboat, and a helicopter. "The Lord's going to rescue me," he tells them all the while. When the flood takes his life and he gets to heaven, he yells at God. "I trusted you," he says, "and you let me down." The Lord looks at him and says, "I sent two boats and a helicopter. What more can I do?" We often miss the signs of God in this life because we are too busy looking for the big miracles as a sign of God's presence. We forget that God speaks in many ways, including the opportunities we have to care for the least among us.

Such was the case with the rich man in Luke's Gospel. Dives had everything he wanted and failed to notice (or simply ignored) the poor man outside his gate. Lazarus was God's invitation to Dives to look beyond himself and share what he had, just as Moses and all the prophets had told him to do in their writings. Throughout the Old Testament, the care for the poor, widows, and orphans are commandments built into the law. In Isaiah, an entire chapter (58) is devoted to social justice and sharing what we have with those who have less. When Dives, who finally realizes what he did, asks Abraham to warn his relatives, Abraham gives a variation on what God said to the preacher. "They didn't listen to Moses and the prophets. They won't listen even if someone rises from the dead." The message for us is clear. Through the poor, through prophets and teachers, and through Christ himself, God invites, even commands us to share what we have and care for those who have less. All we have to do is listen and act.

A Fight for Justice

Among the prophets, Amos is well known for his demand for justice, particularly when it comes to inequities between the rich and the poor. In our first reading, the catalogue of creature comforts enjoyed by the rich is contrasted with just one word for the—collapse. Amos was writing when Assyria was laying waste to Israel. The leaders ignored the disaster and continued to live rich lives at the expense of those whom the Assyrians would displace and kill. It's only

fitting that these rich would be the first to go into exile. Psalm 146 which follows this passage might have been written by one of the poor who stand outside the gates. A praise of God is followed by this proclamation of trust: "secures justice for the oppressed, who gives bread to the hungry...."

The Good Fight

While St. Paul addresses Timothy specifically in the second reading, his exhortation is clearly for all of us. As in many of Paul's letters, he holds fast to his understanding of Christian behavior—"pursue righteousness, devotion, faith, love, patience, and gentleness." Paul mentions the good fight of faith. Being Christian isn't always easy. In the first century, persecution was a real risk. Today the risk in our country comes more from peer pressure, scandal in the Church, extremist voices, and even our own apathy. But, as Paul says, we have been called to eternal life. All we have to do is take hold of it.

Good News for All of Us

The Letter to the Hebrew begins: "In times past, God spoke in partial and various ways to our ancestors through the prophets; in these last days, he spoke to us through a son...." God has never stopped speaking to us in many ways. The message is always one of love—for God, for our neighbor, and for ourselves, but it might be disguised as a challenge to do more than we are doing, take time for silence, or walk a particular path. The readings today remind us of our obligation to the corporal works of mercy: feed the hungry, give drink to the thirsty, clothe the naked, shelter the homeless, visit the sick and imprisoned, and bury the dead. If we would follow Jesus, they must be a part of our actions.

Questions for Reflection and Discussion

➤ *What words of advice would you give to those trying to live a Christian life today?*

➤ *What does your church do to engage the corporal acts of mercy? Are there others that you participate in yourself?*

Related Journey of Faith Lesson

M2, "The Role of the Laity"

Themes

Conversion
    Q2, "What Is Faith?"
    M1, "Conversion: A Lifelong Process"
Evangelization
    Q13, "The Church as Community"
    M8, "Evangelization"
Service
    Q12, "Who Shepherds the Church?"
    M2, "The Role of the Laity"
    M3, "Your Spiritual Gifts"

READING 1, HABAKKUK 1:2–3; 2:2–4

How long, O Lord? I cry for help but you do not listen! I cry out to you, "Violence!" but you do not intervene. Why do you let me see ruin; why must I look at misery? Destruction and violence are before me; there is strife, and clamorous discord. Then the Lord answered me and said: Write down the vision clearly upon the tablets, so that one can read it readily. For the vision still has its time, presses on to fulfillment, and will not disappoint; if it delays, wait for it, it will surely come, it will not be late. The rash one has no integrity; but the just one, because of his faith, shall live.

PSALM 95:1-2, 6-7, 8-9

READING 2, 2 TIMOTHY 1:6–8, 13–14

Beloved: I remind you, to stir into flame the gift of God that you have through the imposition of my hands. For God did not give us a spirit of cowardice but rather of power and love and self-control. So do not be ashamed of your testimony to our Lord, nor of me, a prisoner for his sake; but bear your share of hardship for the gospel with the strength that comes from God. Take as your norm the sound words that you heard from me, in the faith and love that are in Christ Jesus. Guard this rich trust with the help of the Holy Spirit that dwells within us.

GOSPEL, LUKE 17:5–10

The apostles said to the Lord, "Increase our faith." The Lord replied, "If you have faith the size of a mustard seed, you would say to this mulberry tree, 'Be uprooted and planted in the sea,' and it would obey you. "Who among you would say to your servant who has just come in from plowing or tending sheep in the field, 'Come here immediately and take your place at table'? Would he not rather say to him, 'Prepare something for me to eat. Put on your apron and wait on me while I eat and drink. You may eat and drink when I am finished'? Is he grateful to that servant because he did what was commanded? So should it be with you. When you have done all you have been commanded, say, 'We are unprofitable servants; we have done what we were obliged to do.'"

Waiting on the Lord

"They that hope in the Lord will renew their strength...." Isaiah spoke these words to the exiles in Babylon as they waited for freedom from captivity (Isaiah 40:31). But waiting on anyone requires patience and trust, and we live in the world where both are often in short supply. We become impatient when problems don't resolve as quickly as we think they should. Think of how impatient people were in the recent pandemic. We are not often sure who to trust in times of trouble, especially if there are conflicting voices advocating different solutions. Isaiah reminds us that faith in God can be a healing balm in times of uncertainty, even if the answers don't come as quickly as we would like. In our first reading, we hear the beginning of Habakkuk's lament about the injustices and sinfulness of Israelite society. He wonders how God can see the suffering of the people and not answer their prayers. What we may not be aware of is that Habakkuk's complaint continues throughout chapter 1. We pick up again in the beginning of chapter 2 where God gives a definitive answer that is coming but is not yet fulfilled. Every act of God must wait for its proper time. God encourages Habakkuk to wait and trust. God will not disappoint.

Increasing Our Faith

Our response to the situation of Habakkuk may well be the apostle's response to Jesus: "Lord increase our faith." They have just learned that they need to forgive people seventy times seven times—and they believe that requires a measure of grace they are not sure they have. Jesus holds up a mustard seed, which is very small and reminds them that faith has a capacity they may not comprehend. Faith is such a gift that the smallest amount enables the disciples to do great things. As Jesus continues, he addresses their inability to trust they can follow all that Jesus teaches. The servant does what the master asks with no thought of reward. He is simply doing his job. Jesus expects the disciples and us to do ours, whether it's forgiving others, loving our neighbors as ourselves, or loving God with all our hearts. Faith makes all that possible.

A Spirit of Power and Love

Timothy was converted to Christianity at the hand of Paul, who trained him to be an apostle of the Good News. Here Paul reminds his young protégé that the faith he received is a God-given gift—a spirit of power and love. Timothy was likely facing the same kind of persecution that Paul was, so Paul's words were ones of encouragement in the face of hardship. He doesn't want Timothy to water down the teaching or be ashamed of the faith he proclaims because it is a treasure, given through the Holy Spirit. It's the same treasure we were given at baptism.

Good News for All of Us

How much do we trust God to do what must be done? Are we able to hold fast to our faith in times of trouble and be patient when it seems that God is not answering our prayer? The answer might be a little different for each of us and it would be helpful to reflect on the "spirit of power" that comes with faith. But we should also know that even while we are waiting for the vision, God throws us little reminders that he is here. One spiritual director calls them "life preservers." It might be a friend who calls out of the blue, the peace that comes from a beautiful sunset, or the distinct impression that God is here when we sit quietly in prayer. These things break open the little seed of faith we have and let it grow. And in the meantime, we keep doing what Jesus commands.

Questions for Reflection and Discussion

> ➤ *If you had to compare your faith to the size of something, what would it be and why?*

> ➤ *Have you ever had to wait for something or someone without knowing when they would come? Were you patient when that happened? What helped you wait more calmly?*

Related Journey of Faith Lesson

Q6, "Divine Revelation"

Themes

Faith
   Q2, "What Is Faith?"
   M1, "Conversion: A Lifelong Process"
   M5, "Our Call to Holiness"
Interpretation
   Q6, "Divine Revelation"
   M3, "Your Spiritual Gifts"
   Q7, "Your Prayer Life"
Patience
   Q8, "Catholic Prayers and Practices"
   M4, "Discernment"

READING 1, 2 KINGS 5:14–17

Naaman went down and plunged into the Jordan seven times at the word of Elisha, the man of God. His flesh became again like the flesh of a little child, and he was clean of his leprosy. Naaman returned with his whole retinue to the man of God. On his arrival he stood before Elisha and said, "Now I know that there is no God in all the earth, except in Israel. Please accept a gift from your servant." Elisha replied, "As the Lord lives whom I serve, I will not take it;" and despite Naaman's urging, he still refused. Naaman said: "If you will not accept, please let me, your servant, have two mule-loads of earth, for I will no longer offer holocaust or sacrifice to any other god except to the Lord."

PSALM 98:1, 2–3, 3–4

READING 2, 2 TIMOTHY 2:8–13

Beloved: Remember Jesus Christ, raised from the dead, a descendant of David: such is my gospel, for which I am suffering, even to the point of chains, like a criminal. But the word of God is not chained. Therefore, I bear with everything for the sake of those who are chosen, so that they too may obtain the salvation that is in Christ Jesus, together with eternal glory. This saying is trustworthy: If we have died with him, we shall also live with him; if we persevere, we shall also reign with him. But if we deny him he will deny us. If we are unfaithful, he remains faithful, for he cannot deny himself.

GOSPEL, LUKE 17:11–19

As Jesus continued his journey to Jerusalem, he traveled through Samaria and Galilee. As he was entering a village, ten lepers met him. They stood at a distance from him and raised their voices, saying, "Jesus, Master! Have pity on us!" And when he saw them, he said, "Go show yourselves to the priests." As they were going, they were cleansed. And one of them, realizing he had been healed, returned, glorifying God in a loud voice; and he fell at the feet of Jesus and thanked him. He was a Samaritan. Jesus said in reply, "Ten were cleansed, were they not? Where are the other nine? Has none but this foreigner returned to give thanks to God?" Then he said to him, "Stand up and go; your faith has saved you."

Faith and Thanksgiving

How do we offer thanks for gifts received? My mother insisted that we write thank-you notes the day after Christmas to send to our relatives who had sent gifts to the house. The habit is still with me, and I have passed it on to our daughters. With the advent of email, thank-you notes are often sent over computer or text message along with a picture of the clothing or book received. A simple "thank you" expresses our appreciation for a service rendered or a kindness extended to us. It is the polite thing to do and honors the person who did it.

Our readings today tell us about giving thanks. We begin in the middle of a story. Naaman, an Aramean pagan, had leprosy than no doctor could cure. A young servant suggests to the king of Aram that Naaman see Elisha the prophet in Israel. Naaman goes and Elisha tells him to wash himself in the Jordan River seven times. Naaman refuses, no doubt thinking that if Elisha is as powerful as he has heard, he would simply wave his arms to effect a cure. We pick up the story when Naaman goes to Jordan and is healed. Naaman's first expression of thanks is the recognition of the God of Israel. His second is to offer a gift to Elisha, who does not accept it. His third is a promise to offer a sacrifice to the Lord using the soil of the land where he first believed. His response was a spontaneous welling up of joy over his cure, much the way we might respond to a particularly kind gesture when we least expect it. Luke's Gospel also deals with an unexpected cure. Lepers were under a permanent quarantine. When they were out in public, they had to warn people they were coming which they did by shouting out or wearing bells. Their cry for mercy to Jesus was such a warning and a beggar's plea for money since they could not support themselves. Jesus doesn't say they are cured, he just tells them to show themselves to the priest, one of the steps a leper had to take to be restored to the community after healing. Only one returned, a Samaritan. And his response is much like Naaman's. He praises God and prostrates himself, so great is his joy. Jesus remarked on his faith, declaring it has made him well. Faith, even if it's just in the possibility that God can do more than we can imagine, makes us bathe in rivers and call out for mercy. The thanksgiving that follows signals a faith that has grown deep and embraces a God who is loving and worthy of praise.

This Is My Gospel

The Epistle continues St. Paul's Second Letter to Timothy and his instruction to his young apprentice. It is by turns an exhortation to stay strong in faith and an assurance of the fruits of that faith. Paul repeats what appears to be a traditional teaching—its form is almost poetic. "If we have died with him, we shall also live with him…" Paul takes the Gospel as his own and wants Timothy to do the same, because he believes that those who endure any suffering for the sake of the gospel will reign with Christ at the end of time. Paul's thanks comes through perseverance in preaching and suffering. Paul's faith gives him confidence that Christ will see him through whatever comes.

Good News for All of Us

The thanks that we give is often influenced by the gift we receive. God sent his Son, Jesus, who died that we might live forever. That requires something more than an email or a perfunctory prayer whispered before we sleep. People like Naaman and the leper give us some hints—praise, deep and responsive gratitude, and a promise to extend the love and mercy of God to everyone we meet. We give thanks by worshiping together, loving the stranger, and praying frequently with intention. When we bring our whole self before God, we give praise with our thanks because God is faithful, and so we must be.

Questions for Reflection and Discussion

➤ *What are some of the ways you thank people for what they have done for you?*

➤ *Are there places in your life where God has given you a gift that you didn't expect? How did you express your thanks?*

Related Journey of Faith Lesson

Q8, "Catholic Prayers and Practices"

Themes

Gratitude
    Q8, "Catholic Prayers and Practices"
    M4, "Discernment"
    M5, "Our Call to Holiness"
Praise
    M3, "Your Spiritual Gifts"
    Q7, "Your Prayer Life"

READING 1, EXODUS 17:8–13

In those days, Amalek came and waged war against Israel. Moses, therefore, said to Joshua, "Pick out certain men, and tomorrow go out and engage Amalek in battle. I will be standing on top of the hill with the staff of God in my hand." So Joshua did as Moses told him: he engaged Amalek in battle after Moses had climbed to the top of the hill with Aaron and Hur. As long as Moses kept his hands raised up, Israel had the better of the fight, but when he let his hands rest, Amalek had the better of the fight. Moses' hands, however, grew tired; so they put a rock in place for him to sit on. Meanwhile Aaron and Hur supported his hands, one on one side and one on the other, so that his hands remained steady till sunset. And Joshua mowed down Amalek and his people with the edge of the sword.

PSALM 121:1–2, 3–4, 5–6, 7–8

READING 2, 2 TIMOTHY 3:14—4:2

Beloved: Remain faithful to what you have learned and believed, because you know from whom you learned it, and that from infancy you have known the sacred Scriptures, which are capable of giving you wisdom for salvation through faith in Christ Jesus. All Scripture is inspired by God and is useful for teaching, for refutation, for correction, and for training in righteousness, so that one who belongs to God may be competent, equipped for every good work. I charge you in the presence of God and of Christ Jesus, who will judge the living and the dead, and by his appearing and his kingly power: proclaim the word; be persistent whether it is convenient or inconvenient; convince, reprimand, encourage through all patience and teaching.

GOSPEL, LUKE 18:1–8

Jesus told his disciples a parable about the necessity for them to pray always without becoming weary. He said, "There was a judge in a certain town who neither feared God nor respected any human being. And a widow in that town used to come to him and say,

'Render a just decision for me against my adversary.' For a long time the judge was unwilling, but eventually he thought, 'While it is true that I neither fear God nor respect any human being, because this widow keeps bothering me I shall deliver a just decision for her lest she finally come and strike me.'" The Lord said, "Pay attention to what the dishonest judge says. Will not God then secure the rights of his chosen ones who call out to him day and night? Will he be slow to answer them? I tell you, he will see to it that justice is done for them speedily. But when the Son of Man comes, will he find faith on earth?"

The Virtue of Persistence

"If at first you don't succeed...." Most people can complete that proverb. It is embedded in our culture, urging us to keep trying until we can master a particular task or a bit of knowledge. And most of the time it works. Repeated effort yields better results. Our Scriptures today give us a picture of persistence in the spiritual life from both in the Old and New Testaments. Each example helps us see how persistence helps beat a path to God's door.

Steady Hands

After the Israelites left Egypt, they wandered in the desert for forty years. The journey was not without its problems. The people suffered from a lack of food and water, both of which were answered with a miracle from God. They also encountered enemies and were forced to fight for survival. The Amalekites were fierce warriors, and Moses knew they could not be defeated without divine intervention. At the top of the hill, Moses holds up his hand with God's staff in it. We don't know how long the battle lasted, but we can imagine what it would be like to hold our hands outstretched for hours at a time. When Moses got tired, Aaron and Hur held up his hands, and the story says his hands remained steady. The word that is used for steady comes from the same root as the word for faith. We actually say it at the end of our prayers— *Amen.* Moses was confident that God would give him the grace to persevere. When we pray "amen," we are expressing our faith that God hears our prayers and will give us what we need.

Faithful Preaching

Saint Paul encourages Timothy to be persistent in his learning, in his teaching, and in his preaching. "Remain faithful," Paul says, "to what you have learned and believed." Paul also wants him to be persistent in preaching whether it's convenient or not. The word of God demands our attention, and the world is sorely in need of it. Between these two readings, the responsorial psalm speaks about God's persistence who never "slumbers nor sleeps" (verse 4) and who "guards our going and our coming" (verse 8). Because our God continually watches over us, we can continually turn to his for comfort, challenge, and peace.

Persistence in Prayer

Today's passage in Luke's Gospel seeks to draw a comparison between the unjust judge and God. Even the unjust judge finally capitulates to the widow who continually pleads her case. Jesus is quick to ask how much more God will respond to those who cry out to him. His listeners probably figured out the answer. But a wise spiritual director I knew once pointed out that sometimes what keeps us from God is that the path has not been worn down enough for God to get to us. Our persistence in prayer is what will wear down the path between our house and God's. The more we pray, the easier it is to walk there.

Good News for All of Us

A steady heart, faithfulness in what we learn and believe, a willingness to invite others to believe it as well, and persistence in prayer are hallmarks of the Christian life. Of course, none of it is possible without the grace that God has already given us. We feel it in our desire to know God more intimately and to follow him more closely every day of our lives. Where can we demonstrate our faith and our faithfulness today?

Questions for Reflection and Discussion

➤ *Has there been anything in your life that has made you beat a path to God's door over and over? If so, how did God answer that prayer? If not, what would make you do that?*

➤ *Has there ever been a time when you have remained steady in your convictions or your actions in spite of naysayers or conflict? What kept you going?*

Related Journey of Faith Lesson

M1, "Conversion: A Lifelong Process"

Themes

Perseverance
    Q13, "The Church as Community"
    M1, "Conversion: A Lifelong Process"
Prayer
    Q7, "Your Prayer Life"
    M4, "Discernment"

READING 1, SIRACH 35:12–14, 16–18

The LORD is a God of justice, who knows no favorites. Though not unduly partial toward the weak, yet he hears the cry of the oppressed. The Lord is not deaf to the wail of the orphan, nor to the widow when she pours out her complaint. The one who serves God willingly is heard; his petition reaches the heavens. The prayer of the lowly pierces the clouds; it does not rest till it reaches its goal, nor will it withdraw till the Most High responds, judges justly and affirms the right, and the Lord will not delay.

PSALM 34:2–3, 17–18, 19, 23

READING 2, 2 TIMOTHY 4:6–8, 16–18

Beloved: I am already being poured out like a libation, and the time of my departure is at hand. I have competed well; I have finished the race; I have kept the faith. From now on the crown of righteousness awaits me, which the Lord, the just judge, will award to me on that day, and not only to me, but to all who have longed for his appearance. At my first defense no one appeared on my behalf, but everyone deserted me. May it not be held against them! But the Lord stood by me and gave me strength, so that through me the proclamation might be completed and all the Gentiles might hear it. And I was rescued from the lion's mouth. The Lord will rescue me from every evil threat and will bring me safe to his heavenly kingdom. To him be glory forever and ever. Amen.

GOSPEL, LUKE 18:9–14

Jesus addressed this parable to those who were convinced of their own righteousness and despised everyone else. "Two people went up to the temple area to pray; one was a Pharisee and the other was a tax collector. The Pharisee took up his position and spoke this prayer to himself, 'O God, I thank you that I am not like the rest of humanity—greedy, dishonest, adulterous—or even like this tax collector. I fast twice a week, and I pay tithes on my whole income.' But the tax collector stood off at a distance and would not even raise his eyes to heaven but beat his breast and prayed, 'O God, be merciful to me a sinner.' I tell you, the latter went home justified, not the former; for whoever exalts himself will be humbled, and the one who humbles himself will be exalted."

Role Models

Who is our role model? The answers that we give vary greatly. It might be an admired teacher, one of our parents, or a well-known figure like the pope, the president, or an athlete. Our Scriptures today give us three role models of the Christian life for our consideration. Each is a little bit different from the others but taken together they give us a fairly accurate picture of how we live this life.

A Service Pleasing to the Lord

Jesus Ben Sira's advice begins with a description of God as judge over creation. Sirach makes it clear that, while God will judge all impartially, he has a special concern for the poor, the widow, and the orphan, and he listens to their pleading. In Israel these three groups had no means of support other than the few coins they received from begging. If there is any service that is pleasing to the Lord, it is caring for those who cannot support themselves and God promises to hear those prayers as well and to do justice for those who are righteous. Psalm 34 underscores the point. "The LORD is close to the brokenhearted and saves those whose spirit is crushed" (verse 19). The psalmist also implies that the righteous include not only the poor, but the one who acts justly and compassionately toward them.

The Good Fight

In the second reading, Paul, sensing that his martyrdom is near, gives one of his last addresses to Timothy. For him, the good fight is one that keeps faith front and center in spite of hardship or trouble. Paul understood his mission to the Gentiles clearly. Preach to the Gentiles so they also could hear the gospel and turn to Christ. He has no regrets, though he was imprisoned and beaten. It was the Lord who gave him the strength to continue his good fight.

Have Mercy on Me, a Sinner

By the time we get to the Gospel, we already have a good idea of the kind of person who is righteous in God's eyes—one who is humble, who cares for the poor, and who preaches the Good News to all he meets. When the Pharisee shows up at the temple in Jesus' parable, we almost groan at his behavior. He assumes that his wealth and his position as a Pharisee makes him more worthy of God's favor than anyone else. Indeed, he may have thought—as so many did—that his wealth was a sign of God's favor. His prayer was one of sinful pride. The tax collector, on the other hand, was an outcast in society because of abuse in the tax system of which he had taken part. But his prayer for mercy and his admission of sin came from the heart. Jesus has no problem identifying the one who is justified. It isn't the Pharisee. Every one of us is a sinner who has fallen short of God's will for us. No one has cause to feel superior to anyone else.

Good News for All of Us

Today our role models continue to inspire and encourage us to be the best we can be. These three from Scripture remind us that the twin commandments to love God and love our neighbor continue to form the central tenets of the Christian life. When we love God, we do what he asks, and readily admit when we fall short. We practice humility in prayer and extend the same mercy we receive to others. When we love our neighbor, we care for those who are in need with a joyful and generous heart because we remember that God did the same for us when we were lost. By this love, we shall know one another as Christ's children.

Questions for Reflection and Discussion

> *Feeling like we're more important or better than someone else is a very human emotion, even if it's only a fleeting one. What do you do when you feel that way? How do you remember to honor the humanity of that person?*

> *In what ways do you care for the poor, invite others to know Jesus, and humbly seek reconciliation with God?*

Related Journey of Faith Lesson

Q15, "The Saints"

Themes

Humility
    Q15, "The Saints"
    Q14, "Mary"
    M4, "Discernment"
    M5, "Our Call to Holiness"
Justice
    Q12, "Who Shepherds the Church?"
    Q13, "The Church as Community"
    M2, "The Role of the Laity"
    M8, "Evangelization"
Prayer
    Q7, "Your Prayer Life"

READING 1, WISDOM 11:22—12:2

Before the LORD the whole universe is as a grain from a balance or a drop of morning dew come down upon the earth. But you have mercy on all, because you can do all things; and you overlook people's sins that they may repent. For you love all things that are and loathe nothing that you have made; for what you hated, you would not have fashioned. And how could a thing remain, unless you willed it; or be preserved, had it not been called forth by you? But you spare all things, because they are yours, O LORD and lover of souls, for your imperishable spirit is in all things! Therefore you rebuke offenders little by little, warn them and remind them of the sins they are committing, that they may abandon their wickedness and believe in you, O LORD!

PSALM 145:1–2, 8–9, 10–11, 13, 14

READING 2, 2 THESSALONIANS 1:11—2:2

Brothers and sisters: We always pray for you, that our God may make you worthy of his calling and powerfully bring to fulfillment every good purpose and every effort of faith, that the name of our Lord Jesus may be glorified in you, and you in him, in accord with the grace of our God and Lord Jesus Christ. We ask you, brothers and sisters, with regard to the coming of our Lord Jesus Christ and our assembling with him, not to be shaken out of your minds suddenly, or to be alarmed either by a "spirit," or by an oral statement, or by a letter allegedly from us to the effect that the day of the Lord is at hand.

GOSPEL, LUKE 19:1–10

At that time, Jesus came to Jericho and intended to pass through the town. Now a man there named Zacchaeus, who was a chief tax collector and also a wealthy man, was seeking to see who Jesus was; but he could not see him because of the crowd, for he was short in stature. So he ran ahead and climbed a sycamore tree in order to see Jesus, who was about to pass that way. When he reached the place, Jesus looked up and said, "Zacchaeus, come down quickly, for today I must stay at your house." And he came down quickly and received him with joy. When they all saw this, they began to grumble, saying, "He has gone to stay at the house of a sinner." But Zacchaeus stood there and said to the Lord, "Behold, half of my possessions, Lord, I shall give to the poor, and if I have extorted anything from anyone I shall repay it four times over." And Jesus said to him, "Today salvation has come to this house because this man too is a descendant of Abraham. For the Son of Man has come to seek and to save what was lost."

Wanting to See God

When popes visit the United States, the crowd lining the streets just to see his car is an amazing sight. People are everywhere—on lamp poles, in trees, crammed into every inch of the parkway. We are drawn by famous people, and this is what we do to get near them and hear what they have to say. We might even hope that they notice us and speak to us. That's what God does. God notices us, small as we are. God talks to us and loves us. What do we do in return?

Merciful and Loving to All

Today we hear from the Book of Wisdom, another piece of wisdom literature that uses human experience to reflect on the reality of God. In this passage, the author recognizes how incredibly small we are compared to the whole of creation. He finds it amazing that God loves us at all. The phrase that stands out is this one: "You would not fashion what you hate." Every piece of creation, every human person is willed into existence by God and God is merciful to all.

Quiet Expectation

While the early Christians did not know when Jesus would come again, most expected he would come in their lifetimes. Paul believed that and his exhortations have a sense of urgency about them. The baptized should live transformed lives in the joyful hope of that coming. But Paul had to balance this expectation with his warnings about false teachers who proclaimed that the day had already arrived. Paul didn't want the new Christians to be swayed by those who claimed to be the Messiah (and there were more than a few). That's why so many of his letters preach faithfulness in troubled times. For instance, in today's reading from 2

Thessalonians, he also expresses his fervent prayer that God will strengthen their sense of purpose and their efforts to spread the faith. For Paul, this is the best way to prepare to see God.

Unexpected Conversation

Zacchaeus was a sinner. He knew it and so did everybody else. Tax collectors lined their own pockets while gathering taxes for Rome. But he wanted to see who Jesus was; he had heard so much about him. Too short to see over the crowd, he climbed the nearest tree, undoubtedly jostled by those who wanted nothing to do with him. He had no expectation that Jesus would even notice him. Suddenly that voice called out to him. "Come down. I'll stay at your house." When the Pope stops his car or pauses in his audiences to talk with someone, their faces soften, and they are overcome with joy for that few moments. I imagine Zacchaeus felt the same way. Others weren't so sure about Jesus talking to this sinner. But the very presence of Jesus and the mercy he showed moves Zacchaeus to divest himself of his ill-gotten money and to welcome Christ into his heart. He saw who Jesus was, and seeing him, wanted to follow him.

Good News for All of Us

Wisdom tells us that God is found in all creation. "The world is charged with the grandeur of God," says the poet Gerard Manley Hopkins. We find the evidence of God's love all around us, and Jesus is the fullest revelation of all. The first step to following Jesus is a sincere desire to know him. Zacchaeus climbed a tree. We might read the Scriptures, engage in daily prayer, listen to spiritual companions or our families and partners in prayer. The more we know Jesus, the more we will desire to be like him and will make a home in our hearts for him.

Questions for Reflection and Discussion

➤ *When you meet someone you would like to know better, what are the things you do to achieve that?*

➤ *Do you think God has a sense of humor? What in creation might lead you to believe that?*

Related Journey of Faith Lesson

C13, "Christian Moral Living"

Themes

Forgiveness
    C13, "Christian Moral Living"
    M4, "Discernment"
Reconciliation
    Q2, "What Is Faith?"
    Q7, "Your Prayer Life"
Repentance
    Q8, "Catholic Prayers and Practices"
    M1, "Conversion: A Lifelong Process"
    M5, "Our Call to Holiness"

READING 1, 2 MACCABEES 7:1–2, 9–14

It happened that seven brothers with their mother were arrested and tortured with whips and scourges by the king, to force them to eat pork in violation of God's law. One of the brothers, speaking for the others, said: "What do you expect to achieve by questioning us? We are ready to die rather than transgress the laws of our ancestors." At the point of death he said: "You accursed fiend, you are depriving us of this present life, but the King of the world will raise us up to live again forever. It is for his laws that we are dying." After him the third suffered their cruel sport. He put out his tongue at once when told to do so, and bravely held out his hands, as he spoke these noble words: "It was from Heaven that I received these; for the sake of his laws I disdain them; from him I hope to receive them again." Even the king and his attendants marveled at the young man's courage, because he regarded his sufferings as nothing. After he had died, they tortured and maltreated the fourth brother in the same way. When he was near death, he said, "It is my choice to die at the hands of men with the hope God gives of being raised up by him; but for you, there will be no resurrection to life."

PSALM 17:1, 5–6, 8, 15

READING 2, 2 THESSALONIANS 2:16—3:5

Brothers and sisters: May our Lord Jesus Christ himself and God our Father, who has loved us and given us everlasting encouragement and good hope through his grace, encourage your hearts and strengthen them in every good deed and word. Finally, brothers and sisters, pray for us, so that the word of the Lord may speed forward and be glorified, as it did among you, and that we may be delivered from perverse and wicked people, for not all have faith. But the Lord is faithful; he will strengthen you and guard you from the evil one. We are confident of you in the Lord that what we instruct you, you are doing and will continue to do. May the Lord direct your hearts to the love of God and to the endurance of Christ.

GOSPEL, LUKE 20:27–38

Some Sadducees, those who deny that there is a resurrection, came forward and put this question to Jesus, saying, "Teacher, Moses wrote for us, If someone's brother dies leaving a wife but no child, his brother must take the wife and raise up descendants for his brother. Now there were seven brothers; the first married a woman but died childless. Then the second and the third married her, and likewise all the seven died childless. Finally the woman also died. Now at the resurrection whose wife will that woman be? For all seven had been married to her." Jesus said to them, "The children of this age marry and remarry; but those who are deemed worthy to attain to the coming age and to the resurrection of the dead neither marry nor are given in marriage. They can no longer die, for they are like angels; and they are the children of God because they are the ones who will rise. That the dead will rise even Moses made known in the passage about the bush, when he called out 'Lord,' the God of Abraham, the God of Isaac, and the God of Jacob; and he is not God of the dead, but of the living, for to him all are alive."

Children of the Resurrection

As we get closer to the end of the Church year, our readings begin to focus on what lies beyond this world. What will happen when we die? What will heaven be like? The persecutions in the last two centuries before Christ had already given rise to a theology of resurrection. It was not an official doctrine, but some Jews accepted the possibility. The readings today give us hints of what resurrection might mean for us.

The Hope of Resurrection

The Catholic canon of the Old Testament contains two books of Maccabees. Both tell the story of Judas Maccabeus and his brothers who staged a revolt against the Seleucid empire and refused to turn their backs on God. The first book recounts the noble battles waged by Judas and his brothers, but it does not reflect on their deaths, seeming to take them in stride. The second book finds meaning in martyrdom and begins to explore a different hope, as the fourth brother declares: "It is my choice to die at the hands of mortals with the hope that God will restore me to life; but for you, there will be no resurrection to life." Resurrection was not part of Jewish thought, but persecution and the need to make meaning out of suffering coupled with the belief that God will punish the wicked and reward the righteous combined to create a new understanding that would become a central tenet of Christian faith.

God of the Living

In Luke's Gospel, the Sadducees use the dispute regarding resurrection to trap Jesus. Since they reject the idea of resurrection, they assume that those who believe in it think that life after death will be the same as life before it. Thus, they pose a question that they think exposes the absurdity of the whole idea. Jesus is quick to set them right. Who will be married to whom is a question that belongs to this world. In the life to come, the children of God will not think of community with one another in the same way. They will have no need for marriage and no need to worry about it. They

will be changed. At the very end of Jesus' answer, he does speak of the fact that the dead are raised and uses Moses' encounter with the burning bush to prove it. Moses addressed the God of Abraham, Isaac, and Jacob because, in God, they are all alive. Jesus' words give us our first understanding of the Communion of Saints.

The Lord Is Faithful

"May the Lord direct your hearts to the love of God," Paul says as he begins the final part of 2 Thessalonians. Paul had such confidence in his faith that it inspires us even today. He saw God's grace as a gift given to all who seek it and believed that it was the source of hope, strength, and love for every Christian. Moreover, Christians had a duty to pass that love onto others— another facet of the Good News. Above all, Paul rested secure in the knowledge that the Lord was faithful, even if people weren't. Such certainty was enough for Paul to carry out his mission. Is it enough for us?

Good News for All of Us

In the Nicene Creed, we say, "I look forward to the resurrection of the dead and the life of the world to come." Our joyful hope is that we will be one with God from whom we came and to whom we long to return. With God's help, we shall do so.

Questions for Reflection and Discussion

➤ *What were your images of heaven, hell, and purgatory when you were a child? How have they changed?*

➤ *What is the purpose of suffering? Why doesn't God stop suffering in the world?*

Related Journey of Faith Lesson

Q2, "What Is Faith?"

Themes

Death
    Q2, "What Is Faith?"
Personhood
    Q15, "The Saints"
    M1, "Conversion: A Lifelong Process"
    M2, "The Role of the Laity"
    M3, "Your Spiritual Gifts"
Resurrection
    Q2, "What Is Faith?"
    M5, "Our Call to Holiness"

READING 1, MALACHI 3:19–20A

Lo, the day is coming, blazing like an oven, when all the proud and all evildoers will be stubble, and the day that is coming will set them on fire, leaving them neither root nor branch, says the LORD of hosts. But for you who fear my name, there will arise the sun of justice with its healing rays.

PSALM 98:5–6, 7–8, 9

READING 2, 2 THESSALONIANS 3:7–12

Brothers and sisters: You know how one must imitate us. For we did not act in a disorderly way among you, nor did we eat food received free from anyone. On the contrary, in toil and drudgery, night and day we worked, so as not to burden any of you. Not that we do not have the right. Rather, we wanted to present ourselves as a model for you, so that you might imitate us. In fact, when we were with you, we instructed you that if anyone was unwilling to work, neither should that one eat. We hear that some are conducting themselves among you in a disorderly way, by not keeping busy but minding the business of others. Such people we instruct and urge in the Lord Jesus Christ to work quietly and to eat their own food.

GOSPEL, LUKE 21:5–19

While some people were speaking about how the temple was adorned with costly stones and votive offerings, Jesus said, "All that you see here—the days will come when there will not be left a stone upon another stone that will not be thrown down." Then they asked him, "Teacher, when will this happen? And what sign will there be when all these things are about to happen?" He answered, "See that you not be deceived, for many will come in my name, saying, 'I am he,' and "The time has come.' Do not follow them! When you hear of wars and insurrections, do not be terrified; for such things must happen first, but it will not immediately be the end." Then he said to them, "Nation will rise against nation,

and kingdom against kingdom. There will be powerful earthquakes, famines, and plagues from place to place; and awesome sights and mighty signs will come from the sky. "Before all this happens, however, they will seize and persecute you, they will hand you over to the synagogues and to prisons, and they will have you led before kings and governors because of my name. It will lead to your giving testimony. Remember, you are not to prepare your defense beforehand, for I myself shall give you a wisdom in speaking that all your adversaries will be powerless to resist or refute. You will even be handed over by parents, brothers, relatives, and friends, and they will put some of you to death. You will be hated by all because of my name, but not a hair on your head will be destroyed. By your perseverance you will secure your lives."

The Day of the Lord

At the end of Luke's story of the ascension (Acts 1:1–11), two men in white robes (presumably angels) tell the apostles that Jesus will "come in the same way as you saw him go into heaven." The expectation of the return of Jesus as ruler and judge drew on and melded with the "Day of the Lord" in the Old Testament. That day was alternately described as one of joy and feasting for the righteous and one of terror for the wicked. Christians drew their hope from this day when the world would become subject to Christ. And while they didn't know exactly when it would come, they expected it sooner rather than later.

Our readings today present some aspect of that hoped-for day. The mysterious prophet Malachi (the name means "my messenger") addresses the concerns of the post-exilic Jews, whose return to Judah did not solve every problem. Instead, they saw wicked people becoming rich and powerful while the poor suffered. Malachi calls their attention to the coming day of the Lord which will burn the wicked with fire (often a symbol and means of purification) but will heal the suffering believers like the warm rays of the sun.

Mind Your Own Business

Of course, Paul could not be everywhere at once. His letters were a way of speaking to problems that arose in specific Christian communities because of the context in which they found themselves. In Thessalonica, there were those false teachers who insisted that the day of the Lord was already here or was so imminent that they didn't need to do anything to get ready for it. Instead, they spent their time being busybodies and expecting others to serve them. Paul was not impressed. Being Christian meant actively living a Christian life and teaching and preaching the Good News as Paul had done. The day of the Lord was coming, but the signs of its coming had not yet appeared, and in any case, it was not an excuse to stop working or make trouble for anyone. Paul urges the Thessalonians not to fall prey to the false teacher, but to hold fast to his example and those of his missionary companions.

Do Not Be Afraid

In the Gospel, Jesus offers three prophetic visions of the *Parousia* (the Greek word for the Second Coming. It means presence or official visit). All of them are challenging and a little uncomfortable.

The first prophecies about the destruction of the Second Temple (which the Romans destroyed in the year 70). Jesus warns people not to listen to false teachers who claim to be the Messiah or to know exactly when Christ would come again.

The second prophecy describes the wars, earthquakes, famines, and the heavenly signs that will signal the coming day of the Lord. These descriptions are straight out of apocalyptic literature (see the second half of Daniel or the Book of Revelation, for examples). It was the absence of these signs that told Paul the day of the Lord had not come yet.

The third prophecy involves Christian persecution at the hands of the Jews and the Romans, and betrayal by families and friends. While frightening, Jesus points out that this is also an opportunity to give witness and promises that he will give the words needed for such a testimony.

Good News for All of Us

We are fortunate in this country. We are not persecuted as the early Christians were and as many Christians around the world continue to be. So it's hard for us to imagine what it would be like to give witness to Christ when our bodies were being hurt or death was imminent. There's one thing to remember, though. That's what happened to Jesus. He was tortured and killed for telling us the truth about God's love and showing us how to live in that truth. Whatever slights we suffer, we can be assured that Christ walks with us now and always.

Questions for Reflection and Discussion

> ➤ How do people react when they find out that you are Catholic or are becoming a Catholic? Does the portrayal of Catholics in movies or in the media raise any questions for you?

> ➤ "Imitation is the sincerest form of flattery." Saint Paul would think this saying was true and would try to be worthy of being imitated. Is your practice of faith worthy of being imitated?

Related Journey of Faith Lesson

M5, "Our Call to Holiness"

Themes

Fidelity
    Q15, "The Saints"
    Q14, "Mary"
    M4, "Discernment"
    M5, "Our Call to Holiness"
Ministry
    Q12, "Who Shepherds the Church?"
    M2, "The Role of the Laity"
    M3, "Your Spiritual Gifts"
Perseverance
    M6, "Living the Virtues"
    M1, "Conversion: A Lifelong Process"
Death and Life
    Q16, "Eschatology: The 'Last Things'"

READING 1, 2 SAMUEL 5:1–3

In those days, all the tribes of Israel came to David in Hebron and said:"Here we are, your bone and your flesh. In days past, when Saul was our king, it was you who led the Israelites out and brought them back. And the Lord said to you, 'You shall shepherd my people Israel and shall be commander of Israel.'" When all the elders of Israel came to David in Hebron, King David made an agreement with them there before the Lord, and they anointed him king of Israel.

PSALM 122:1–2, 3–4, 4–5

READING 2, COLOSSIANS 1:12–20

Brothers and sisters: Let us give thanks to the Father, who has made you fit to share in the inheritance of the holy ones in light. He delivered us from the power of darkness and transferred us to the kingdom of his beloved Son, in whom we have redemption, the forgiveness of sins. He is the image of the invisible God, the firstborn of all creation. For in him were created all things in heaven and on earth, the visible and the invisible, whether thrones or dominions or principalities or powers; all things were created through him and for him. He is before all things, and in him all things hold together. He is the head of the body, the church. He is the beginning, the firstborn from the dead, that in all things he himself might be preeminent. For in him all the fullness was pleased to dwell, and through him to reconcile all things for him, making peace by the blood of his cross through him, whether those on earth or those in heaven.

GOSPEL, LUKE 23:35–43

The rulers sneered at Jesus and said, "He saved others, let him save himself if he is the chosen one, the Christ of God." Even the soldiers jeered at him. As they approached to offer him wine they called out, "If you are King of the Jews, save yourself." Above him there was an inscription that read, "This is the King of the Jews." Now one of the criminals hanging there reviled Jesus, saying, "Are you not the Christ? Save yourself and us." The other, however, rebuking him, said in reply, "Have you no fear of God, for you are subject to the same condemnation? And indeed, we have been condemned justly, for the sentence we received corresponds to our crimes, but this man has done nothing criminal." Then he said, "Jesus, remember me when you come into your kingdom." He replied to him, "Amen, I say to you, today you will be with me in Paradise."

A King Like No Other

When we think of kings today, we either have visions of rulers who have varying degrees of power over their countries or we think of fairy tale monarchs who lead armies into battle, make laws, and marry in order to form alliances. The king in the Old Testament had one job. He was to be the example of obedience to the law of God for all the people. Making laws and leading armies might also happen, but that wasn't his main concern. Israel had one allegiance and that was to the Lord. The king was to show that allegiance always. In today's readings, we see that idea of kingship play out in David and in Jesus, the one a shepherd-ruler; the other the perfection of kingship in the fullest sense of the word.

Shepherd King

In the first centuries after Moses led the people out of Egypt, Israel did not have a king. Leadership was passed down from Moses to Joshua, to the Judges. The people, who saw that the surrounding nations had kings who could raise up armies to attack, entreated the prophet Samuel to anoint one for Israel. Because God was king, Samuel was reluctant, but eventually gave in and anointed Saul. Saul ultimately disobeyed God and fell into madness. God instructed Samuel to search out Jesse's youngest son, whom God had chosen to be anointed in Saul's place. David was just a shepherd. Not even Samuel expected such a lowly figure to be chosen. But David grew in age and grace and eventually all the tribes of Israel recognized that he was the king who would shepherd Israel by God's command. They anointed him in Hebron, and though David was not perfect, he was held up as the example of obedience by which other kings were judged. God made a covenant with David to love him and be with him always and it was from the house of David that the Messiah would come.

The Last Temptation of the King

Just before Jesus begins his public ministry, he is tempted in the desert. We hear the devil say: "If you are the Son of God…" as he urges Jesus to turn stone into bread or fall down and worship him. As Jesus is dying on the cross, the tempter returns looking like those who mocked him: "If you are the king of the Jews, save yourself." The soldiers and others who taunt him saw only the sign that Pilate put on the cross: "The King of the Jews," and they took it to mean an earthly king like all the others they knew. Even Pilate meant it as a humiliation. This king had no power; look at what was happening to him. None of them understood the true nature of kingship as obedience to the one true King who was God. Jesus alone knew that the life of the world to come depended on him being obedient to his Father even to death on the cross. The good thief caught a glimpse of the power inherent in that obedience and the kingdom it signified. His faith brought him to his reward.

Good News for All of Us

Jesus' obedience to his Father earned us redemption and reconciliation with God. In his Letter to the Colossians, Paul talks about it as our deliverance from darkness by Christ who is himself the fullness of light and the complete revelation of God. The words we say about Jesus in our Creed echo the words of the hymn that Paul includes in his letter. This is the miracle of our lives: that God so loved us, he chose to dwell with us in the person of Jesus. The best gift we could give in return is our own obedience as we follow the example of Jesus.

Questions for Reflection and Discussion

> *When you think of Jesus as king, what images come to mind? What commands do you imagine Jesus giving you?*

> *We are at the end of the Church year. How has your faith grown in the last year? Do you see things differently than you did a year ago?*

Related Journey of Faith Lesson

E5, "The Way of the Cross"

Themes

Crucifixion
    E5, "The Way of the Cross"
Kingdom
    M4, "Discernment"
    M8, "Evangelization"
Service
    M2, "The Role of the Laity"
    M3, "Your Spiritual Gifts"

READING 1, GENESIS 3:9–15, 20

After the man, Adam, had eaten of the tree, the LORD God called to the man and asked him, "Where are you?" He answered, "I heard you in the garden; but I was afraid, because I was naked, so I hid myself." Then he asked, "Who told you that you were naked? You have eaten, then, from the tree of which I had forbidden you to eat!" The man replied, "The woman whom you put here with me—she gave me fruit from the tree, and so I ate it." The LORD God then asked the woman, "Why did you do such a thing?" The woman answered, "The serpent tricked me into it, so I ate it." Then the LORD God said to the serpent: "Because you have done this, you shall be banned from all the animals and from all the wild creatures; on your belly shall you crawl, and dirt shall you eat all the days of your life. I will put enmity between you and the woman, and between your offspring and hers; he will strike at your head, while you strike at his heel." The man called his wife Eve, because she became the mother of all the living.

PSALM 98:1, 2–3, 3–4

READING 2, EPHESIANS 1:3–6, 11–12

Brothers and sisters: Blessed be the God and Father of our Lord Jesus Christ, who has blessed us in Christ with every spiritual blessing in the heavens, as he chose us in him, before the foundation of the world, to be holy and without blemish before him. In love he destined us for adoption to himself through Jesus Christ, in accord with the favor of his will, for the praise of the glory of his grace that he granted us in the beloved. In him we were also chosen, destined in accord with the purpose of the One who accomplishes all things according to the intention of his will, so that we might exist for the praise of his glory, we who first hoped in Christ.

GOSPEL, LUKE 1:26–38

The angel Gabriel was sent from God to a town of Galilee called Nazareth, to a virgin betrothed to a man named Joseph, of the house of David, and the virgin's name was Mary. And coming to her, he said, "Hail, full of grace! The Lord is with you." But she was greatly troubled at what was said and pondered what sort of greeting this might be. Then the angel said to her, "Do not be afraid, Mary, for you have found favor with God. Behold, you will conceive in your womb and bear a son, and you shall name him Jesus. He will be great and will be called Son of the Most High, and the Lord God will give him the throne of David his father, and he will rule over the house of Jacob forever, and of his Kingdom there will be no end." But Mary said to the angel, "How can this be, since I have no relations with a man?" And the angel said to her in reply, "The Holy Spirit will come upon you, and the power of the Most High will overshadow you. Therefore the child to be born will be called holy, the Son of God. And behold, Elizabeth, your relative, has also conceived a son in her old age, and this is the sixth month for her who was called barren; for nothing will be impossible for God." Mary said, "Behold, I am the handmaid of the Lord. May it be done to me according to your word." Then the angel departed from her.

Nothing Is Impossible for God

In Paul's epistle today, he praises God who "chose us in [Christ]…to be holy and without blemish before him" (Ephesians 1:4). When we look around the world today and in our own lives it might seem like God has made a mistake in doing so. We're sinful—as individuals and as nations. We don't always care for the poor, promote peace and justice, or revere life in all its stages. We like to be right, sometimes to the detriment of being compassionate, merciful, or just. We try and often fail. How can God possibly have chosen us? Paul continues: "In love, [God] destined us for adoption to himself through Jesus Christ…" (verse 5). That says everything we need to know. God loves us even though we are flawed, sinful, and broken. God can work with us because nothing is impossible for him. Because we belong to God, we rejoice and strive to live lives of holiness through his grace.

I am reminded of this because the feast of the Immaculate Conception of Mary is frequently experienced as somewhat removed from our experience. We understand that it honors Mary as being conceived without sin, and perhaps we sometimes wonder why that's important enough for us to observe another holy day of obligation in her honor. The reasons are in the story itself.

When the angel Gabriel appears to Mary, he doesn't call her by her name. Instead, he addresses her as "full of grace." Name changes in Scripture reveal a particular identity and vocation in God's eyes. Simon becomes Peter (rock) and is told, "on this rock I will build my Church" (Matthew 16:18). Mary is revealed as the one so filled with God's grace that she can respond wholeheartedly to God's command. When the Church reflected on this in later years, it understood Mary to have been miraculously preserved from the effects of original sin. That means she was always able to say yes to God with her whole being, even in difficult or puzzling circumstances. Far from being removed from our experience, she is the first and best example of what can happen when God does what we think is impossible—fills us with the grace to be holy and to do his will. Growth in understanding and embracing that kind of freedom is precisely what the Lord wants for us. That growth comes when we say our own yes to the Holy Spirit again and again, at ever deeper levels.

Mother of All the Living

Just as Christ is called the "New Adam," Mary is frequently referred to as the "New Eve." The analogy isn't perfect, but the thought behind it carries the concept of the new creation ushered in by the death and resurrection of Jesus. Saint Paul says: "So whoever is in Christ is a new creation: the old things have passed away; behold, new things have come" (2 Corinthians 5:17). Eve's name means "living one" or "source of life," and so Adam calls her the mother of all the living. In the new creation, Mary assumes that role not only as the mother of Jesus, but as the mother of all those who have found life in Christ.

Good News for All of Us

What would it be like to hear the word of God and obey it with a glad and willing heart? What would it be like to acknowledge our fears, our personal desires, and the temptation of worldly goods and still follow Jesus as adopted brothers and sisters into the fullness of divine life? Mary was the first to do so, and we look to her as an example. "Oh," we might say, "she was born without sin, so it was easy." It wasn't easy. But we know our baptism frees us from original sin and gives us the grace to make the same decision to obey God because nothing is impossible for God.

Questions for Reflection and Discussion

> Our Lady of the Immaculate Conception is the patron saint of the United States. How might Mary's example guide us in making our country a more just, merciful, and holy place to live?

> Have you ever been tempted to do (or have you done) something you know isn't right because of a temporary good or because of the pressure of friends? What kept you from doing what God might have wanted you to do?

> Not many of us have angels visiting us. How do you think God speaks to you? Where do you hear the voice of God the loudest?

Related Journey of Faith Lesson

Q14, "Mary"

Themes

Immaculate Conception, Mary
  C10, "The People of God"
  Q4, "Who Is Jesus Christ?"
  Q14, "Mary"
Life
  C3, "The Sacrament of Baptism"
  C7, "The Sacrament of Anointing of the Sick"
  C15, "A Consistent Ethic of Life"
  C14, "The Dignity of Life"
Sin
  C6, "The Sacrament of Penance and
      Reconciliation"

READING 1, ISAIAH 9:1–6

The people who walked in darkness have seen a great light; upon those who dwelt in the land of gloom a light has shone. You have brought them abundant joy and great rejoicing, as they rejoice before you as at the harvest, as people make merry when dividing spoils. For the yoke that burdened them, the pole on their shoulder, and the rod of their taskmaster you have smashed, as on the day of Midian. For every boot that tramped in battle, every cloak rolled in blood, will be burned as fuel for flames. For a child is born to us, a son is given us; upon his shoulder dominion rests. They name him Wonder-Counselor, God-Hero, Father-Forever, Prince of Peace. His dominion is vast and forever peaceful, from David's throne, and over his kingdom, which he confirms and sustains by judgment and justice, both now and forever. The zeal of the LORD of hosts will do this!

PSALM 96: 1–2, 2–3, 11–12, 13

READING 2, TITUS 2:11–14

Beloved: The grace of God has appeared, saving all and training us to reject godless ways and worldly desires and to live temperately, justly, and devoutly in this age, as we await the blessed hope, the appearance of the glory of our great God and savior Jesus Christ, who gave himself for us to deliver us from all lawlessness and to cleanse for himself a people as his own, eager to do what is good.

GOSPEL, LUKE 2:1–14

In those days a decree went out from Caesar Augustus that the whole world should be enrolled. This was the first enrollment, when Quirinius was governor of Syria. So all went to be enrolled, each to his own town. And Joseph too went up from Galilee from the town of Nazareth to Judea, to the city of David that is called Bethlehem, because he was of the house and family of David, to be enrolled with Mary, his betrothed, who was with child. While they were there, the time came for her to have her child, and she gave birth to her firstborn son. She wrapped him in swaddling clothes and laid him in a manger, because there was no room for them in the inn. Now there were shepherds in that region living in the fields and keeping the night watch over their flock. The angel of the Lord appeared to them and the glory of the Lord shone around them, and they were struck with great fear. The angel said to them, "Do not be afraid; for behold, I proclaim to you good news of great joy that will be for all the people. For today in the city of David a savior has been born for you who is Christ and Lord. And this will be a sign for you: you will find an infant wrapped in swaddling clothes and lying in a manger." And suddenly there was a multitude of the heavenly host with the angel, praising God and saying: "Glory to God in the highest and on earth peace to those on whom his favor rests."

Prince of Peace

For as long as I can remember, every Christmas has included multiple variations on the wish for peace. From the titles of the child in Isaiah's prophecy to the song of the angels in Luke's Gospel, the hope for peace on earth rings out. Even today people of every faith and none often wish one another peace in this season, finding a common bond in their desire for an end to the divisions that threaten to consume us.

Isaiah's vision of light at the end of a dark age in Israel rested on the newborn child whose authority is from God. I am intrigued by the titles that Isaiah employs. They don't begin with anything having to do with war. They begin with two nouns: Wonder-Counselor, which suggest what the child is—a wonder or miracle and one who is wise, compassionate, and just. They continue with names that speak to the child's relationship with the people—God-Hero (the mighty one, champion of his people) and Father-Forever (bound in a family relationship with his people). The last name—Prince of Peace—tells us that this child will usher in the peace that accompanies the reign of God. At the end of this passage, Isaiah envisions this peace as a time when justice and righteousness will fill the earth. Elsewhere, he speaks of a great banquet (Isaiah 25:6–9) and a time of restoration when the wolf and lamb shall lie down together (Isaiah 11:1–9).

Many in Israel expected a Messiah who would vanquish Israel's enemies and bring the peace that is the absence of war. When Jesus came, many did not recognize him as the Messiah because he did not conquer the Roman oppressors in the way they expected. They were fixated on a vision of the Messiah as the mighty warrior and forgot that justice and righteousness meant correcting even those in authority when they misinterpreted God's commands. They didn't realize that peace can come in the heart when one lives according to the law of love which comes from God regardless of the world's pressure.

A Savior Is Born this Day

Isaiah never used the term *Messiah* when he proclaimed his prophecy. When Luke remembers the birth of Jesus, he starts with the birth of a child and puts his identity in the mouths of the angels. This is the Savior (deliverer) who is Christ (the anointed one—Messiah in Hebrew) the Lord (a name used for God in the Hebrew Scriptures). No wonder the angels announced peace on earth. This child was the fulfillment of Isaiah's prophecy. We came to understand that he was God who became incarnate to conquer our true enemies, sin and death, and to reconcile us to God.

Good News for All of Us

The Christmas season is generally a time of hope and goodwill toward all people. For many though, it can also be a time of loneliness if they have suffered the loss of family or friends or if they feel that hope has passed them by. In the spirit of the Christ Child and the vision of the world he brings, we can reach out to anyone who needs encouragement to go on another day. We can contribute or work for a food pantry, buy a present for a family in need, or simply go out of our way to talk to a homeless person. We can work for justice for all people and bring a little peace into our daily lives. Jesus can help us do this.

Questions for Reflection and Discussion

> *Does someone in your church or your town need a helping hand or a friendly smile? How can you help that person today?*

> *Where do you find peace in the midst of a busy or stressful time? How do you share it with others?*

Related Journey of Faith Lesson

C16, "Social Justice"

Themes

Christmas, Savior
  C5, "The Sacrament of the Eucharist"
  Q4, "Who Is Jesus Christ?"
  C14, "The Dignity of Life"
Commitment
  C4, "The Sacrament of Confirmation"
  C8, "The Sacrament of Matrimony"
  C9, "The Sacrament of Holy Orders"
  C10, "The People of God"
  C13, "Christian Moral Living"

READING 1, NUMBERS 6:22–27

The Lord said to Moses: "Speak to Aaron and his sons and tell them: This is how you shall bless the Israelites. Say to them: The Lord bless you and keep you! The Lord let his face shine upon you, and be gracious to you! The Lord look upon you kindly and give you peace! So shall they invoke my name upon the Israelites, and I will bless them."

PSALM 67:2–3, 5, 6, 8

READING 2, GALATIANS 4:4–7

Brothers and sisters: When the fullness of time had come, God sent his Son, born of a woman, born under the law, to ransom those under the law, so that we might receive adoption as sons. As proof that you are sons, God sent the Spirit of his Son into our hearts, crying out, "Abba, Father!" So you are no longer a slave but a son, and if a son then also an heir, through God.

GOSPEL, LUKE 2:16–21

The shepherds went in haste to Bethlehem and found Mary and Joseph, and the infant lying in the manger. When they saw this, they made known the message that had been told them about this child. All who heard it were amazed by what had been told them by the shepherds. And Mary kept all these things, reflecting on them in her heart. Then the shepherds returned, glorifying and praising God or all they had heard and seen, just as it had been told to them. When eight days were completed for his circumcision, he was named Jesus, the name given him by the angel before he was conceived in the womb.

Mother of God, Mother of Us All

With reverence and affection, the Church opens the calendar year by honoring the woman who bore Jesus and rightly deserves the name *Theotokos* ("God-bearer"). I have often wondered what Mary thought in those early weeks after Jesus was born. She was no doubt exhausted, as new mothers often are, and perhaps overwhelmed at the thought of bringing up a child in the middle of the Roman occupation. Gabriel's prophecy was a long nine months ago, but I am sure his words about Jesus were still in her heart: "He will be great and the Son of the Most High…he will be holy and called the Son of God" (Luke 1:26–38). She probably asked herself, "What will that be like, to raise such a child?" But, like most new parents, Mary was also filled with wonder at the precious life lying in the manger. She marveled that something so small could have come from her womb, a place of warmth, nourishment, and shelter.

In the years and centuries after the death and resurrection of Christ, the place of Mary in the theology of the Church continued to grow. She received the first fruits of our reconciliation with God. She was assumed into heaven upon her death. She has been a constant intercessor for all people. Her reputation and queen of the universe is seen in the many names under which she is known—"Star of the Sea," "Untier of Knots," "Our Lady of…" (put any one of hundreds of place names here). She is seen as a source of mercy and kindness. She is Our Mother of Perpetual Help and Our Lady of Good Counsel. She is the Mother of all the Church by whatever other name she is known.

A Visit from the Shepherds

After Jesus was born, Luke records that shepherds heard the news from an angel, and they eagerly came to the stable (more likely a cave) where the Holy Family found shelter. Shepherds were largely hired hands who spent their days and nights tending the master's flock. They smelled. They were likely dirty from being outside. They would not have been welcome in many places. But in that stable they eagerly shared the message of the angels which contained an additional name for Jesus. This is a Savior who is Christ (the Messiah) the Lord. Everyone, including Mary was amazed as the shepherds shared their good news. Luke is careful to state that Mary treasured what she heard and held it in her heart. This was her child, born to set all people free. This knowledge surely stayed with her for her entire life. At the end of his life, Jesus would name the beloved disciple, John, as Mary's new family. "Behold your son," he tells Mary, and, "Behold your mother," he says to John from the cross. In this way, Jesus let go of his mother that she might be known as the mother of all of us.

Good News for All of Us

Mary is one of two people mentioned in the Creed. Pontius Pilate is the other. We might have thought that our confession of faith would include Peter or the other disciples, but only these two make the cut. Why? Mary gave birth to Christ; Pontius Pilate presided over his execution. Someone once noted that there are two ways to respond to Christ when he comes. One is to welcome him in and give him a home. Mary's yes to God made space for Christ. The other way to respond is to try and get rid of him, even if it means killing him. Jesus challenges the power and the status quo of the self-righteous and the self-important. Those who are unwilling to change will forever be threatened by his presence. Through the intercession of Mary, we can find the courage to open our minds and hearts to the Lord.

Questions for Reflections and Discussion

➤ *Do you welcome Jesus into every facet of your life? What happens when you are challenged to change?*

➤ *Mary's life and open welcome of the Holy Spirit helps us reflect on how open we are to Jesus. How can reflection on Mary in prayers like the Hail Mary help us to follow Jesus more closely every day?*

Related Journey of Faith Lesson

Q14, "Mary"

Themes

Mary
    Q14, "Mary"
    Q4, "Who Is Jesus Christ?"
Parenthood
    C8, "The Sacrament of Matrimony"
    C14, "The Dignity of Life"
Shepherd
    C9, "The Sacrament of Holy Orders"
    C16, "Social Justice"

READING 1 (ABC), MALACHI 3:1–4

Thus says the LORD God: Lo, I am sending my messenger to prepare the way before me; And suddenly there will come to the temple the LORD whom you seek, And the messenger of the covenant whom you desire. Yes, he is coming, says the LORD of hosts. But who will endure the day of his coming? And who can stand when he appears? For he is like the refiner's fire, or like the fuller's lye. He will sit refining and purifying silver, and he will purify the sons of Levi, Refining them like gold or like silver that they may offer due sacrifice to the LORD. Then the sacrifice of Judah and Jerusalem will please the LORD, as in the days of old, as in years gone by.

PSALM 24:7, 8, 9, 10

READING 2 (ABC), HEBREWS 2:14–18

Since the children share in blood and flesh, Jesus likewise shared in them, that through death he might destroy the one who has the power of death, that is, the Devil, and free those who through fear of death had been subject to slavery all their life. Surely he did not help angels but rather the descendants of Abraham; therefore, he had to become like his brothers and sisters in every way, that he might be a merciful and faithful high priest before God to expiate the sins of the people. Because he himself was tested through what he suffered, he is able to help those who are being tested.

GOSPEL (ABC), LUKE 2:22–40

When the days were completed for their purification according to the law of Moses, Mary and Joseph took Jesus up to Jerusalem to present him to the Lord, just as it is written in the law of the Lord, "Every male that opens the womb shall be consecrated to the Lord," and to offer the sacrifice of "a pair of turtledoves or two young pigeons," in accordance with the dictate in the law of the Lord. Now there was a man in Jerusalem whose name was Simeon. This man was righteous and devout, awaiting the consolation of Israel, and the Holy Spirit was upon him. It had been revealed to him by the Holy Spirit that he should not see death before he had seen the Messiah of the Lord. He came in the Spirit into the temple; and when the parents brought in the child Jesus to perform the custom of the law in regard to him, he took him into his arms and blessed God, saying: "Now, Master, you may let your servant go in peace, according to your word, for my eyes have seen your salvation, which you prepared in the sight of all the peoples: a light for revelation to the Gentiles, and glory for your people Israel."

The child's father and mother were amazed at what was said about him; and Simeon blessed them and said to Mary his mother, "Behold, this child is destined for the fall and rise of many in Israel, and to be a sign that will be contradicted—and you yourself a sword will pierce—so that the thoughts of many hearts may be revealed." There was also a prophetess, Anna, the daughter of Phanuel, of the tribe of Asher. She was advanced in years, having lived seven years with her husband after her marriage, and then as a widow until she was eighty-four. She never left the temple, but worshiped night and day with fasting and prayer. And coming forward at that very time, she gave thanks to God and spoke about the child to all who were awaiting the redemption of Jerusalem. When they had fulfilled all the prescriptions of the law of the Lord, they returned to Galilee, to their own town of Nazareth. The child grew and became strong, filled with wisdom; and the favor of God was upon him.

A Prophecy Come True

The feast of the Presentation on February 2 marked the traditional end of the Christmas season. The liturgical calendars of some churches like the Anglican Church still reflect that practice. Why the discrepancy? February 2 is about forty days after Christmas. In the Jewish ritual of the time, the woman who gave birth was to present herself for purification at the temple at that time. The visit usually included a ritual bath and a sacrifice. A different ritual presented the first-born son and dedicated him to the Lord (the ritual did not apply to those of the tribe of Levi). Gradually, the Church combined the two celebrations into one and dropped the purification of Mary.

As Luke tells it, two holy people, Simeon and Anna, were witnesses on the day Mary brought Jesus to the temple. Simeon is described as a righteous and devout man on whom the Holy Spirit rests. He was looking for the "consolation of Israel"—the promise God had made through the prophets to send a messiah. His faith made him able to see this child as the fulfillment of that promise. His words might have given Mary and Joseph pause, however. I'm not sure they knew what it meant that their baby would be a sign that would be contradicted. And Mary, who had pondered everything that Gabriel and the shepherds told her about Jesus, would now bear a challenge as well. All parents want to protect their children from harm or trouble. Simeon was telling Mary that she couldn't interfere with Jesus' mission and that would be painful for her.

Anna is a prophet—one who speaks for God and can see God at work in the world. Her response to Jesus is immediate. She begins to proclaim the glory of God and the redemption of Israel to anyone who would listen to her. Her desire to tell everyone about the Child Jesus cannot be contained. This makes her one of the first evangelizers. She needed only a glimpse of Jesus to recognize the presence of the Messiah. She could do nothing else but announce the news. Meanwhile, Jesus is taken home to grow in wisdom and favor before God until the time of his mission comes. The word used for favor here is the same as the one for grace, echoing what Gabriel said to Mary, who is both full of grace and favored of God.

A Messenger Who Purifies the World

Simeon's vision of Jesus was not drawn out of thin air. Isaiah spoke of a servant who brings justice to the earth. Malachi speaks of a messenger who will purify the descendants of Levi like fire purifies gold and silver. The smelting process eliminated impurities from metal. What would it be like to have our own impurities burned away until we are worthy to enter the courts of the Lord? None of us know. But we know that growing is painful, and acknowledging sin is often painful emotionally, if not physically. Will we fall or will we rise? Only God knows the answer to that. We simply do our best to follow God's Son.

Good News for All of Us

Luke's extended birth narrative reminds us that Jesus was born as we all are—vulnerable, naked, and dependent on others for our well-being. The Letter to the Hebrews also reminds us that at the Incarnation, God took flesh as Jesus Christ and became like us in every way—tempted, suffering, even dying so that he might show us the way back to God. Our belief in the Incarnation sets Christianity apart from every other religion. We believe that God walked among us, at once fully human and fully divine. Jesus died for us so that we might become reconciled to God and devote our lives to becoming more fully like him. As the season of Lent approaches, we might think about the ways in which we can begin to do that.

Questions for Reflection and Discussion

➤ *When and how do you talk about your faith with others? Do you feel the joy and excitement that Anna has?*

➤ *What are some of the Christian disciplines you will practice in the Lenten season? How will these help you draw closer to God?*

Related Journey of Faith Lesson

Q4, "Who Is Jesus Christ?"

Themes

Incarnation
    C2, "The Sacraments: An Introduction"
    C3, "The Sacrament of Baptism"
    C5, "The Sacrament of the Eucharist"
    Q4, "Who Is Jesus Christ?"
Mary
    C8, "The Sacrament of Matrimony"
Prophecy
    C4, "The Sacrament of Confirmation"

St. Joseph, Husband of Mary, March 19

READING 1 (ABC), 2 SAMUEL 7:4–5A, 12–14A, 16

The LORD spoke to Nathan and said: "Go, tell my servant David, 'When your time comes and you rest with your ancestors, I will raise up your heir after you, sprung from your loins, and I will make his kingdom firm. It is he who shall build a house for my name. And I will make his royal throne firm forever. I will be a father to him, and he shall be a son to me. Your house and your kingdom shall endure forever before me; your throne shall stand firm forever.'"

PSALM 89:2–3, 4–5, 27, 29

READING 2 (ABC), ROMANS 4:13, 16–18, 22

Brothers and sisters: It was not through the law that the promise was made to Abraham and his descendants that he would inherit the world, but through the righteousness that comes from faith. For this reason, it depends on faith, so that it may be a gift, and the promise may be guaranteed to all his descendants, not to those who only adhere to the law but to those who follow the faith of Abraham, who is the father of all of us, as it is written, I have made you father of many nations. He is our father in the sight of God, in whom he believed, who gives life to the dead and calls into being what does not exist. He believed, hoping against hope, that he would become the father of many nations, according to what was said, Thus shall your descendants be. That is why it was credited to him as righteousness.

GOSPEL (ABC), MATTHEW 1:16, 18–21, 24A

Jacob was the father of Joseph, the husband of Mary. Of her was born Jesus who is called the Christ.

Now this is how the birth of Jesus Christ came about. When his mother Mary was betrothed to Joseph, but before they lived together, she was found with child through the Holy Spirit. Joseph her husband, since he was a righteous man, yet unwilling to expose her to shame, decided to divorce her quietly. Such was his intention when, behold, the angel of the Lord appeared to him in a dream and said, "Joseph, son of David, do not be afraid to take Mary your wife into your home.

For it is through the Holy Spirit that this child has been conceived in her. She will bear a son and you are to name him Jesus, because he will save his people from their sins." When Joseph awoke, he did as the angel of the Lord had commanded him and took his wife into his home.

A Silent Presence

We know little about Joseph. He is mentioned only in the beginning of Matthew and Luke, the two Gospels that carry the birth narratives of Jesus. We know he was a righteous, compassionate man. Matthew describes his unwillingness to expose Mary to shame after she was found pregnant before their marriage. Joseph, already betrothed to Mary, simply resolved to leave her. Then he was awakened in a dream. In many stories in the Old Testament, either God or God's angel (both the Hebrew and Greek words mean "messenger") appears in a dream to give a command or a warning to the dreamer.

In Matthew's Gospel, an angel awakens Joseph three times—when he finds out Mary is pregnant, when he is warned to flee from Herod and go to Egypt, and when he is told to return to Israel where the three of them settle in Nazareth. Joseph's example points to the importance of listening for the voice of God whenever and wherever it might be found.

In Luke's Gospel, we learn that Joseph dutifully took his family to Jerusalem for Passover. When they could not find Jesus on the way back, they returned to find him in the temple. Joseph does not speak, but Mary scolds Jesus telling him: "Your father and I have been searching for you with great anxiety." Joseph and Mary knew the worry any parent feels when their child might be in danger. I also think Joseph was proud when Jesus was referred to as "the son of Joseph."

All of this is to say that Joseph took this Child of God and Mary and loved him as his own. He cared for him and taught him what he knew. Joseph loved and cared for Mary. So, while we don't know much about him, we celebrate his strong and silent presence in the lives of Jesus and Mary and in our own life.

Hoping on the Promise of God

Our first and second readings today are the promises of God as they were given to David and Abraham. Each one is a promise of many descendants, but each gives a unique look at the relationship of those descendants with God. In 2 Samuel, David is relieved to find that his son will have a great kingdom and build the temple where God's name is. It is God's own definition of their relationship that draws us: "I will be a father to him, and he shall be a son to me." The word for *father* is the same as that used by Jesus, suggesting that at least part of the reason Jesus identified God as Father is because God identified himself that way to the descendants of David. In inviting his followers to do the same, Jesus welcomed them into this privileged relationship as sons and daughters of God, as he was.

In Romans, Paul recalls the faith of Abraham, who believed God's promise that he would have many descendants, even though he was old. For Paul, faith is a gift which helps us see that God brings life where there is death and existence to things that don't exist. Abraham had no way of knowing for a fact that God's promise would come true. He couldn't see the generations that would spring from his children and grandchildren. But his faith allowed him to hope for what he couldn't yet see and trust that God would fulfill his promise.

Good News for All of Us

Abraham's faith, David's covenant and relationship with God, Joseph's constant silent presence in the life of Jesus—these paint a picture of lives attuned to the voice and will of God. When things seemed impossible or circumstances turned from good to bad, these three tried to follow what God told them. Were they perfect at it? No, and neither are we. God chose to be in a relationship with them anyway and God calls us to the faith and hope they displayed that we might be his children forever.

Questions for Reflection and Discussion

➤ *What is your relationship with God? Do you see God as Father, friend, Giver of Life, or would you describe it in a different way?*

➤ *OCIA is a process which began before you came to class and will continue after your baptism, confirmation, and first Communion. When did you first experience faith and who has helped form you in it?*

Related Journey of Faith Lesson

E1, "Election: Saying Yes to Jesus"

Themes

Faith
    E1, "Election: Saying Yes to Jesus"
    E4, "The Creed"
Family
    E7, "The Meaning of Holy Week"
    E8, "Easter Vigil Retreat"
Future
    E3, "Scrutinies: Looking Within"
    E5, "The Way of the Cross"

READING 1 (ABC), ISAIAH 7:10–14; 8:10

The LORD spoke to Ahaz, saying: Ask for a sign from the LORD, your God; let it be deep as the nether world, or high as the sky! But Ahaz answered, "I will not ask! I will not tempt the LORD!" Then Isaiah said: Listen, O house of David! Is it not enough for you to weary people, must you also weary my God? Therefore the Lord himself will give you this sign: the virgin shall be with child, and bear a son, and shall name him Emmanuel, which means "God is with us!"

PSALM 40:7–8A, 8B–9, 10, 11

READING 2 (ABC), HEBREWS 10:4–10

Brothers and sisters: It is impossible that the blood of bulls and goats take away sins. For this reason, when Christ came into the world, he said: "Sacrifice and offering you did not desire, but a body you prepared for me; in holocausts and sin offerings you took no delight. Then I said, 'As is written of me in the scroll, behold, I come to do your will, O God.'" First he says, "Sacrifices and offerings, holocausts and sin offerings, you neither desired nor delighted in." These are offered according to the law. Then he says, "Behold, I come to do your will." He takes away the first to establish the second. By this "will," we have been consecrated through the offering of the Body of Jesus Christ once for all.

GOSPEL (ABC), LUKE 1:26–38

The angel Gabriel was sent from God to a town of Galilee called Nazareth, to a virgin betrothed to a man named Joseph, of the house of David, and the virgin's name was Mary. And coming to her, he said, "Hail, full of grace! The Lord is with you." But she was greatly troubled at what was said and pondered what sort of greeting this might be. Then the angel said to her, "Do not be afraid, Mary, for you have found favor with God. Behold, you will conceive in your womb and bear a son, and you shall name him Jesus. He will be great and will be called Son of the Most High, and the Lord God will give him the throne of David his father, and he will rule over the house of Jacob forever, and of his Kingdom there will be no end." But Mary said to the angel, "How can this be, since I have no relations with a man?" And the angel said to her in reply, "The Holy Spirit will come upon you, and the power of the Most High will overshadow you. Therefore the child to be born will be called holy, the Son of God. And behold, Elizabeth, your relative, has also conceived a son in her old age, and this is the sixth month for her who was called barren; for nothing will be impossible for God." Mary said, "Behold, I am the handmaid of the Lord. May it be done to me according to your word." Then the angel departed from her.

Here I Am Lord; I Come to Do Your Will

The refrain of our psalm today makes us echo again and again, "Here I am Lord, I come to do your will." The prophet Samuel used these words when he heard the voice of God in the night (1 Samuel 3:4–10). Isaiah the prophet responds to God in the same way after his vision of the temple (Isaiah 6:8). In a well-known prayer by St. Ignatius, he invites God to take everything he is and everything he has. He simply asks God for God's love and grace because they will be enough. All of these are the exclamations of those who have found their freedom in doing God's commands and following the divine path wherever it leads.

Today we read the story of the annunciation once again (this is the third time this year), and we remind ourselves that when Mary heard the message of God, she listened carefully, asked a good question, and then said, "Behold," which is another way of saying, "Here I am." She obeys God with all her heart and shows us that we can do that as well.

In the Letter to the Hebrews, the author writes about Jesus, our Savior who was "obedient to his father, even unto death, death on a cross" (Philippians 2:8). Jesus said, "I have come to do your will." And we remember Jesus in the garden of Gethsemane, saying to his Father, "Not my will, but yours be done" (Luke 22:42). The author of Hebrews establishes that Jesus offered his own body as a sacrifice for us so we might be reconciled to God, and consecrated (that is, set apart as holy) for his service.

A Sign from God

Long before Gabriel visited Mary, two kings from Aram and Ephraim tried to conquer Jerusalem. They were unsuccessful, but the people, including King Ahaz were afraid they would try it again. Isaiah brought a message to Ahaz telling him that the Lord says, "Remain calm," and prophesying that the two kingdoms would be crushed in defeat. God's message concluded: "Unless your faith is firm, you shall not be firm!" (Isaiah 7:9). Faith gives us courage and strength to stand when trouble comes. Ahaz was doubtful. God commanded him to ask for a sign and he refused to do it. He was thinking of asking the King of Assyria for help, not realizing that Assyria would become an oppressor. Ahaz did not trust the Lord to deliver the people of Judah. When God hears Ahaz refuse to ask for a sign, God gives one anyway: "The young woman, pregnant and about to bear a son, shall name him Emmanuel." The child's name says everything we need to know about God's faithfulness: The name means "God is with us."

Centuries later, when early Christians heard the stories of Jesus and his Mother Mary who had not known a man, they remembered Isaiah's prophecy and believed that Mary was the sign, and that God was indeed with them. Luke's story is made all the more interesting when we note that Gabriel tells her of another sign of God's power just before she says yes. Elizabeth, who was barren, is pregnant. Her baby is due in three months. By this Mary knows that nothing is impossible for God. If only Ahaz had listened as well.

Good News for All of Us

In many and various ways, says the Letter to the Hebrews, God speaks to us. Sometimes it's through the words of sacred Scripture, sometimes through a homily, and sometimes through family and friends, art and music, and other signs of his presence. God never stops talking to us. That may be because we don't always hear what God says and God needs to keep trying.

The stories of the virgin in Isaiah and Elizabeth and Mary in the Gospel are God-signs—places where God is trying to show us the wonders of his love and presence in our lives. Jesus is God himself in flesh and blood, sacrificing his body for us that we might find our way back to God. All of them invite, even compel, us to turn to the Lord and give our lives to him without knowing what that means for us or where we will go. In our prayer, we can ask Jesus to show us the path we are to travel. We may not see what's around every corner, but our faith makes us confident that Jesus travels with us and we can say with a glad heart, "Here I am; I have come to do your will."

Questions for Reflection and Discussion

> ➤ *We often speak of God's call in relation to our vocation (what we do and how we make a difference) and our state of life (who are our closest traveling companions and how do we share our lives with them). Our discernment involves prayer, awareness of our gifts, conversation with friends and mentors, and, more often than not, a leap of faith. How did you get to this place and time in your life and what do you think God had to do with that?*

> ➤ *Is there any vocation or state of life to which your answer to God would be: "I need to get back to you on that?" Why?*

Related Journey of Faith Lesson

E3, "Scrutinies: Looking Within"

Themes

Annunciation, Discipleship, Mary
    Q14, "Mary"
    E1, "Election: Saying Yes to Jesus"
Redemption
    E2, "Living Lent"
    E3, "Scrutinies: Looking Within"
    E5, "The Way of the Cross"
    E7, "The Meaning of Holy Week"

READING 1, EXODUS 17:3–7

In those days, in their thirst for water, the people grumbled against Moses, saying, "Why did you ever make us leave Egypt? Was it just to have us die here of thirst with our children and our livestock?" So Moses cried out to the LORD, "What shall I do with [these] people? [A] little more and they will stone me!" The LORD answered Moses, "Go over there in front of the people, along with some of the elders of Israel, holding in your hand, as you go, the staff with which you struck the river. I will be standing there in front of you on the rock in Horeb. Strike the rock, and the water will flow from it for the people to drink." This Moses did, in the presence of the elders of Israel. The place was called Massah and Meribah, because the Israelites quarreled there and tested the LORD, saying, "Is the LORD in our midst or not?"

PSALM 95:1–2, 6–7, 8–9

READING 2, ROMANS 5:1–2, 5–8

Brothers and sisters: Since we have been justified by faith, we have peace with God through our Lord Jesus Christ, through whom we have gained access by faith to this grace in which we stand, and we boast in hope of the glory of God. And hope does not disappoint, because the love of God has been poured out into our hearts through the Holy Spirit who has been given to us. For Christ, while we were still helpless, died at the appointed time for the ungodly. Indeed, only with difficulty does one die for a just person, though perhaps for a good person one might even find courage to die. But God proves his love for us in that while we were still sinners Christ died for us.

GOSPEL, JOHN 4:5–42

Jesus came to a town of Samaria called Sychar, near the plot of land that Jacob had given to his son Joseph. Jacob's well was there. Jesus, tired from his journey, sat down there at the well. It was about noon. A woman of Samaria came to draw water. Jesus said to her, "Give me a drink." His disciples had gone into the town to buy food. The Samaritan woman said to him, "How can you, a Jew, ask me, a Samaritan woman, for a drink?"— For Jews use nothing in common with Samaritans.—

Jesus answered and said to her, "If you knew the gift of God and who is saying to you, 'Give me a drink, 'you would have asked him and he would have given you living water. The woman said to him, "Sir, you do not even have a bucket and the cistern is deep; where then can you get this living water? Are you greater than our father Jacob, who gave us this cistern and drank from it himself with his children and his flocks?"

Jesus answered and said to her, "Everyone who drinks this water will be thirsty again; but whoever drinks the water I shall give will never thirst; the water I shall give will become in him a spring of water welling up to eternal life." The woman said to him, "Sir, give me this water, so that I may not be thirsty or have to keep coming here to draw water."

Jesus said to her, "Go call your husband and come back." The woman answered and said to him, "I do not have a husband." Jesus answered her, "You are right in saying, 'I do not have a husband.' For you have had five husbands, and the one you have now is not your husband. What you have said is true." The woman said to him, "Sir, I can see that you are a prophet. Our ancestors worshiped on this mountain; but you people say that the place to worship is in Jerusalem." Jesus said to her, "Believe me, woman, the hour is coming when you will worship the Father neither on this mountain nor in Jerusalem. You people worship what you do not understand; we worship what we understand, because salvation is from the Jews. But the hour is coming, and is now here, when true worshipers will worship the Father in Spirit and truth; and indeed the Father seeks such people to worship him. God is Spirit, and those who worship him must worship in Spirit and truth." The woman said to him, "I know that the Messiah is coming, the one called the Christ; when he comes, he will tell us everything."

Jesus said to her, "I am he, the one speaking with you."

At that moment his disciples returned, and were amazed that he was talking with a woman, but still no one said, "What are you looking for?" or "Why are you talking with her?" The woman left her water jar and went into the town and said to the people, "Come see a man who told me everything I have done. Could he possibly be the Christ?" They went out of the town and came to him. Meanwhile, the disciples urged him, "Rabbi, eat." But he said to them, "I have food to eat of which you do not know." So the disciples said to one another, "Could someone have brought him something to eat?" Jesus said to them, "My food is to do the will of the one who sent me and to finish his work. Do you not say, 'In four months the harvest will be here'? I tell you, look up and see the fields ripe for the harvest. The reaper is already receiving payment and gathering crops for eternal life, so that the sower and reaper can rejoice together. For here the saying is verified that 'One sows and another reaps.' I sent you to reap what you have not worked for; others have done the work, and you are sharing the fruits of their work."

Many of the Samaritans of that town began to believe in him because of the word of the woman who testified, "He told me everything I have done." When the Samaritans came to him, they invited him to stay with them; and he stayed there two days. Many more began to believe in him because of his word, and they said to the woman, "We no longer believe because of your word; for we have heard for ourselves, and we know that this is truly the savior of the world."

Waters of Life

Whenever I teach a baptism class, we talk at length about the significance of water in Judeo-Christian history and in our own lives. The Spirit of God hovered over the waters at creation (Genesis 1:2), and forty days and nights of rain flooded the earth in the time of Noah (Genesis 7:4). The Israelites passed through the waters of the Red Sea (see Exodus 14:21 and following verses), and Jesus was baptized in the waters of the Jordan (Matthew 3:13). We need water to live and know that water can be a source of death for us.

In the first reading, the lack of water makes the Israelites fear death. They begin to doubt that they will make it through the wilderness and regret leaving Egypt (it won't be the first time such doubts creep in). When they complain to Moses, Moses complains to God. It's hard to trust that God will give you everything you need when you are hot and thirsty. The miraculous water from the hard rock reminds the Israelites that they must depend on God for everything. The responsorial psalm reminds us not to harden our hearts in difficult times. It's not a bad lesson for any of us.

Living Water

The ability to draw water from a deep well brings a Samaritan woman and Jesus to the same spot in the Gospel. Jews and Samaritans were different branches of the same ancestor. Jews looked down on Samaritans and did not consider them full members of Judaism. In any case, the Samaritan woman is surprised that Jesus would even speak to her and ask for a drink. Jews and Samaritans would never have taken a drink from the same bucket. But Jesus tells her if she just asks, he would give her living water. She doesn't understand at first, but after his description, she does ask: "Give me this water." Afterward, a remarkable exchange happens. The woman reveals her true self to Jesus as one who knows she is in an irregular relationship. She recognizes him as a prophet and confesses her belief in the coming Messiah. Jesus then reveals his true self as the Messiah who is to come. This is the living water for which she longed, and she leaves her water jar to proclaim the encounter in the village.

The last part of the Gospel alternates two scenes. The woman preaches to the villagers and the disciples return and question Jesus about talking to a woman (they are more surprised about that than about the fact she is a Samaritan). The woman's words are so powerful that the villagers go in search of Jesus. In the meantime, Jesus tells the disciples, "I sent you to reap that for which you did not labor." We can imagine the disciples looking up and seeing the crowd coming to Jesus ready for the harvesting, all because a Samaritan woman was filled with the living water that Jesus gave.

While We Were Still Sinners

God's love for us is something of a mystery. We are mortal and we mess things up. There is nothing that God needs from us and nothing we can give him that could equal what he has given us. When the Israelites had been in the desert for a while after they left Egypt, they began to complain about the heat and their thirst and hunger. They wondered if they made a mistake following Moses and Moses had had enough. Moses, of course, complained to God. For most of us, this is our history as well. God brings us to a new place in our lives and we complain because it doesn't have exactly what we think we need. When Moses strikes the rock and water flows out, the people were no doubt overjoyed, but it wouldn't be long before they started complaining again (see Numbers 11).

Third Sunday of Lent, Year A

This is our pattern. We see it throughout the Bible and into our world today. We start fresh, sure that we will not go astray this time, and then something happens—call it the human condition or original sin—but we turn away from God who has been with us all along. That God notices us at all is amazing. But more amazing still is that he loves us. When Jesus was born, God didn't say, "I sent my only Son into the world because you are rotten." As the Gospel of John puts it, "God so loved the world that he sent his only Son, so that everyone who believes in him may not perish but may have eternal life" (John 3:16).

When St. Paul talks about justification by faith and our hope of sharing in God's glory, he reminds us of the mystery of God's love. We were sinners and Christ came anyway. We were ungodly and Christ died for us. And to help us continue the journey, God poured his love—that same love—in our hearts through the power of the Holy Spirit. This is the reason for our hope—that confident expectation that we will see God face to face and share in divine glory.

Living Water

On the campus of the University of Notre Dame in South Bend, Indiana, there is a sculpture of the woman at the well. Jesus sits on the edge of the well and the woman holds her water jar with her head cocked to one side as she listens intently. The sculpture begs us to listen in on the conversation or imagine ourselves in the woman's place. Their conversation is personal and theological as he probes the openness of her heart and the depth of her faith. Two things stand out. She tells Jesus the truth about herself and her husband and she believes the Messiah will come who will reveal everything. Her honesty gives Jesus the opening to reveal his true self as the Messiah in whom she has believed.

The disciples intrude on the conversation, and the woman leaves as they scold Jesus for speaking to her in the first place. He tells them that they will reap what they did not sow. Meanwhile the woman preaches about the encounter to anyone who will listen, and they all come to hear Jesus. I imagine that at the moment Jesus tells the disciples to look around, they suddenly see the many people coming across the fields from the town to see Jesus because of the power of the woman's witness.

Good News for All of Us

Pope Francis, in his first interview after becoming Pope, was asked who he was. "I am a sinner," he said. Like the woman at the well, he revealed his true self before all. We are all sinners. Our baptism also tells us that we are freed from the bondage of (original sin) and have been given the grace to choose a different path—to be a beloved child of God and find our freedom as disciples of Jesus Christ. We don't always follow that path, but in the mystery of God's enduring love, we were given a savior who waits patiently for us to return to him.

Questions for Reflection and Discussion

➤ *Imagine you are at the well with Jesus. What are some of the things you would tell him about yourself and what you believe? Is there anything you would hold back?*

➤ *How has God's love been revealed in your life and who have you told about it?*

Related *Journey of Faith* Lesson

E2, "Living Lent"

Themes

   E2, "Living Lent"
   E4, "The Creed"
Love
   E1, "Election: Saying Yes to Jesus"
Water
   E3, "Scrutinies: Looking Within"

Fourth Sunday of Lent, Year A

READING 1, 1 SAMUEL 16:1B, 6–7, 10–13A

The LORD said to Samuel: "Fill your horn with oil, and be on your way. I am sending you to Jesse of Bethlehem, for I have chosen my king from among his sons." As Jesse and his sons came to the sacrifice, Samuel looked at Eliab and thought, "Surely the LORD's anointed is here before him." But the LORD said to Samuel: "Do not judge from his appearance or from his lofty stature, because I have rejected him. Not as man sees does God see, because man sees the appearance but the LORD looks into the heart." In the same way Jesse presented seven sons before Samuel, but Samuel said to Jesse, "The LORD has not chosen any one of these." Then Samuel asked Jesse, "Are these all the sons you have?" Jesse replied, "There is still the youngest, who is tending the sheep." Samuel said to Jesse, "Send for him; we will not begin the sacrificial banquet until he arrives here." Jesse sent and had the young man brought to them. He was ruddy, a youth handsome to behold and making a splendid appearance. The LORD said, "There—anoint him, for this is the one!" Then Samuel, with the horn of oil in hand, anointed David in the presence of his brothers; and from that day on, the spirit of the LORD rushed upon David.

PSALM 23:1–3A, 3B–4, 5, 6

READING 2, EPHESIANS 5:8–14

Brothers and sisters: You were once darkness, but now you are light in the Lord. Live as children of light, for light produces every kind of goodness and righteousness and truth. Try to learn what is pleasing to the Lord. Take no part in the fruitless works of darkness; rather expose them, for it is shameful even to mention the things done by them in secret; but everything exposed by the light becomes visible, for everything that becomes visible is light. Therefore, it says: "Awake, O sleeper, and arise from the dead, and Christ will give you light."

GOSPEL, JOHN 9:1–41

As Jesus passed by he saw a man blind from birth. His disciples asked him, "Rabbi, who sinned, this man or his parents, that he was born blind?" Jesus answered, "Neither he nor his parents sinned; it is so that the works of God might be made visible through him. We have to do the works of the one who sent me while it is day. Night is coming when no one can work. While I am in the world, I am the light of the world." When he had said this, he spat on the ground and made clay with the saliva, and smeared the clay on his eyes, and said to him, "Go wash in the Pool of Siloam" —which means Sent—so he went and washed, and came back able to see. His neighbors and those who had seen him earlier as a beggar said, "Isn't this the one who used to sit and beg?" Some said, "It is," but others said, "No, he just looks like him." He said, "I am." So they said to him, "How were your eyes opened?" He replied, "The man called Jesus made clay and anointed my eyes and told me, 'Go to Siloam and wash.' So I went there and washed and was able to see." And they said to him, "Where is he?" He said, "I don't know."

They brought the one who was once blind to the Pharisees. Now Jesus had made clay and opened his eyes on a sabbath. So then the Pharisees also asked him how he was able to see. He said to them, "He put clay on my eyes, and I washed, and now I can see." So some of the Pharisees said, "This man is not from God, because he does not keep the sabbath." But others said, "How can a sinful man do such signs?" And there was a division among them. So they said to the blind man again, "What do you have to say about him, since he opened your eyes?" He said, "He is a prophet." Now the Jews did not believe that he had been blind and gained his sight until they summoned the parents of the one who had gained his sight. They asked them, "Is this your son, who you say was born blind? How does he now see?" His parents answered and said, "We know that this is our son and that he was born blind. We do not know how he sees now, nor do we know who opened his eyes. Ask him, he is of age; he can speak for himself." His parents said this because they were afraid of the Jews, for the Jews had already agreed that if anyone acknowledged him as the Christ, he would be expelled from the synagogue. For this reason his parents said, "He is of age; question him."

So a second time they called the man who had been blind and said to him, "Give God the praise! We know that this man is a sinner." He replied, "If he is a sinner, I do not know.

One thing I do know is that I was blind and now I see." So they said to him, "What did he do to you? How did he open your eyes?" He answered them, "I told you already and you did not listen. Why do you want to hear it again? Do you want to become his disciples, too?" They ridiculed him and said, "You are that man's disciple; we are disciples of Moses! We know that God spoke to Moses, but we do not know where this one is from." The man answered and said to them, "This is what is so amazing, that you do not know where he is from, yet he opened my eyes. We know that God does not listen to sinners, but if one is devout and does his will, he listens to him. It is unheard of that anyone ever opened the eyes of a person born blind. If this man were not from God, he would not be able to do anything." They answered and said to him, "You were born totally in sin, and are you trying to teach us?" Then they threw him out.

When Jesus heard that they had thrown him out, he found him and said, "Do you believe in the Son of Man?" He answered and said, "Who is he, sir, that I may believe in him?" Jesus said to him, "You have seen him, and the one speaking with you is he." He said, "I do believe, Lord," and he worshiped him. Then Jesus said, "I came into this world for judgment, so that those who do not see might see, and those who do see might become blind."

Some of the Pharisees who were with him heard this and said to him, "Surely we are not also blind, are we?" Jesus said to them, "If you were blind, you would have no sin; but now you are saying, 'We see,' so your sin remains.

Not as We See, but as God Sees

An old saying tells us that we do not see the world as we are; we see it as we are. Our attitudes, prejudices, emotions, and experience all color what we see and we when we remember an experience, we tend to retell it from our viewpoint which makes it hard to see anyone else's. Our readings today are about two points of view. The first is the human point of view. Each reading tells the way humans read a situation. The second is God's point of view. And clearly God sees something different than we do. The people in question either change their view or continue to think that the only right way to see is theirs.

Consider the first reading. The prophet Samuel has received a message that he is to anoint a new king for Israel. God gives very explicit instructions to go to Jesse from Bethlehem. As 7 of the 8 sons of Jesse line up, Samuel is impressed with their size and apparent strength. He believes in his heart that the eldest was the chosen king. It made sense. In Israelite culture, the eldest inherited the father's property and had a privileged place in the family. God had other plans. And Samuel realizes that the youngest, David, is the king God chose. Were the other brothers unworthy? Not necessarily. But as God saw it, David, this shepherd who might have been overlooked because he was young, would be instrumental in continuing the plan of salvation for the world.

Darkness into Light

Paul's vision is very close to God's vision. "Once you were darkness," he says. God would not have disagreed. The people were caught in a trap of their own making. They embraced the way the world saw things and believed they had no other choice. When that happens, it's easy to walk away from God, especially if God seems absent. But the Incarnation changed that. Jesus showed his followers a different path that would bring them back to God. Jesus' way was so significant that John's Gospel talked about Jesus as the light, and that light shone so brightly that everything else seemed dark. Paul appeals here to our identity as children of light that we might show forth everything that is good.

Fourth Sunday of Lent, Year A

I Was Blind, but Now I See

John's story of the man born blind is a wonderful healing that speaks to blindness of the heart, which is a result of the way we see, and the miraculous process we undergo to see as God sees. The Pharisees, like so many of us at times, are stubborn and refuse to believe that this itinerant preacher from Nazareth could heal someone who was born blind. They remained willfully blind to the power of God standing right in front of them, preferring to attack those who saw differently. On the other hand, the man, when questioned by his neighbors, thinks of Jesus as a man. Questioned again by the Pharisees, he calls Jesus a prophet. Questioned a third time, he acknowledges that Jesus has disciples and implies that he is one of them. When Jesus finds him again and is able to see him clearly for the first time, he calls Jesus "Lord" and worships him. Jesus doesn't condemn blindness that comes from accident or ignorance. Gaining sight is a process with many steps. The willful refusal to see anything different from the way we have always seen is far more difficult to deal with.

Good News for All of Us

Faith is a gift AND a process. Who God was for us when we were young is different than who God is for us now—not because God changes, but because we do. The more open we are to God's presence in our lives, to the words of Scripture, and in prayer, the closer we are to seeing as God does at least some of the time. Those are the times we can root out injustice, bring peace among nations and neighborhoods, love our brothers and sisters wherever we find them, and see the world in the light of God's grace.

Questions for Reflection and Discussion

➤ *Have you ever heard one person's version of a past event and said to yourself, "That's not what I remember"? Share some of the difference between your memories.*

➤ *Which identity of Jesus that the man born blind uses do you resonate with? (Jesus is man, prophet, teacher with disciples, Lord.)*

Related *Journey of Faith* Lesson

E1, "Election: Saying Yes to Jesus"

Themes

Blindness
    E1, "Election: Saying Yes to Jesus"
Conversion
    E3, "Scrutinies: Looking Within"
Light
    E2, "Living Lent"

READING 1, EZEKIEL 37:12–14

Thus says the Lord GOD: O my people, I will open your graves and have you rise from them, and bring you back to the land of Israel. Then you shall know that I am the LORD, when I open your graves and have you rise from them, O my people! I will put my spirit in you that you may live, and I will settle you upon your land; thus you shall know that I am the LORD. I have promised, and I will do it, says the LORD.

PSALM 130:1–2, 3–4, 5–6, 7–8

READING 2, ROMANS 8:8–11

Brothers and sisters: Those who are in the flesh cannot please God. But you are not in the flesh; on the contrary, you are in the spirit, if only the Spirit of God dwells in you. Whoever does not have the Spirit of Christ does not belong to him. But if Christ is in you, although the body is dead because of sin, the spirit is alive because of righteousness. If the Spirit of the one who raised Jesus from the dead dwells in you, the one who raised Christ from the dead will give life to your mortal bodies also, through his Spirit dwelling in you.

GOSPEL, JOHN 11:1–45

Now a man was ill, Lazarus from Bethany, the village of Mary and her sister Martha. Mary was the one who had anointed the Lord with perfumed oil and dried his feet with her hair; it was her brother Lazarus who was ill. So the sisters sent word to him saying, "Master, the one you love is ill." When Jesus heard this he said, "This illness is not to end in death, but is for the glory of God, that the Son of God may be glorified through it." Now Jesus loved Martha and her sister and Lazarus. So when he heard that he was ill, he remained for two days in the place where he was. Then after this he said to his disciples, "Let us go back to Judea." The disciples said to him, "Rabbi, the Jews were just trying to stone you, and you want to go back there?"

Jesus answered, "Are there not twelve hours in a day? If one walks during the day, he does not stumble, because he sees the light of this world. But if one walks at night, he stumbles, because the light is not in him." He said this, and then told them,

"Our friend Lazarus is asleep, but I am going to awaken him." So the disciples said to him, "Master, if he is asleep, he will be saved." But Jesus was talking about his death, while they thought that he meant ordinary sleep. So then Jesus said to them clearly, "Lazarus has died. And I am glad for you that I was not there, that you may believe. Let us go to him." So Thomas, called Didymus, said to his fellow disciples, "Let us also go to die with him."

When Jesus arrived, he found that Lazarus had already been in the tomb for four days. Now Bethany was near Jerusalem, only about two miles away. And many of the Jews had come to Martha and Mary to comfort them about their brother. When Martha heard that Jesus was coming, she went to meet him; but Mary sat at home. Martha said to Jesus, "Lord, if you had been here, my brother would not have died. But even now I know that whatever you ask of God, God will give you."

Jesus said to her, "Your brother will rise." Martha said to him, "I know he will rise, in the resurrection on the last day."

Jesus told her, "I am the resurrection and the life; whoever believes in me, even if he dies, will live, and everyone who lives and believes in me will never die. Do you believe this?" She said to him, "Yes, Lord. I have come to believe that you are the Christ, the Son of God, the one who is coming into the world." When she had said this, she went and called her sister Mary secretly, saying, "The teacher is here and is asking for you."

As soon as she heard this, she rose quickly and went to him. For Jesus had not yet come into the village, but was still where Martha had met him. So when the Jews who were with her in the house comforting her saw Mary get up quickly and go out, they followed her, presuming that she was going to the tomb to weep there. When Mary came to where Jesus was and saw him, she fell at his feet and said to him, "Lord, if you had been here, my brother would not have died." When Jesus saw her weeping and the Jews who had come with her weeping, he became perturbed and deeply troubled, and said, "Where have you laid him?" They said to him, "Sir, come and see." And Jesus wept. So the Jews said, "See how he loved him." But some of them said, "Could not the one who opened the eyes of the blind man have done something so that this man would not have died?"

So Jesus, perturbed again, came to the tomb. It was a cave, and a stone lay across it. Jesus said, "Take away the stone." Martha, the dead man's sister, said to him, "Lord, by now there will be a stench; he has been dead for four days." Jesus said to her, "Did I not tell you that if you believe you will see the glory of God?" So they took away the stone. And Jesus raised his eyes and said, Father, I thank you for hearing me. I know that you always hear me; but because of the crowd here I have said this, that they may believe that you sent me." And when he had said this, He cried out in a loud voice, "Lazarus, come out!"

The dead man came out, tied hand and foot with burial bands, and his face was wrapped in a cloth. So Jesus said to them, "Untie him and let him go."

Now many of the Jews who had come to Mary and seen what he had done began to believe in him.

The Spirit that Dwells in You

Even after the ascension, the early Christians experienced Jesus as alive in their midst. They had seen his death; they knew of his resurrection and he appeared to some of them; and they heard from the disciples about his ascension. But they experienced him as present still through the teachings of the apostles, the breaking of the bread, and the change they witnessed in themselves and others who had been baptized. This life was different—joyful, peaceful, even when they seemed surrounded by trouble. Paul called this new attitude "being in the Spirit," which was another way of saying that God had taken up residence in your heart and soul. Paul saw his mission to bring that Good News to as many places as possible and exhort the people to live into the fullness of that life.

Opening the Graves

Paul's understanding of the Spirit that gives life was undoubtedly influenced by his knowledge of the Hebrew Scriptures such as the passage from our first reading today. Ezekiel's vision of a graveyard described the people of Israel in exile—far away from their homeland and undoubtedly feeling buried by their Babylonian conquerors. The promise that God would open their graves and bring them back to the land must have provided some sorely needed hope in a time of despair. And God also promised to send his Spirit into the people that they might live. When that happened, God said, everyone would know the Lord.

Taking Away the Stone

The story of Lazarus invites all who hear it to imagine themselves in the drama. Are we Mary and Martha, mourning our dead brother? Are we crowd members who see a dead man walking and are told to untie him and let him go? Are we Lazarus, dead in a grave called sin, power, or hopelessness? In many ways, the Lazarus story is Ezekiel's prophecy come to life. Jesus opened the grave and Lazarus lived again. Even Jesus' prayer echoes Ezekiel. In the prophecy, God promised that the people would "know that I am the Lord." Jesus tells the crowd, "Did I not tell you that if you believe you will see the glory of God? 'God is with us.'" The prophecy comes true. Our story ends with many of the Jews who witnessed the miracle came to believe in Jesus.

Fifth Sunday of Lent, Year A

Good News for All of Us

In the Rite of Christian Initiation for Adults, the story of Lazarus is the last of three scrutinies—rituals designed to lead those awaiting baptism deeper into the process of conversion. According to the *Catechism of the Catholic Church*, the scrutinies help uncover and heal whatever is weak or sinful in the hearts of the elect and strengthen all that is upright, strong, and good. Each of the Gospels for the three scrutinies present Jesus as the answer to our prayers. He is Living Water to the woman at the well, the Light of the World to the man born blind, and the resurrection and life to Lazarus. In turn, we sometimes find ourselves marginalized—dead and buried in our sin—because of our way of life, blinded by circumstance or our own refusal to see. Accompanying the elect as they enter the scrutinies gives us a chance to renew our own faith in Jesus as Savior. It gives us the opportunity to examine ourselves and see what holds us back from accepting the gift of life that Jesus gives us. As we approach Holy Week, let us strive to open our hearts so that Christ, the Light, might fill us completely.

Questions for Reflection and Discussion

> *Lazarus' friends needed to untie the burial clothes before Lazarus could be fully freed. What do you need to untie so that you might be free from whatever might be holding you back?*

> *In times of great despair, we might feel abandoned by God and say, "Lord, if you had been here, such and so wouldn't have happened." Have you ever felt like this? What do you think Jesus would say to you?*

Related *Journey of Faith* Lesson

E7, "The Meaning of Holy Week"

Themes

Death
    E2, "Living Lent"
    E6, "The Lord's Prayer"
Spirit
    E7, "The Meaning of Holy Week"

The Lord's Supper (Holy Thursday), the Easter Triduum

READING 1 (ABC), EXODUS 12:1–8, 11–14

The LORD said to Moses and Aaron in the land of Egypt, "This month shall stand at the head of your calendar; you shall reckon it the first month of the year. Tell the whole community of Israel: On the tenth of this month every one of your families must procure for itself a lamb, one apiece for each household. If a family is too small for a whole lamb, it shall join the nearest household in procuring one and shall share in the lamb in proportion to the number of persons who partake of it. The lamb must be a year-old male and without blemish. You may take it from either the sheep or the goats. You shall keep it until the fourteenth day of this month, and then, with the whole assembly of Israel present, it shall be slaughtered during the evening twilight. They shall take some of its blood and apply it to the two doorposts and the lintel of every house in which they partake of the lamb. That same night they shall eat its roasted flesh with unleavened bread and bitter herbs. "This is how you are to eat it: with your loins girt, sandals on your feet and your staff in hand, you shall eat like those who are in flight. It is the Passover of the LORD. For on this same night I will go through Egypt, striking down every firstborn of the land, both man and beast, and executing judgment on all the gods of Egypt—I, the LORD! But the blood will mark the houses where you are. Seeing the blood, I will pass over you; thus, when I strike the land of Egypt, no destructive blow will come upon you. "This day shall be a memorial feast for you, which all your generations shall celebrate with pilgrimage to the LORD, as a perpetual institution."

PSALM 116:12–13, 15–16BC, 17–18

READING 2 (ABC), 1 CORINTHIANS 11:23–26

Brothers and sisters: I received from the Lord what I also handed on to you, that the Lord Jesus, on the night he was handed over, took bread, and, after he had given thanks, broke it and said, "This is my body that is for you. Do this in remembrance of me." In the same way also the cup, after supper, saying, "This cup is the new covenant in my blood. Do this, as often as you drink it, in remembrance of me." For as often as you eat this bread and drink the cup, you proclaim the death of the Lord until he comes.

GOSPEL (ABC), JOHN 13:1–15

Before the feast of Passover, Jesus knew that his hour had come to pass from this world to the Father. He loved his own in the world and he loved them to the end. The devil had already induced Judas, son of Simon the Iscariot, to hand him over. So, during supper, fully aware that the Father had put everything into his power and that he had come from God and was returning to God, he rose from supper and took off his outer garments. He took a towel and tied it around his waist. Then he poured water into a basin and began to wash the disciples' feet and dry them with the towel around his waist. He came to Simon Peter, who said to him, "Master, are you going to wash my feet?" Jesus answered and said to him, "What I am doing, you do not understand now, but you will understand later." Peter said to him, "You will never wash my feet." Jesus answered him, "Unless I wash you, you will have no inheritance with me." Simon Peter said to him, "Master, then not only my feet, but my hands and head as well." Jesus said to him, "Whoever has bathed has no need except to have his feet washed, for he is clean all over; so you are clean, but not all." For he knew who would betray him; for this reason, he said, "Not all of you are clean." So when he had washed their feet and put his garments back on and reclined at table again, he said to them, "Do you realize what I have done for you? You call me 'teacher' and 'master,' and rightly so, for indeed I am. If I, therefore, the master and teacher, have washed your feet, you ought to wash one another's feet. I have given you a model to follow, so that as I have done for you, you should also do."

Handing on Our Faith

The Corinthians had some problems. In his letters, Paul worked hard to help them by changing how they thought about things and giving them practical details. When Paul heard that the Corinthian community didn't share their bread when they gathered with each other on Sundays and that some of them even got drunk, he knew he had to do something. In what is probably the first eucharistic formula recorded in the New Testament, Paul recalls for the Corinthians the story of the last supper and its solemn and sacred meaning. Paul's conversion and experience of Christianity was so powerful that he understood that in some way it was Jesus himself who was present at every gathering of Christians to celebrate the "breaking of the bread" and the telling of the story. Paul's retelling of this sacred rite was his attempt to restore the dignity of the celebration and refocus the Corinthians on the presence of Christ in their midst. In this way, he reminded them that every time they gathered at the table, they gave witness, "proclaiming the Lord's death, until he comes."

A Passover Celebration

Long before Jesus was born, when the Israelites were enslaved in Egypt, God sent the last of ten plagues designed to convince Pharaoh to let the Israelites go. The angel of death would strike down the first-born son of every family. Moses commanded the people to slaughter a lamb and sprinkle its blood on their doorposts, then roast the lamb and eat it. When the angel of death came and saw the blood, he would pass over those houses and they would be spared from the plague. Every year after that, the Israelites celebrated the Passover by eating the same foods and telling the story. Even today, each Jew remembers as if it were happening to them today recalling that "We were slaves in the land of Egypt." In a similar way, when Christians tell the story of the Last Supper at the consecration, the priest looks at the congregation and says: "Take this all of you and eat of it…" drawing us into the story personally." Many biblical scholars believe the Last Supper was a Passover meal. And in Corinthians 5:7, Paul refers to Jesus as the Passover lamb (*pascha*).

A Memory of Servanthood

On this day when we celebrate both the sacrament of Eucharist and priesthood, John's Gospel stands out for its emphasis on servant leadership. The washing of the feet reminds all Christians that both leadership and service come from a place of love and humility and that if we would serve, we have to be open to being served. Before this evening, even Jesus was willing to have his feet washed (see Luke 7:36–50). Peter, the leader of the apostles, objects, but Jesus is firm, "Unless I wash you, you have no inheritance with me." Jesus washed them all—the one who would deny him, the ones who would run, abandon him, even the one who would betray him. And then he looked at all of them and said, "As I have washed your feet, you ought to wash one another's feet." When we remember Jesus' service, it compels all of us to do the same in love and humility to friend and enemy, a fitting way to give thanks for all Christ has done for us.

Good News for All of Us

We close out Lent by gathering at the altar, proclaiming the Good News of Jesus Christ, sharing in the Eucharist, and loving and serving one another as we prepare for the days to come. Even now, we believe it is Christ himself who invites us to the table. We tell the same story; we share the same actions, and in doing so we remember who we are and commit ourselves to follow Christ through death to life. Paul described it as "proclaiming the death of the Lord until he comes." At Mass we get a little foretaste of what that coming might be like.

Questions for Reflection and Discussion

> ➤ *We don't become Christian by passing a test; we become Christian by having someone give us a bath. We begin by being washed. Have there been other times in your life where someone has served you in a way that made you know you were loved?*

> ➤ *We can't always be literal in our service. Name some specific ways in which you have or might "wash someone else's feet."*

Related Journey of Faith Lesson

E4, "The Creed"

Themes

Community
    E4, "The Creed"
    E8, "Easter Vigil Retreat"
Eucharist
    E1, "Election: Saying Yes to Jesus"
    E7, "The Meaning of Holy Week"
Service
    E3, "Scrutinies: Looking Within"

READING 1 (ABC), ISAIAH 52:13—53:12

See, my servant shall prosper, he shall be raised high and greatly exalted. Even as many were amazed at him—so marred was his look beyond human semblance and his appearance beyond that of the sons of man—so shall he startle many nations, because of him kings shall stand speechless; for those who have not been told shall see, those who have not heard shall ponder it.

Who would believe what we have heard? To whom has the arm of the LORD been revealed? He grew up like a sapling before him, like a shoot from the parched earth; there was in him no stately bearing to make us look at him, nor appearance that would attract us to him. He was spurned and avoided by people, a man of suffering, accustomed to infirmity, one of those from whom people hide their faces, spurned, and we held him in no esteem.

Yet it was our infirmities that he bore, our sufferings that he endured, while we thought of him as stricken, as one smitten by God and afflicted. But he was pierced for our offenses, crushed for our sins; upon him was the chastisement that makes us whole, by his stripes we were healed. We had all gone astray like sheep, each following his own way; but the LORD laid upon him the guilt of us all.

Though he was harshly treated, he submitted and opened not his mouth; like a lamb led to the slaughter or a sheep before the shearers, he was silent and opened not his mouth. Oppressed and condemned, he was taken away, and who would have thought any more of his destiny? When he was cut off from the land of the living, and smitten for the sin of his people, a grave was assigned him among the wicked and a burial place with evildoers, though he had done no wrong nor spoken any falsehood. But the LORD was pleased to crush him in infirmity.

If he gives his life as an offering for sin, he shall see his descendants in a long life, and the will of the LORD shall be accomplished through him.

Because of his affliction he shall see the light in fullness of days; through his suffering, my servant shall justify many, and their guilt he shall bear. Therefore I will give him his portion among the great, and he shall divide the spoils with the mighty, because he surrendered himself to death and was counted among the wicked; and he shall take away the sins of many, and win pardon for their offenses.

PSALM 31:2, 6, 12–13, 15–16, 17, 25

READING 2 (ABC), HEBREWS 4:14–16; 5:7–9

Brothers and sisters: Since we have a great high priest who has passed through the heavens, Jesus, the Son of God, let us hold fast to our confession. For we do not have a high priest who is unable to sympathize with our weaknesses, but one who has similarly been tested in every way, yet without sin. So let us confidently approach the throne of grace to receive mercy and to find grace for timely help. In the days when Christ was in the flesh, he offered prayers and supplications with loud cries and tears to the one who was able to save him from death, and he was heard because of his reverence. Son though he was, he learned obedience from what he suffered; and when he was made perfect, he became the source of eternal salvation for all who obey him.

GOSPEL (ABC), JOHN 18:1—19:42

Jesus went out with his disciples across the Kidron valley to where there was a garden, into which he and his disciples entered. Judas his betrayer also knew the place, because Jesus had often met there with his disciples. So Judas got a band of soldiers and guards from the chief priests and the Pharisees and went there with lanterns, torches, and weapons. Jesus, knowing everything that was going to happen to him, went out and said to them, "Whom are you looking for?" They answered him, "Jesus the Nazorean." He said to them, "I AM." Judas his betrayer was also with them. When he said to them, "I AM," they turned away and fell to the ground. So he again asked them, "Whom are you looking for?" They said, "Jesus the Nazorean." Jesus answered, "I told you that I AM. So if you are looking for me, let these men go." This was to fulfill what he had said, "I have not lost any of those you gave me."

Then Simon Peter, who had a sword, drew it, struck the high priest's slave, and cut off his right ear. The slave's name was Malchus. Jesus said to Peter, "Put your sword into its scabbard. Shall I not drink the cup that the Father gave me?"

So the band of soldiers, the tribune, and the Jewish guards seized Jesus, bound him, and brought him to Annas first. He was the father-in-law of Caiaphas, who was high priest that year. It was Caiaphas who had counseled the Jews that it was better that one man should die rather than the people.

Simon Peter and another disciple followed Jesus. Now the other disciple was known to the high priest, and he entered the courtyard of the high priest with Jesus. But Peter stood at the gate outside. So the other disciple, the acquaintance of the high priest, went out and spoke to the gatekeeper and brought Peter in. Then the maid who was the gatekeeper said to Peter, "You are not one of this man's disciples, are you?" He said, "I am not." Now the slaves and the guards were standing around a charcoal fire that they had made, because it was cold, and were warming themselves. Peter was also standing there keeping warm.

The high priest questioned Jesus about his disciples and about his doctrine. Jesus answered him, "I have spoken publicly to the world. I have always taught in a synagogue or in the temple area where all the Jews gather, and in secret I have said nothing. Why ask me? Ask those who heard me what I said to them. They know what I said." When he had said this, one of the temple guards standing there struck Jesus and said, "Is this the way you answer the high priest?" Jesus answered him, "If I have spoken wrongly, testify to the wrong; but if I have spoken rightly, why do you strike me?" Then Annas sent him bound to Caiaphas the high priest.

Now Simon Peter was standing there keeping warm. And they said to him, "You are not one of his disciples, are you?" He denied it and said, "I am not." One of the slaves of the high priest, a relative of the one whose ear Peter had cut off, said, "Didn't I see you in the garden with him?" Again Peter denied it. And immediately the cock crowed.

Then they brought Jesus from Caiaphas to the praetorium. It was morning. And they themselves did not enter the praetorium, in order not to be defiled so that they could eat the Passover. So Pilate came out to them and said, "What charge do you bring against this man?" They answered and said to him, "If he were not a criminal, we would not have handed him over to you." At this, Pilate said to them, "Take him yourselves, and judge him according to your law." The Jews answered him, "We do not have the right to execute anyone," in order that the word of Jesus might be fulfilled that he said indicating the kind of death he would die. So Pilate went back into the praetorium and summoned Jesus and said to him, "Are you the King of the Jews?" Jesus answered, "Do you say this on your own or have others told you about me?" Pilate answered, "I am not a Jew, am I? Your own nation and the chief priests handed you over to me. What have you done?" Jesus answered, "My kingdom does not belong to this world. If my kingdom did belong to this world, my attendants would be fighting to keep me from being handed over to the Jews. But as it is, my kingdom is not here." So Pilate said to him, "Then you are a king?" Jesus answered, "You say I am a king. For this I was born and for this I came into the world, to testify to the truth. Everyone who belongs to the truth listens to my voice." Pilate said to him, "What is truth?"

When he had said this, he again went out to the Jews and said to them, "I find no guilt in him. But you have a custom that I release one prisoner to you at Passover. Do you want me to release to you the King of the Jews?" They cried out again, "Not this one but Barabbas!" Now Barabbas was a revolutionary.

Then Pilate took Jesus and had him scourged. And the soldiers wove a crown out of thorns and placed it on his head, and clothed him in a purple cloak, and they came to him and said, "Hail, King of the Jews!" And they struck him repeatedly. Once more Pilate went out and said to them, "Look, I am bringing him out to you, so that you may know that I find no guilt in him." So Jesus came out, wearing the crown of thorns and the purple cloak. And he said to them, "Behold, the man!" When the chief priests and the guards saw him they cried out, "Crucify him, crucify him!" Pilate said to them, "Take him yourselves and crucify him. I find no guilt in him." The Jews answered, "We have a law, and according to that law he ought to die, because he made himself the Son of God." Now when Pilate heard this statement, he became even more afraid, and went back into the praetorium and said to Jesus, "Where are you from?" Jesus did not answer him. So Pilate said to him, "Do you not speak to me? Do you not know that I have power to release you and I have power to crucify you?" Jesus answered him, "You would have no power over me if it had not been given to you from above. For this reason the one who handed me over to you has the greater sin." Consequently, Pilate tried to release him; but the Jews cried out, "If you release him, you are not a Friend of Caesar. Everyone who makes himself a king opposes Caesar."

When Pilate heard these words he brought Jesus out and seated him on the judge's bench in the place called Stone Pavement, in Hebrew, Gabbatha. It was preparation day for Passover, and it was about noon. And he said to the Jews, "Behold, your king!" They cried out, "Take him away, take him away! Crucify him!" Pilate said to them, "Shall I crucify your king?" The chief priests answered, "We have no king but Caesar." Then he handed him over to them to be crucified.

So they took Jesus, and, carrying the cross himself, he went out to what is called the Place of the Skull, in Hebrew, Golgotha. There they crucified him, and with him two others, one on either side, with Jesus in the middle. Pilate also had an inscription written and put on the cross. It read, "Jesus the Nazorean, the King of the Jews." Now many of the Jews read this inscription, because the place where Jesus was crucified was near the city; and it was written in Hebrew, Latin, and Greek. So the chief priests of the Jews said to Pilate, "Do not write 'The King of the Jews,' but that he said, 'I am the King of the Jews'." Pilate answered, "What I have written, I have written." When the soldiers had crucified Jesus, they took his clothes and divided them into four shares, a share for each soldier. They also took his tunic, but the tunic was seamless, woven in one piece from the top down. So they said to one another, "Let's not tear it, but cast lots for it to see whose it will be," in order that the passage of Scripture might be fulfilled that says: *They divided my garments among them, and for my vesture they cast lots.* This is what the soldiers did. Standing by the cross of Jesus were his mother and his mother's sister, Mary the wife

of Clopas, and Mary of Magdala. When Jesus saw his mother and the disciple there whom he loved he said to his mother, "Woman, behold, your son." Then he said to the disciple, "Behold, your mother." And from that hour the disciple took her into his home. After this, aware that everything was now finished, in order that the Scripture might be fulfilled, Jesus said, "I thirst." There was a vessel filled with common wine. So they put a sponge soaked in wine on a sprig of hyssop and put it up to his mouth. When Jesus had taken the wine, he said, "It is finished." And bowing his head, he handed over the spirit.

Here all kneel and pause for a short time.

Now since it was preparation day, in order that the bodies might not remain on the cross on the sabbath, for the sabbath day of that week was a solemn one, the Jews asked Pilate that their legs be broken and that they be taken down. So the soldiers came and broke the legs of the first and then of the other one who was crucified with Jesus. But when they came to Jesus and saw that he was already dead, they did not break his legs, but one soldier thrust his lance into his side, and immediately blood and water flowed out. An eyewitness has testified, and his testimony is true; he knows that he is speaking the truth, so that you also may come to believe. For this happened so that the Scripture passage might be fulfilled: *Not a bone of it will be broken.* And again another passage says: *They will look upon him whom they have pierced.*

After this, Joseph of Arimathea, secretly a disciple of Jesus for fear of the Jews, asked Pilate if he could remove the body of Jesus. And Pilate permitted it. So he came and took his body. Nicodemus, the one who had first come to him at night, also came bringing a mixture of myrrh and aloes weighing about one hundred pounds. They took the body of Jesus and bound it with burial cloths along with the spices, according to the Jewish burial custom. Now in the place where he had been crucified there was a garden, and in the garden a new tomb, in which no one had yet been buried. So they laid Jesus there because of the Jewish preparation day; for the tomb was close by.

A Suffering Servant

We end this Holy Week in our Church as we began it, with a reading of the passion and death of Jesus. The event itself was so profound that when the evangelists told of it, they reached into their sacred texts to find the words that described their experience. They found them in the prophet Isaiah, who spoke of a servant of God willing to suffer for the sins of Israel. The servant endured shame and spitting; he was bruised beyond recognition and yet he quietly endured his injuries. Isaiah adds: "The Lord laid on him the guilt of us all." The early Christians saw Jesus in the image of the suffering servant. It was the only thing that made sense of Jesus' death. He died for us and did it in obedience to God, his Father. Jesus was the Lamb of God who gave his life as a sin offering for the world. It's hard to imagine that someone could love us so much that he would gladly bear all our sin for a chance to restore our relationship with God. But Isaiah's vision is clear: "because he surrendered himself to death...he shall take away the sins of many and win pardon for their offenses" (Isaiah 53:12).

A Death that Leads to Life

The servant in Isaiah surrenders himself to death. In John's Gospel, Jesus is in full control of the events. He knows what's going to happen. He tells Peter that he is to drink the cup the Father has given him. And he declares to Pilate that he would have no power over him had it not been given by the Father. Nearly everything that took place, John says, was to fulfill the words of Scripture. In the end, Jesus simply says: "It is finished," bows down his head, and gives up his Spirit. Jesus' passion and death plunged him into the mystery of human suffering and death. He, who was God, experienced the pain of rejection and the cruelty human beings can inflict on one another. He experienced denial and betrayal and what we might have labeled failure in the eyes of others. His death was a criminal's death—it hardly seemed like the death of a great hero. And yet, this is the death that shapes our entire experience and is deemed so important that we have to tell the story every year both as a preparation for and a prelude to the ending of Holy Week.

Why does this story never wear out? The Letter to the Hebrews has the answer. Jesus is our high priest who has been tested as we are, suffered as we do, and who has died as we will die. His death to the eyes of outsiders looked like a failure, but his death was the source of eternal salvation for the world. His death meant spiritual life for us. At the end of these three days (this is what the word Triduum means) we will finish the story and realize that the death of Christ is not the end for us—it is a beginning of new life in the Spirit.

The Lord's Passion (Good Friday), the Easter Triduum

Good News for All of Us

We might say that death is what gets Christians up in the morning. If we're doing it right, we practice a little death each day when we make time to talk to a friend in need or sacrifice a pleasure in order to take care of a family member. We go through our own hardships—the death of loved ones or the loss of a job and we die a little inside. When we find life again, we also find we have changed. We may appreciate small things more or love others more deeply. And we cherish our memories. This is the paschal mystery. Life comes from death. Jesus taught us that. And there is no place we experience that more than in following him. "To whom would we go," Peter once asked Jesus, "you have the words of eternal life" (John 6:68).

Questions for Reflection and Discussion

➤ *Did Jesus have to suffer and die in order to save us? Why or why not?*

➤ *Good Friday is the only day that Mass is not celebrated. The main liturgy involves telling the passion story followed by veneration of the cross and the reception of communion that was consecrated on Holy Thursday. Catholics aren't required to attend, but why might it be important to attend?*

Related Journey of Faith Lesson

E4, "The Creed"

Themes

Death
    E4, "The Creed"
    E7, "The Meaning of Holy Week"
Pain, Suffering
    E5, "The Way of the Cross"
Sin
    E2, "Living Lent"
    E3, "Scrutinies: Looking Within"
    E8, "Easter Vigil Retreat"

READING 1 (ABC), GENESIS 1:1—2:2

In the beginning, when God created the heavens and the earth, the earth was a formless wasteland, and darkness covered the abyss, while a mighty wind swept over the waters.

Then God said, "Let there be light," and there was light. God saw how good the light was. God then separated the light from the darkness. God called the light "day," and the darkness he called "night." Thus evening came, and morning followed—the first day.

Then God said, "Let there be a dome in the middle of the waters, to separate one body of water from the other." And so it happened: God made the dome, and it separated the water above the dome from the water below it. God called the dome "the sky." Evening came, and morning followed—the second day.

Then God said, "Let the water under the sky be gathered into a single basin, so that the dry land may appear." And so it happened: the water under the sky was gathered into its basin, and the dry land appeared. God called the dry land "the earth, " and the basin of the water he called "the sea." God saw how good it was. Then God said, "Let the earth bring forth vegetation: every kind of plant that bears seed and every kind of fruit tree on earth that bears fruit with its seed in it." And so it happened: the earth brought forth every kind of plant that bears seed and every kind of fruit tree on earth that bears fruit with its seed in it. God saw how good it was. Evening came, and morning followed—the third day.

Then God said: "Let there be lights in the dome of the sky, to separate day from night. Let them mark the fixed times, the days and the years, and serve as luminaries in the dome of the sky, to shed light upon the earth." And so it happened: God made the two great lights, the greater one to govern the day, and the lesser one to govern the night; and he made the stars. God set them in the dome of the sky, to shed light upon the earth, to govern the day and the night, and to separate the light from the darkness. God saw how good it was. Evening came, and morning followed—the fourth day.

Then God said, "Let the water teem with an abundance of living creatures, and on the earth let birds fly beneath the dome of the sky." And so it happened: God created the great sea monsters and all kinds of swimming creatures with which the water teems, and all kinds of winged birds. God saw how good it was, and God blessed them, saying, "Be fertile, multiply, and fill the water of the seas; and let the birds multiply on the earth." Evening came, and morning followed—the fifth day.

Then God said, "Let the earth bring forth all kinds of living creatures: cattle, creeping things, and wild animals of all kinds." And so it happened: God made all kinds of wild animals, all kinds of cattle, and all kinds of creeping things of the earth. God saw how good it was. Then God said: "Let us make man in our image, after our likeness. Let them have dominion over the fish of the sea, the birds of the air, and the cattle, and over all the wild animals and all the creatures that crawl on the ground." God created man in his image; in the image of God he created him; male and female he created them. God blessed them, saying: "Be fertile and multiply; fill the earth and subdue it. Have dominion over the fish of the sea, the birds of the air, and all the living things that move on the earth." God also said: "See, I give you every seed-bearing plant all over the earth and every tree that has seed-bearing fruit on it to be your food; and to all the animals of the land, all the birds of the air, and all the living creatures that crawl on the ground, I give all the green plants for food." And so it happened. God looked at everything he had made, and he found it very good. Evening came, and morning followed—the sixth day.

Thus the heavens and the earth and all their array were completed. Since on the seventh day God was finished with the work he had been doing, he rested on the seventh day from all the work he had undertaken.

PSALM 104: 1–2, 5–6, 10, 12, 13–14, 24, 35

READING 3 (ABC), EXODUS 14:15—15:1

The LORD said to Moses, "Why are you crying out to me? Tell the Israelites to go forward. And you, lift up your staff and, with hand outstretched over the sea, split the sea in two, that the Israelites may pass through it on dry land. But I will make the Egyptians so obstinate that they will go in after them. Then I will receive glory through Pharaoh and all his army, his chariots and charioteers. The Egyptians shall know that I am the LORD, when I receive glory through Pharaoh and his chariots and charioteers." The angel of God, who had been leading Israel's camp, now moved and went around behind them. The column of cloud also, leaving the front, took up its place behind them, so that it came between the camp of the Egyptians and that of Israel. But the cloud now became dark, and thus the night passed without the rival camps coming any closer together all night long. Then Moses stretched out his hand over the sea, and the LORD swept the sea with a strong east wind throughout the night and so turned it into dry land. When the water was thus divided, the Israelites marched into the midst of the sea on dry land, with the water like a wall to their right and to their left. The Egyptians followed in pursuit; all Pharaoh's horses and chariots and charioteers went after them right into the midst of the sea. In the night watch just before dawn the LORD cast through the column of the fiery cloud upon the Egyptian force a glance that threw it into a panic; and he so clogged their chariot wheels that they could hardly drive. With that the Egyptians sounded the retreat before Israel, because the LORD was fighting for them against the Egyptians. Then the LORD told Moses, "Stretch out your hand over the sea, that the water may flow back upon the Egyptians, upon their chariots and their charioteers." So Moses stretched out his hand over the sea, and at dawn the sea flowed back to its normal depth. The Egyptians were fleeing head on toward the sea, when the LORD hurled them into its midst. As the water flowed back, it covered the chariots and the charioteers of Pharaoh's whole army which had followed the Israelites into the sea. Not a single one of them escaped. But the Israelites had marched on dry land through the midst of the sea, with the water like a wall to their right and to their left. Thus the LORD saved Israel on that day from the power of the Egyptians. When Israel saw the Egyptians lying dead on the seashore and beheld the great power that the LORD had shown against the Egyptians, they feared the LORD and believed in him and in his servant Moses. Then Moses and the Israelites sang this song to the LORD: I will sing to the LORD, for he is gloriously triumphant; horse and chariot he has cast into the sea.

EPISTLE (ABC), ROMANS 6:3–11

Brothers and sisters: Are you unaware that we who were baptized into Christ Jesus were baptized into his death? We were indeed buried with him through baptism into death, so that, just as Christ was raised from the dead by the glory of the Father, we too might live in newness of life. For if we have grown into union with him through a death like his, we shall also be united with him in the resurrection. We know that our old self was crucified with him, so that our sinful body might be done away with, that we might no longer be in slavery to sin. For a dead person has been absolved from sin. If, then, we have died with Christ, we believe that we shall also live with him. We know that Christ, raised from the dead, dies no more; death no longer has power over him. As to his death, he died to sin once and for all; as to his life, he lives for God. Consequently, you too must think of yourselves as being dead to sin and living for God in Christ Jesus.

PSALM 118:1–2, 16–17, 22–23

GOSPEL (A), MATTHEW 28:1–10

After the sabbath, as the first day of the week was dawning, Mary Magdalene and the other Mary came to see the tomb. And behold, there was a great earthquake; for an angel of the Lord descended from heaven, approached, rolled back the stone, and sat upon it. His appearance was like lightning and his clothing was white as snow. The guards were shaken with fear of him and became like dead men. Then the angel said to the women in reply, "Do not be afraid! I know that you are seeking Jesus the crucified. He is not here, for he has been raised just as he said. Come and see the place where he lay. Then go quickly and tell his disciples, 'He has been raised from the dead, and he is going before you to Galilee; there you will see him.' Behold, I have told you." Then they went away quickly from the tomb, fearful yet overjoyed, and ran to announce this to his disciples. And behold, Jesus met them on their way and greeted them. They approached, embraced his feet, and did him homage. Then Jesus said to them, "Do not be afraid. Go tell my brothers to go to Galilee, and there they will see me."

GOSPEL (B), MARK 16:1–7

When the sabbath was over, Mary Magdalene, Mary, the mother of James, and Salome bought spices so that they might go and anoint him. Very early when the sun had risen, on the first day of the week, they came to the tomb. They were saying to one another, "Who will roll back the stone for us from the entrance to the tomb?" When they looked up, they saw that the stone had been rolled back; it was very large. On entering the tomb they saw a young man sitting on the right side, clothed in a white robe, and they were utterly amazed. He said to them, "Do not be amazed! You seek Jesus of Nazareth, the crucified. He has been raised; he is not here. Behold the place where they laid him. But go and tell his disciples and Peter, 'He is going before you to Galilee; there you will see him, as he told you.'"

GOSPEL (C), LUKE 24:1–12

At daybreak on the first day of the week the women who had come from Galilee with Jesus took the spices they had prepared and went to the tomb. They found the stone rolled away from the tomb; but when they entered, they did not find the body of the Lord Jesus. While they were puzzling over this, behold, two men in dazzling garments appeared to them. They were terrified and bowed their faces to the ground. They said to them, "Why do you seek the living one among the dead? He is not here, but he has been raised. Remember what he said to you while he was still in Galilee, that the Son of Man must be handed over to sinners and be crucified, and rise on the third day." And they remembered his words. Then they returned from the tomb and announced all these things to the eleven and to all the others. The women were Mary Magdalene, Joanna, and Mary the mother of James; the others who accompanied them also told this to the apostles, but their story seemed like nonsense and they did not believe them. But Peter got up and ran to the tomb, bent down, and saw the burial cloths alone; then he went home amazed at what had happened.

Scripture readings for the Easter Vigil:
Genesis 1:1—2:2 or 1:1, 26–31a;
Psalm 104:1–2, 5–6, 10, 12, 13–14, 24, 35 or
Psalm 33:4–5, 6–7, 12–13 20–22;
Genesis 22:1–18 or 22:1–2, 9a, 10–13, 15–18;
Psalm 16:5, 8, 9–10, 11;
Exodus 14:15—15:1;
Exodus 15:1–2, 3–4, 5–6, 17–18;
Isaiah 54:5–14/
Psalm 30:2, 4, 5–6, 11–12, 13;
Isaiah 55:1–11;
Isaiah 12:2–3, 4, 5–6;
Baruch 3:9–15, 32—4:4;
Psalm 19:8, 9, 10, 11;
Ezekiel 36:16–17a, 18–28;
Psalm 42:3, 5 and 43:3, 4 or
Isaiah 12:2–3, 4bcd, 5–6 or
Psalm 51:12–13, 14–15, 18–19;
Romans 6:3–11;
Psalm 118:1–2, 16–17, 22–23;
Matthew 28:1–10;
Mark 16:1–7;
Luke 24:1–12

Alleluia, He Is Risen

The third day of the Triduum begins at sunset on Holy Saturday. Since Holy Thursday we have been walking with the disciples into these last days of Jesus' life, we have witnessed his death, and we have been left with a Church stripped of its music, decoration, and its Eucharist. When the darkness comes at the end of that second day, a sense of anticipation begins to build. The service begins in darkness outside the Church doors, but a new fire is kindled and the light of Christ, symbolized by the Easter candle, is lit and from that light all the baptized receive the light of Christ and enter the church to hear the great proclamation of Easter which calls us all to rejoice. This is the service in which those who seek the sacrament of baptism and the completion of initiation will be welcomed in to receive their sacraments. It is the time when the entire body of the faithful will repeat their baptismal promises and be sprinkled again with newly blessed water. Once you have been to an Easter Vigil, it's hard to imagine celebrating Easter in any other way.

Many people ask why there are so many readings at the Vigil. These readings trace the story of God's care for his people from creation to the passion, death and resurrection of Jesus. They are our last instruction to the elect and a reminder of God's blessing to the faithful. The readings from Genesis and Exodus represent the Law. The readings from Isaiah, Baruch, and Ezekiel represent the Prophets. In our understanding of Scripture, Jesus is the fulfillment of promises contained in the Law and the Prophets. Those readings give us the words to talk about Jesus. Paul's epistle reminds us that Jesus' death and life is our death and life. And in the telling of the story, the Gospel proclaims that he is risen. The service which began in darkness ends in glorious light. We welcome those who have been baptized and received. We are blessed with the grace to follow Jesus in the years to come.

The Paschal Mystery

Paul's Letter to the Romans summons us all to a mystery. Death leads to life. What Jesus suffered at the end of his life for our sake was a far cry from the image of the great warrior that many imagined the Messiah to be. Many people, including some disciples, thought their hope died with him. But somehow, Jesus' death was overturned. "Why do you seek the living among the dead?" the angels asked those who visited the tomb in Luke's Gospel. "He isn't here," they said in Mark's version of the story. The one they saw dead and buried had been raised from the dead. New life was his. And Paul says that if we are baptized into Christ, then we are also baptized into his death (the death of anything that keeps us from following him) and just as he was raised from the dead, so we shall have new life and have it abundantly in the grace of God. This is our Good News to share with anyone who will listen.

Good News for All of Us

John, the Gospel writer whose stories we will hear throughout the Easter season, was convinced that those who had faith in Jesus had eternal life already. Those who did not were already dead. For John it was simple. Jesus was life and everything else was death. Moses said something similar in the Hebrew Scriptures: "I have set before you life and death, the blessing and the curse. Choose life, then, that you and your descendants may live" (Deuteronomy 30:19). While the choice may seem stark (no shades of gray) it was clear that for John and the early Christians, the experience of the risen Christ was so life-giving that anything else seemed like death. At the Easter vigil, we get a glimpse of that experience. And we hope that it carries us through the rest of the Easter season and beyond.

Questions for Reflection and Discussion

➤ *How do you experience the life of Christ in your life?*

➤ *What have you had to "die to" in order to live as a Catholic in this society?*

Related Journey of Faith Lesson

E4, "The Creed"

Themes

Life, Resurrection
    M1, "Conversion: A Lifelong Process"
    M3, "Your Spiritual Gifts"
    M4, "Discernment"
    M5, "Our Call to Holiness"
Relationships
    M2, "The Role of the Laity"
    M7, "Family Life"
    Q7, "Your Prayer Life"
    M8, "Evangelization"

READING 1, ACTS 1:1–11

In the first book, Theophilus, I dealt with all that Jesus did and taught until the day he was taken up, after giving instructions through the Holy Spirit to the apostles whom he had chosen. He presented himself alive to them by many proofs after he had suffered, appearing to them during forty days and speaking about the kingdom of God. While meeting with the them, he enjoined them not to depart from Jerusalem, but to wait for "the promise of the Father about which you have heard me speak; for John baptized with water, but in a few days you will be baptized with the Holy Spirit." When they had gathered together they asked him, "Lord, are you at this time going to restore the kingdom to Israel?" He answered them, "It is not for you to know the times or seasons that the Father has established by his own authority. But you will receive power when the Holy Spirit comes upon you, and you will be my witnesses in Jerusalem, throughout Judea and Samaria, and to the ends of the earth." When he had said this, as they were looking on, he was lifted up, and a cloud took him from their sight. While they were looking intently at the sky as he was going, suddenly two men dressed in white garments stood beside them. They said, "Men of Galilee, why are you standing there looking at the sky? This Jesus who has been taken up from you into heaven will return in the same way as you have seen him going into heaven."

PSALM 47:2–3, 6–7, 8–9

READING 2, EPHESIANS 1:17–23

Brothers and sisters: May the God of our Lord Jesus Christ, the Father of glory, give you a Spirit of wisdom and revelation resulting in knowledge of him. May the eyes of your hearts be enlightened, that you may know what is the hope that belongs to his call, what are the riches of glory in his inheritance among the holy ones, and what is the surpassing greatness of his power for us who believe, in accord with the exercise of his great might, which he worked in Christ, raising him from the dead and seating him at his right hand in the heavens, far above every principality, authority, power, and dominion, and every name that is named not only in this age but also in the one to come. And he put all things beneath his feet and gave him as head over all things to the church, which is his body, the fullness of the one who fills all things in every way.

GOSPEL (A), MATTHEW 28:16–20

The eleven disciples went to Galilee, to the mountain to which Jesus had ordered them. When they saw him, they worshiped, but they doubted. Then Jesus approached and said to them, "All power in heaven and on earth has been given to me. Go, therefore, and make disciples of all nations, baptizing them in the name of the Father, and of the Son, and of the Holy Spirit, teaching them to observe all that I have commanded you. And behold, I am with you always, until the end of the age."

GOSPEL (B), MARK 16:15–20

Jesus said to his disciples: "Go into the whole world and proclaim the gospel to every creature. Whoever believes and is baptized will be saved; whoever does not believe will be condemned. These signs will accompany those who believe: in my name they will drive out demons, they will speak new languages. They will pick up serpents with their hands, and if they drink any deadly thing, it will not harm them. They will lay hands on the sick, and they will recover." So then the Lord Jesus, after he spoke to them, was taken up into heaven and took his seat at the right hand of God. But they went forth and preached everywhere, while the Lord worked with them and confirmed the word through accompanying signs.

GOSPEL (C), LUKE 24:46–53

Jesus said to his disciples: "Thus it is written that the Christ would suffer and rise from the dead on the third day and that repentance, for the forgiveness of sins, would be preached in his name to all the nations, beginning from Jerusalem. You are witnesses of these things. And behold I am sending the promise of my Father upon you; but stay in the city until you are clothed with power from on high." Then he led them out as far as Bethany, raised his hands, and blessed them. As he blessed them he parted from them and was taken up to heaven. They did him homage and then returned to Jerusalem with great joy, and they were continually in the temple praising God.

I Will Be with You Always

There can be no doubt that those who followed Jesus after the crucifixion and resurrection and the early Church as a whole experienced Jesus as alive in their midst. They knew of his death on the cross (or had experienced it personally). They heard about the good news of his resurrection and his appearances among the disciples and others, and they understood that he was no longer with them in the same way their friends and neighbors were, but they experienced his living presence in the community.

The Gospels each told a slightly different version of the risen Christ. Three of them talk about the ascension. All of them contain Jesus' promise to be present with them. Matthew includes the great commandment to all of us to go and make disciples of all nations and the promise that Jesus will be with us always. In Mark's Gospel, Jesus commands the apostles to proclaim the Good News—to evangelize. His Gospel ends with the words: "They went forth and preached everywhere, while the Lord worked with them and confirmed the word through accompanying signs" (Mark 16:20). Luke's Gospel has Jesus direct the disciples to proclaim repentance and forgiveness of sins to all nations and includes the promise to clothe them with "power" from on high, by which Jesus meant the Holy Spirit. Luke (who also wrote the Book of Acts and our first reading)

alone records the actual ascension. The disciples represent all of us. They stood staring at the sky until two men (probably angels) asked them what they were looking at. There was work to be done. Even though they had seen Jesus ascend into heaven, they continued to worship him and preach as he had commanded them.

A Spirit of Wisdom and Revelation

Paul's letters frequently begin with gratitude and prayer for the communities to whom he writes. Many of those openings are beautiful, and the first chapter of Ephesians is no exception. We sense Paul's genuine care for the community. As he moves into prayer, he asks not for faith, which they already have, but for a spirit of wisdom and revelation. Wisdom is the discernment of the truth; revelation is the knowledge of God that God gives us in many and various ways. When we begin with faith, these gifts can open our hearts to embrace three things: hope in God's call (the Greek word has the force of certainty that carries us through difficult times); the riches of our inheritance among the saints (the freedom and love we find in doing the will of God with gladness and devotion); and the greatness of God's power (which was manifested in fullness with Jesus Christ, but which has been with us from the very beginning). All of these form the foundation of the Christian life and all are worth celebrating and passing on to others.

Ascension of the Lord, Seventh Sunday of Easter, or Sixth Thursday of Easter

Good News for All of Us

If we were to read further in the epistle (or hear the alternate reading for today), we would find Paul exhorting all of us to "live in a manner worthy of the call you have received" with humility, gentleness, patience, and love (Ephesians 4:1–2). There are two things to think about when we hear that. The first is that we are not perfect, and every day is a chance to grow into the person God has called us to be. We can live this life in a worthy fashion with God's grace. The second less obvious thought is that God didn't wait for us to be worthy before he called us. Jesus reached out to sinners and a tax collector, the sick and the possessed, and invited them all in. The change happens when we accept the invitation to live a life of faith. We don't always remember that. When we talk to others about faith, it's important to let people know we didn't and still don't always follow God perfectly. We ask instead for wisdom and guidance to know what God wants and then do our best to follow it. Our humility comes in being willing to start over when we fail.

Questions for Reflection and Discussion

➤ *What is God calling you to in your life or your work? What are you doing to make your life worthy of that call?*

➤ *If you were asked why you are (or want to become) Catholic, how would you answer?*

Related Journey of Faith Lesson

M3, "Your Spiritual Gifts"

Themes

Ascension, Christ, Holy Spirit
  M3, "Your Spiritual Gifts"
  M4, "Discernment"
Church
  M2, "The Role of the Laity"
  M7, "Family Life"
  M5, "Our Call to Holiness"
  M8, "Evangelization"

READING 1 (ABC), ISAIAH 49:1–6

Hear me, O coastlands, listen, O distant peoples. The LORD called me from birth, from my mother's womb he gave me my name. He made of me a sharp-edged sword and concealed me in the shadow of his arm. He made me a polished arrow, in his quiver he hid me. You are my servant, he said to me, Israel, through whom I show my glory. Though I thought I had toiled in vain, and for nothing, uselessly, spent my strength, yet my reward is with the LORD, my recompense is with my God. For now the LORD has spoken who formed me as his servant from the womb, that Jacob may be brought back to him and Israel gathered to him; and I am made glorious in the sight of the LORD, and my God is now my strength! It is too little, he says, for you to be my servant, to raise up the tribes of Jacob, and restore the survivors of Israel; I will make you a light to the nations, that my salvation may reach to the ends of the earth.

PSALM 139:1B–3, 13–14AB, 14C–15

READING 2 (ABC), ACTS 13:22–26

In those days, Paul said: "God raised up David as king; of him God testified, *I have found David, son of Jesse, a man after my own heart; he will carry out my every wish.* From this man's descendants God, according to his promise, has brought to Israel a savior, Jesus. John heralded his coming by proclaiming a baptism of repentance to all the people of Israel; and as John was completing his course, he would say, 'What do you suppose that I am? I am not he. Behold, one is coming after me; I am not worthy to unfasten the sandals of his feet.' "My brothers, sons of the family of Abraham, and those others among you who are God-fearing, to us this word of salvation has been sent."

GOSPEL (ABC), LUKE 1:57–66, 80

When the time arrived for Elizabeth to have her child she gave birth to a son. Her neighbors and relatives heard that the Lord had shown his great mercy toward her, and they rejoiced with her. When they came on the eighth day to circumcise the child, they were going to call him Zechariah after his father, but his mother said in reply, "No. He will be called John." But they answered her, "There is no one among your relatives who has this name." So they made signs, asking his father what he wished him to be called. He asked for a tablet and wrote, "John is his name," and all were amazed. Immediately his mouth was opened, his tongue freed, and he spoke blessing God. Then fear came upon all their neighbors, and all these matters were discussed throughout the hill country of Judea. All who heard these things took them to heart, saying, "What, then, will this child be?" For surely the hand of the Lord was with him. The child grew and became strong in spirit, and he was in the desert until the day of his manifestation to Israel.

One Is Coming after Me

A friend of mine who is a priest once compared his ministry to that of John the Baptist. "I point to Jesus and I get out of the way." I've thought about that often since, wondering what John felt about being the "opening act," so to speak. But in every account of John in the Gospels, he finds his mission to prepare people for the coming of Christ to be the very definition of living a purpose-driven life. He preaches a baptism of repentance, urging people to change their hearts and their lives so they would be ready for the one who was to come.

In the Gospel of John, the Baptist is called the witness to the light (John 1:7). In Matthew, Mark, and Luke, John comes out of the wilderness and is compared to the voice of one crying, "Prepare the way of the LORD." (Isaiah 40:3). In physical appearance, John resembles the great prophet Elijah who will come before the day of the Lord (Malachi 4:5). In all this, John does not waver from his call. He doesn't set himself up as the one to follow. In fact, he consistently points to Jesus and humbly remarks that he is not worthy to untie Jesus' sandals.

Formed to Be God's Servant

Today's prophecy from Isaiah could apply to several figures in both the Old and New Testaments. It is one of the four so-called Servant Songs that speak of a servant of God who is given as a light to the nations (Isaiah 42:6) and is called to establish justice on the earth (Isaiah 42:3) and to sustain the weary (Isaiah

50:4). Perhaps most remarkable, the servant will suffer on behalf of others (Isaiah 52:1—53:12 and other passages). It's easy to see why Christians read these passages and immediately think of Jesus. Today the Church uses the passage to talk about John the Baptist, who, in Luke's Gospel, heralded the coming of Jesus. Luke signals this in many ways. The conception itself is miraculous (Elizabeth had been barren). An angel delivers the message of the upcoming birth to Zechariah. The Holy Spirit is involved. Luke even uses language that echoes Isaiah's servant song. Zechariah had a few doubts and was made mute until the birth. When the child is born, Zechariah gives his assent to the name, John, his voice returns, and he praises God. Everyone around John saw the Spirit of God in him from the beginning.

What Do You Suppose that I Am?

The desert is a place of revelation and temptation. We believe John spent his time there in prayer and fasting and in listening to God's call in his heart. When he began his public ministry of baptism, he was, by all accounts, passionate and sometimes fiery in his words. He didn't hesitate to call out religious authorities. He was certain of his mission to bring people to repentance. He had his own followers. None of that mattered when it came to Jesus. John was humbled to be in his presence. He understood that this was the one promised by God. He might even have smiled to hear that Luke and the Church had used Isaiah's prophecy to describe him. He had one job and he knew it well— point to Jesus and get out of the way.

Good News for All of Us

God knew and loved all of us before we were conceived. God was with us in the womb. And God is with us now, calling us to be instruments of his will. We will not all have the same job. God won't call us to be something we are not. But God will use our talents and gifts and the circumstances in which we find ourselves to help spread good (and challenging) news into the world. We begin simply by living lives in accordance with God's will. We radiate the peace that comes from Christ and helps us treat one another as brothers and sisters in Christ. We stand up to injustice and for those who are marginalized. We are not John the Baptist, but we are all witnesses to God's Light in Jesus.

Questions for Reflection and Discussion

➤ *Who first told you about Jesus? How have you grown in faith since then?*

➤ *How is what you are doing a response to God's call? What's your next step if you want to respond more fully?*

Related Journey of Faith Lesson

M8, "Evangelization"

Themes

Baptism
    Q2, "What Is Faith?"
    M1, "Conversion: A Lifelong Process"
Prophet
    Q13, "The Church as Community"
    M3, "Your Spiritual Gifts"
    M4, "Discernment"
Service
    Q12, "Who Shepherds the Church?"
    Q14, "Mary"
    Q15, "Saints"
    M2, "The Role of the Laity"
    M8, "Evangelization"

Sts. Peter and Paul, June 29

READING 1 (ABC), ACTS 12:1–11

In those days, King Herod laid hands upon some members of the Church to harm them. He had James, the brother of John, killed by the sword, and when he saw that this was pleasing to the Jews he proceeded to arrest Peter also. (It was the feast of Unleavened Bread.) He had him taken into custody and put in prison under the guard of four squads of four soldiers each. He intended to bring him before the people after Passover. Peter thus was being kept in prison, but prayer by the Church was fervently being made to God on his behalf. On the very night before Herod was to bring him to trial, Peter, secured by double chains, was sleeping between two soldiers, while outside the door guards kept watch on the prison. Suddenly the angel of the Lord stood by him and a light shone in the cell. He tapped Peter on the side and awakened him, saying, "Get up quickly." The chains fell from his wrists. The angel said to him, "Put on your belt and your sandals." He did so. Then he said to him, "Put on your cloak and follow me." So he followed him out, not realizing that what was happening through the angel was real; he thought he was seeing a vision. They passed the first guard, then the second, and came to the iron gate leading out to the city, which opened for them by itself. They emerged and made their way down an alley, and suddenly the angel left him. Then Peter recovered his senses and said, "Now I know for certain that the Lord sent his angel and rescued me from the hand of Herod and from all that the Jewish people had been expecting."

PSALM 34:2–3, 4–5, 6–7, 8–9

READING 2 (ABC), 2 TIMOTHY 4:6–8, 17–18

I, Paul, am already being poured out like a libation, and the time of my departure is at hand. I have competed well; I have finished the race; I have kept the faith. From now on the crown of righteousness awaits me, which the Lord, the just judge, will award to me on that day, and not only to me, but to all who have longed for his appearance. The Lord stood by me and gave me strength, so that through me the proclamation might be completed and all the Gentiles might hear it. And I was rescued from the lion's mouth. The Lord will rescue me from every evil threat and will bring me safe to his heavenly Kingdom. To him be glory forever and ever. Amen.

GOSPEL (ABC), MATTHEW 16:13–19

When Jesus went into the region of Caesarea Philippi he asked his disciples, "Who do people say that the Son of Man is?" They replied, "Some say John the Baptist, others Elijah, still others Jeremiah or one of the prophets." He said to them, "But who do you say that I am?" Simon Peter said in reply, "You are Christ, the Son of the living God." Jesus said to him in reply, "Blessed are you, Simon son of Jonah. For flesh and blood has not revealed this to you, but my heavenly Father. And so I say to you, you are Peter, and upon this rock I will build my Church, and the gates of the netherworld shall not prevail against it. I will give you the keys to the Kingdom of heaven. Whatever you bind on earth shall be bound in heaven; and whatever you loose on earth shall be loosed in heaven."

Transformed in Christ

Peter was a fisherman when a chance encounter with Jesus took him from his boats to follow an itinerant preacher who was unlike anyone he had ever met. When the time came to stand up and say what he had suspected for a long time, Peter took a breath and said to Jesus, "You are the Messiah, the Son of the living God." And at that moment, when Peter stated who Jesus was, his name was changed, and his life altered forever because Jesus also showed Peter who Peter really was in the eyes of God. After Peter was freed from prison by the angel and led out of the city, the text reads that Peter "recovered his senses." Other translations say, "he came to himself." The Scripture implies that he became fully aware of the miracle that just happened to him. I think he also realized that Jesus wasn't kidding when he said, "You are Peter and, on this rock, I will build my church."

From Persecutor to Poured Out

Paul persecuted the early Christians. As a zealot, Paul considered this new sect to be a threat to orthodox Judaism. In order to keep the religion pure, he took it on himself to imprison and kill all the followers of "the Way," as Christianity was known at first. But something happened to him on the road to Damascus. He encountered Jesus in a vision, and Jesus asked him, "Saul, why do you persecute me?" Blinded by the light, Saul asks Jesus who he is. And Jesus tells him, "I am Jesus whom you persecute." In that moment, Saul's life was changed. He became Paul and turned his life over to Christ. Toward the end, he tells Timothy, one of his missionaries, that he has given his life to the service of Christ. In well-known words, Paul talks about finishing the race, a metaphor for doing his best to preach the Good News to the world in spite of imprisonment and beatings. He gives credit to the Lord who gave him the strength to preach to all who would hear him. Ultimately, Paul was martyred in Rome in 65.

Good News for All of Us

Peter and Paul are examples of the power of Christ to change our lives. Most of us will not experience as dramatic a conversion as Paul or have our names changed like Peter. But the encounter with Christ who is present with us even now can transform us in ways we cannot begin to imagine. The followers of Jesus may have thought or even hoped he was John the Baptist or one of the prophets. If he's just a man, they can carry on as they always have. Nothing had to be any different. When Peter correctly stated Jesus' identity, everything changed.

The same goes for us. When we acknowledge who Jesus truly is—the Son of God—he calls us to be truly who we are: the children of God who reflect the peace and joy of the Spirit and who live lives of faithful obedience to God's love. For most of us, that will require some changes, and the process of becoming a child of God and disciple of Christ will take a lifetime. The good news is, it's never too late to start, and Sts. Peter and Paul—along with the great communion of saints—have paved the way for us.

Questions for Reflection and Discussion

➤ God called on Peter's talents as a fisherman and Paul's fierce passion for the truth to build the church. What gifts do you have that God might like to use to build up the community of faith?

➤ What kind of courage does it take to say to Christ, "I give you my whole life; show me what you would like me to do?" Have you been able to do that yet? Do you want to?

Related Journey of Faith Lesson

Q13, "The Church as Community"

Themes

Authority
    Q12, "Who Shepherds the Church?"
Gifts
    M3, "Your Spiritual Gifts"
Ministry
    Q13, "The Church as Community"
    M2, "The Role of the Laity"
    M8, "Evangelization"

READING 1 (ABC), DANIEL 7:9–10, 13–14

As I watched: Thrones were set up and the Ancient One took his throne. His clothing was bright as snow, and the hair on his head as white as wool; his throne was flames of fire, with wheels of burning fire. A surging stream of fire flowed out from where he sat; Thousands upon thousands were ministering to him, and myriads upon myriads attended him. The court was convened and the books were opened. As the visions during the night continued, I saw: One like a Son of man coming, on the clouds of heaven; When he reached the Ancient One and was presented before him, The one like a Son of man received dominion, glory, and kingship; all peoples, nations, and languages serve him. His dominion is an everlasting dominion that shall not be taken away, his kingship shall not be destroyed.

PSALM 97:1–2, 5–6, 9

READING 2 (ABC), 2 PETER 1:16–19

Beloved: We did not follow cleverly devised myths when we made known to you the power and coming of our Lord Jesus Christ, but we had been eyewitnesses of his majesty. For he received honor and glory from God the Father when that unique declaration came to him from the majestic glory, "This is my Son, my beloved, with whom I am well pleased." We ourselves heard this voice come from heaven while we were with him on the holy mountain. Moreover, we possess the prophetic message that is altogether reliable. You will do well to be attentive to it, as to a lamp shining in a dark place, until day dawns and the morning star rises in your hearts.

GOSPEL (A), MATTHEW 17:1–9

Jesus took Peter, James, and his brother, John, and led them up a high mountain by themselves. And he was transfigured before them; his face shone like the sun and his clothes became white as light. And behold, Moses and Elijah appeared to them, conversing with him. Then Peter said to Jesus in reply, "Lord, it is good that we are here. If you wish, I will make three tents here, one for you, one for Moses, and one for Elijah." While he was still speaking, behold, a bright cloud cast a shadow over them, then from the cloud came a voice that said, "This is my beloved Son, with whom I am well pleased; listen to him." When the disciples heard this, they fell prostrate and were very much afraid. But Jesus came and touched them, saying, "Rise, and do not be afraid." And when the disciples raised their eyes, they saw no one else but Jesus alone. As they were coming down from the mountain, Jesus charged them, "Do not tell the vision to anyone until the Son of Man has been raised from the dead."

GOSPEL (B), MARK 9:2–10

Jesus took Peter, James, and his brother John, and led them up a high mountain apart by themselves. And he was transfigured before them, and his clothes became dazzling white, such as no fuller on earth could bleach them. Then Elijah appeared to them along with Moses, and they were conversing with Jesus. Then Peter said to Jesus in reply, "Rabbi, it is good that we are here! Let us make three tents: one for you, one for Moses, and one for Elijah." He hardly knew what to say, they were so terrified. Then a cloud came, casting a shadow over them; from the cloud came a voice, "This is my beloved Son. Listen to him." Suddenly, looking around, they no longer saw anyone but Jesus alone with them. As they were coming down from the mountain, he charged them not to relate what they had seen to anyone, except when the Son of Man had risen from the dead. So they kept the matter to themselves, questioning what rising from the dead meant.

GOSPEL (C), LUKE 9:28B–36

Jesus took Peter, John, and James and went up a mountain to pray. While he was praying his face changed in appearance and his clothing became dazzling white. And behold, two men were conversing with him, Moses and Elijah, who appeared in glory and spoke of his exodus that he was going to accomplish in Jerusalem. Peter and his companions had been overcome by sleep, but becoming fully awake, they saw his glory and the two men standing with him. As they were about to part from him, Peter said to Jesus, "Master, it is good that we are here; let us make three tents, one for you, one for Moses, and one for Elijah."

But he did not know what he was saying. While he was still speaking, a cloud came and cast a shadow over them, and they became frightened when they entered the cloud. Then from the cloud came a voice that said, "This is my chosen Son; listen to him." After the voice had spoken, Jesus was found alone. They fell silent and did not at that time tell anyone what they had seen.

Son, Beloved, Chosen

In the three accounts of the transfiguration (the story is absent in John's Gospel), Peter, James, and John experience a vision of Jesus they could never have expected, and don't quite know what to do with it. On that mountaintop, Jesus seemed bathed in light brighter than anything they knew. Those two archetypes of the Law and the Prophets, Moses and Elijah, appeared with him, indicating that he was the fulfillment of both. Peter, perhaps reminded that the ancient Israelites carried the Ark of the Covenant in a tent as they traveled, suggested they build three tents for Jesus and the others. I wonder if his impulse was driven a little bit by fear. When God, in the form of a cloud, settled in the tent, even Moses could not enter, and all the others would have been too afraid to see God face to face (Exodus 40:34–38). It's possible Peter wanted to contain the glory he was seeing just a little bit.

But even more important than the appearance of Moses and Elijah was the appearance of the cloud and the voice like thunder that came from it identifying Jesus as "My Son" (three Gospels), my Beloved (two Gospels), and my Chosen (one Gospel), followed by the command to "listen to him" (three Gospels). With those words, the disciples who already followed Jesus because of his teaching and his actions and identified him as the Messiah as Peter did, coming to understand he was more than Moses or Elijah or even the Messiah. They might not have been able to say that Jesus was God in that moment, but they knew he was connected with God in a way no one else had ever been. That knowledge would carry them through the horror of the crucifixion. The memory of the transfiguration would help reveal the truth about Jesus after the resurrection, not only to the disciples, but to the whole Church.

A Lamp Shining in the Dark

After the resurrection, there were many self-identified prophets and messiahs who claimed to have the cure for various ailments or the plans that would defeat the Romans. With so many voices begging for attention, the preaching of the apostles was hard to hear. In our second reading today, Peter, along with the other disciples, claimed something the false prophets could not. Peter was an eyewitness to the power of Jesus. He remembered the mountaintop and the transfiguration of Jesus. He remembered the voice coming from the cloud. In the light of the resurrection, he embraced the event for what it was—the revelation of Christ's glory. The world might be a dark place now, Peter says, but this is "a lamp shining in a dark place" until Christ himself (the morning star) rises in the hearts of every person.

Good News for All of Us

Looking back, we may realize that we have had "mountaintop" experiences—those moments when God's presence is nearly overwhelming. This can happen on retreat, in prayer, listening to a beautiful piece of music, or in a quiet moment with a friend. Our first impulse likely is to hold on. We don't want the moment to end. Our second could be that there's work to be done and we have to leave that moment to live our lives a little closer to the ground. It's our openness to the experience that determines what happens when we reach the bottom. The disciples could have left Jesus and gone their own way, especially when he talked about the suffering he would endure. Peter even tried to discourage him from talking about it. Ultimately, they stayed, spurred on by vision and a command to listen to Jesus, the beloved and chosen of God. What we do depends on what we have seen and heard. It may not be as spectacular as the Gospel experience, but we remember that God also speaks in silence (see 1 Kings 19:12). And God remains with us along the way.

Questions for Reflection and Discussion

➤ *Daniel's apocalyptic vision of one like "a son of man" (meaning human being) being given dominion, glory, and kingship by the "Ancient One," is quoted in the New Testament referring to Jesus (in capital letters). It's easy to see the comparison. What do you imagine Jesus would look like if he appeared to you?*

➤ *If you have had a mountaintop experience, please share it with the group.*

Related Journey of Faith Lesson

M5, "Our Call to Holiness"

Themes

Revelation
   Q13, "The Church as Community"
   Q16, "Eschatology: The 'Last Things'"
   M1, "Conversion: A Lifelong Process"
Second Coming
   Q2, "What Is Faith?"
   M8, "Evangelization"
Transfiguration
   Q5, "The Bible"
   M5, "Our Call to Holiness"

**READING 1 (ABC),
REVELATION 11:19A; 12:1–6A, 10AB**

God's temple in heaven was opened, and the ark of his covenant could be seen in the temple. A great sign appeared in the sky, a woman clothed with the sun, with the moon under her feet and on her head a crown of twelve stars. She was with child and wailed aloud in pain as she labored to give birth. Then another sign appeared in the sky; it was a huge red dragon, with seven heads and ten horns, and on its heads were seven diadems. Its tail swept away a third of the stars in the sky and hurled them down to the earth. Then the dragon stood before the woman about to give birth, to devour her child when she gave birth. She gave birth to a son, a male child, destined to rule all the nations with an iron rod. Her child was caught up to God and his throne. The woman herself fled into the desert where she had a place prepared by God. Then I heard a loud voice in heaven say: "Now have salvation and power come, and the Kingdom of our God and the authority of his Anointed One."

PSALM 45:10, 11, 12, 16

READING 2 (ABC), 1 CORINTHIANS 15:20–27

Brothers and sisters: Christ has been raised from the dead, the firstfruits of those who have fallen asleep. For since death came through man, the resurrection of the dead came also through man. For just as in Adam all die, so too in Christ shall all be brought to life, but each one in proper order: Christ the firstfruits; then, at his coming, those who belong to Christ; then comes the end, when he hands over the Kingdom to his God and Father, when he has destroyed every sovereignty and every authority and power. For he must reign until he has put all his enemies under his feet. The last enemy to be destroyed is death, for "he subjected everything under his feet."

GOSPEL (ABC), LUKE 1:39–56

Mary set out and traveled to the hill country in haste to a town of Judah, where she entered the house of Zechariah and greeted Elizabeth. When Elizabeth heard Mary's greeting, the infant leaped in her womb, and Elizabeth, filled with the Holy Spirit, cried out in a loud voice and said, "Blessed are you among women, and blessed is the fruit of your womb. And how does this happen to me, that the mother of my Lord should come to me? For at the moment the sound of your greeting reached my ears, the infant in my womb leaped for joy. Blessed are you who believed that what was spoken to you by the Lord would be fulfilled." And Mary said: "My soul proclaims the greatness of the Lord; my spirit rejoices in God my Savior for he has looked with favor on his lowly servant. From this day all generations will call me blessed: the Almighty has done great things for me and holy is his Name. He has mercy on those who fear him in every generation. He has shown the strength of his arm, and has scattered the proud in their conceit. He has cast down the mighty from their thrones, and has lifted up the lowly. He has filled the hungry with good things, and the rich he has sent away empty. He has come to the help of his servant Israel for he has remembered his promise of mercy, the promise he made to our fathers, to Abraham and his children forever." Mary remained with her about three months and then returned to her home.

A Feast of Faith

Dogmas are divinely revealed truths and the most serious of church teachings. In 1950, the assumption of Mary was the last dogma proclaimed by the Catholic Church, but its origins go back to the first centuries of the Church, when Christians already recognized the special place of Mary as the *Theotokos*, the God-bearer or Mother of God. As early as the fifth century, we have evidence of Christians celebrating the dormition (falling asleep) of Mary. They believed that Mary died and her body was assumed into heaven, never to suffer the corruption of death. She was immediately and wholly brought into the presence of God.

The belief continued over the centuries until Pope Pius XII declared it as dogma. It makes sense. In Paul's Letter to the Corinthians, he declares that since death came through a human being (Adam), so the resurrection of the dead will come through a human being (Jesus). Paul also talks about the order of resurrection—first, Jesus who is the first fruit, then when he comes again, those who belong to him. It makes sense that of all of those who belong to

Christ, his Mother would be at the head of the line to experience resurrection in such an amazing fashion. In that, she is our foretaste of what we hope will happen to all of us. By God's grace, we will all get there in the end.

A Woman Clothed with the Sun

John's revelation of the great battle between God and evil (here depicted as the dragon) provides a dramatic backdrop for the appearance of the woman clothed with the sun. The roots of the vision go all the way back to Genesis when God tells Eve that there will be enmity between her offspring and the serpent's. The child will strike at the head of the serpent while the serpent will strike at his heel (Genesis 3:14–15). Revelation's more terrifying image of the dragon appears shortly after the woman who is pregnant. The dragon waits to devour the child but is thwarted by divine intervention, while the woman is given a place of safety.

The appearance of the woman suggests royalty. A crown is on her head and the moon is under her feet. The sun is a sign of importance and a symbol of divine favor. This image was associated with Mary fairly early in the Church's history, though biblical scholars have also thought it could represent the Church. In any case, the Marian appellation Queen of Heaven draws its source from Revelation, and many paintings were based on the text. Her Son is most often considered to be Jesus, though again, some scholars differ.

An Inspired Prayer

Mary's beautiful Magnificat has been a model of prayer and proclamation since the earliest days of the Church. In it she praises the way in which God does what is least expected. He chooses a lowly girl to bear his Son; he lifts the lowly and takes down the powerful. The hungry will eat their fill and the rich will be empty. She also draws our attention to this coming child as the fulfillment of God's promise to Abraham and the entire people of Israel. When Elizabeth recognizes Mary as the "Mother of my Lord," it is a movement of the Holy Spirit and exactly what Mary needs to calm any anxiety and rejoice in what is happening. In the Divine Office, this canticle is recited every evening at vespers.

Good News for All of Us

No one knows what death will be like, and that might be unsettling to you. But our faith says that Christ conquered death and that we who have been baptized have eternal life. This doesn't mean our bodies will never die. It means we will live and meet God face to face. The assumption of Mary shows us that.

Questions for Reflection and Discussion

> *Pray the Magnificat aloud slowly. What lines stand out to you? What does it say about God and Mary?*

> *Mary is known by many names: Queen of Heaven, Star of the Sea, Our Lady of... (fill in the blank). If you had to give Mary a name, what would it be?*

Related Journey of Faith Lesson

Q14, "Mary"

Themes

Assumption, Mary
    Q14, "Mary"
    M5, "Our Call to Holiness"
Redemption
    Q2, "What Is Faith?"
    M1, "Conversion: A Lifelong Process"

Exaltation of the Holy Cross (Triumph of the Cross), September 14

READING 1 (ABC), NUMBERS 21:4B–9

With their patience worn out by the journey, the people complained against God and Moses, "Why have you brought us up from Egypt to die in this desert, where there is no food or water? We are disgusted with this wretched food!" In punishment the LORD sent among the people saraph serpents, which bit the people so that many of them died. Then the people came to Moses and said, "We have sinned in complaining against the LORD and you. Pray the LORD to take the serpents from us."

So Moses prayed for the people, and the LORD said to Moses, "Make a saraph and mount it on a pole, and if any who have been bitten look at it, they will live." Moses accordingly made a bronze serpent and mounted it on a pole, and whenever anyone who had been bitten by a serpent looked at the bronze serpent, he lived.

PSALM 78:1BC–2, 34–35, 36–37, 38

READING 2 (ABC), PHILIPPIANS 2:6–11

Brothers and sisters: Christ Jesus, though he was in the form of God, did not regard equality with God something to be grasped. Rather, he emptied himself, taking the form of a slave, coming in human likeness; and found human in appearance, he humbled himself, becoming obedient to death, even death on a cross. Because of this, God greatly exalted him and bestowed on him the name that is above every name, that at the name of Jesus every knee should bend, of those in heaven and on earth and under the earth, and every tongue confess that Jesus Christ is Lord, to the glory of God the Father.

GOSPEL (ABC), JOHN 3:13–17

Jesus said to Nicodemus: "No one has gone up to heaven except the one who has come down from heaven, the Son of Man. And just as Moses lifted up the serpent in the desert, so must the Son of Man be lifted up, so that everyone who believes in him may have eternal life." For God so loved the world that he gave his only Son, so that everyone who believes in him might not perish but might have eternal life. For God did not send his Son into the world to condemn the world, but that the world might be saved through him.

Looking at the One Who Heals Us

The first reading and Gospel today present stories of miraculous healing but from two very different perspectives. In the Book of Numbers, the people complain to God and Moses, and God punishes them with poisonous serpents. When they repent, they are given a cure for the poison in the form of a bronze serpent lifted up on a pole. The people had only to gaze on what was biting them to be cured. The Gospel turns our gaze to Jesus who was sent into a sinful world to turn our hearts back to God. When Jesus is lifted up on the cross, we look at him in order to be healed as well. But in this case, it means forgiveness of our sin and redemption.

In the first reading, the bronze serpent represents relief from punishment and a chance to start over. In the Gospel, the cross gives us an invitation to eternal life, not by looking at what made us sick, but by looking on Jesus who, humbling himself, gathered up our sins and brokenness and lifted them on the cross as well. That act of love restored our relationship with God and made us, in Paul's words, a new creation (2 Corinthians 5:17).

Jesus Christ Is Lord

Paul frequently quotes the Hebrew Bible in his letters, and Philippians is no exception. A reference to Isaiah 45:23 can be found in the last lines of the reading. In Isaiah, God himself says, "to me every knee shall bend; by me every tongue shall swear... [that only in the Lord are just deeds and power]. Paul uses the phrase to talk about Jesus, even ending the reading with the proclamation that "Jesus Christ is Lord." Two things stand out. The first is the contrast between the title "Lord" and the description of Jesus as emptying himself and taking the form of a slave. It is the great paradox of Christianity that the remarkable victory of Christ (resurrection and redemption) comes out of the greatest weakness (crucifixion). The second thing to stand out is Paul's use of "Lord" as a title for Jesus. In the Hebrew Bible, God is the Lord and no other. By using the title for Jesus, Paul shows us the seeds of our Trinitarian theology and the understanding of Jesus as fully human and fully divine. It would take us three more centuries to fully articulate that theology.

Remember the Works of the Lord

The responsorial psalm today is more than a mere recitation of history. The refrain is our command as well. "Do not forget the works of the Lord." Forgetting and remembering are two of the most important concepts in the Bible. The words are active. If we remember what God has done for us, then we will obey his commandments out of gratitude and faithfulness. If we forget God's wonderful deeds, then we have already committed adultery by finding another god to worship. The psalm is a prayer that makes us remember the wandering in the desert, cautions us not to forget, and anticipates that we will do what God requires of us.

Good News for All of Us

The creation story of Genesis tells us that we are made in the image and likeness of God. We believe that God was incarnate in Jesus Christ, who did not grasp equality with God and did not despise humanity. Rather, he emptied himself that we might be lifted up with him to the Father. What does that mean for us? There is something about having been made in God's image and likeness that calls us to empty ourselves. We should not try to be equal to God but humbly seek the good of all in love, becoming servants of the one true Master. Jesus is both our guide and example.

Questions for Reflection and Discussion

➤ *What has God done for you, and how have you responded to his mercy?*

➤ *Jesus told us to take up our cross and follow him. What is your cross, and who helps you carry it?*

Related Journey of Faith Lesson

Q2, "What Is Faith?"

Themes

Cross, Lord, Salvation
   Q2, "What Is Faith?"
   Q16, "Eschatology: The 'Last Things'"

All Saints, November 1

READING 1 (ABC), REVELATION 7:2–4, 9–14

I, John, saw another angel come up from the East, holding the seal of the living God. He cried out in a loud voice to the four angels who were given power to damage the land and the sea, "Do not damage the land or the sea or the trees until we put the seal on the foreheads of the servants of our God." I heard the number of those who had been marked with the seal, one hundred and forty-four thousand marked from every tribe of the children of Israel. After this I had a vision of a great multitude, which no one could count, from every nation, race, people, and tongue. They stood before the throne and before the Lamb, wearing white robes and holding palm branches in their hands. They cried out in a loud voice: "Salvation comes from our God, who is seated on the throne, and from the Lamb." All the angels stood around the throne and around the elders and the four living creatures. They prostrated themselves before the throne, worshiped God, and exclaimed: "Amen. Blessing and glory, wisdom and thanksgiving, honor, power, and might be to our God forever and ever. Amen." Then one of the elders spoke up and said to me, "Who are these wearing white robes, and where did they come from?" I said to him, "My lord, you are the one who knows." He said to me, "These are the ones who have survived the time of great distress; they have washed their robes and made them white in the Blood of the Lamb."

PSALM 24:1BC–2, 3–4AB, 5–6

READING 2 (ABC), 1 JOHN 3:1–3

Beloved: See what love the Father has bestowed on us that we may be called the children of God. Yet so we are. The reason the world does not know us is that it did not know him. Beloved, we are God's children now; what we shall be has not yet been revealed. We do know that when it is revealed we shall be like him, for we shall see him as he is. Everyone who has this hope based on him makes himself pure, as he is pure.

GOSPEL (ABC), MATTHEW 5:1–12A

When Jesus saw the crowds, he went up the mountain, and after he had sat down, his disciples came to him. He began to teach them, saying: "Blessed are the poor in spirit, for theirs is the Kingdom of heaven. Blessed are they who mourn, for they will be comforted. Blessed are the meek, for they will inherit the land. Blessed are they who hunger and thirst for righteousness, for they will be satisfied. Blessed are the merciful, for they will be shown mercy. Blessed are the clean of heart, for they will see God. Blessed are the peacemakers, for they will be called children of God. Blessed are they who are persecuted for the sake of righteousness, for theirs is the Kingdom of heaven. Blessed are you when they insult you and persecute you and utter every kind of evil against you falsely because of me. Rejoice and be glad, for your reward will be great in heaven."

Servants of God

In the Episcopal seminary in which I taught Scripture, I admired the attention paid to the saints at services each day. Rarely did a weekday go by without some mention of virtues of the saint of the day. One of my former students even developed a way to teach about the saints modeled on the college basketball playoffs called Lent Madness. Saints both well-known and obscure are paired off in brackets with a brief biography attached. People vote on the saint they like best and the winner moves into the next bracket. The winner of the championship round gets the golden halo. I learned about a lot of saints that way.

Catholics, too, revere the great communion of saints, even though we may not talk about them as much. They are the reminder that God's grace does extraordinary things through ordinary human beings—flaws and all. The saints were not perfect; they were open to God's voice and passionate about doing God's will. They were often single minded in their work for the poor and zealous in their preaching of the gospel.

The New Testament doesn't talk about named saints— what my students used to call the capital "S" saints. Saint Paul talks about all baptized Christians as saints (small "s"). The word itself means "holy ones," set apart as God's people. For Paul, that started at baptism. In John's vision in our first reading, they are the servants of God, marked with God's seal who will join the angels and the elders before the throne of God. In the great battle between good and evil, God has prevailed, and these saints have suffered and been purified. In John's vision these saints are wearing white robes and emerge from their suffering to praise God with those who have gone before.

A Code to Live By

The beginning of Jesus' Sermon on the Mount in Matthew has taken its place alongside the Ten Commandments as a code of conduct for Christians. Where the commandments deal with right action toward God and community, the beatitudes deal with right attitudes. The two together suggest that conversion of heart is necessary to do the right thing and that doing the right thing should lead to continuing conversion of heart. It's a lifelong process. Jesus' words are positive reinforcement: "Blessed are the poor in spirit…" Who doesn't want to be blessed? But the words are also challenging because they suggest overturning systems in which power and wealth are more important than faithfulness. It's hard to challenge the status quo. That's why the beatitudes end with, "Blessed are those who are persecuted for righteousness' sake." It takes a lot of courage to be a saint in this Church—whether one is formally recognized or not. Both the psalm and the epistle describe those who would be saints. The psalm repeats the refrain that "this is the people who long to see your face," and reminds us that the one whose heart is clean shall be able to see God. The first epistle of John tells us we are children of God but that what we shall be has not yet been revealed. From John's description, I think we start as children of God at baptism, and we spend our lives growing in our faith and obedience until we see God face to face. The Church canonizes those who have accomplished this, and the saints welcome us when we have been purified as well.

Good News for All of Us

We might think that being a saint is out of reach for us, but in truth, being a saint is the goal for any Christian. Saints are open to hear the voice of God and obey it as we all should be. Saints are particularly attuned to the needs and suffering of others, as we all should be. Saints are humble before God and passionate for God's word; they are God's adult children. But even more than that, saints are living witnesses to God's power and presence in the world and, God willing, we can be that, too.

Questions for Reflection and Discussion

> ➤ Is there a saint of the Church you admire? Why?

> ➤ Who are the saints in your life—those who show you God's presence by the way they live their lives?

Related Journey of Faith Lesson

Q15, "The Saints"

Themes

Freedom
    M3, "Your Spiritual Gifts"
    M5, "Our Call to Holiness"
Revelation
    Q5, "The Bible"
    Q7, "Your Prayer Life"
    Q13, "The Church as Community"
    M4, "Discernment"
Saints
    Q15, "The Saints"
    M2, "The Role of the Laity"

The Commemoration of All the Faithful Departed (All Souls), November 2*

READING 1 (ABC), WISDOM 3:1–9

The souls of the just are in the hand of God, and no torment shall touch them. They seemed, in the view of the foolish, to be dead; and their passing away was thought an affliction and their going forth from us, utter destruction. But they are in peace. For if before men, indeed, they be punished, yet is their hope full of immortality; chastised a little, they shall be greatly blessed, because God tried them and found them worthy of himself. As gold in the furnace, he proved them, and as sacrificial offerings he took them to himself. In the time of their visitation they shall shine, and shall dart about as sparks through stubble; they shall judge nations and rule over peoples, and the LORD shall be their King forever. Those who trust in him shall understand truth, and the faithful shall abide with him in love: because grace and mercy are with his holy ones, and his care is with his elect.

PSALM 23:1–3, 3–4, 5, 6

READING 2 (ABC), ROMANS 5:5–11

Brothers and sisters: Hope does not disappoint, because the love of God has been poured out into our hearts through the Holy Spirit that has been given to us. For Christ, while we were still helpless, died at the appointed time for the ungodly. Indeed, only with difficulty does one die for a just person, though perhaps for a good person one might even find courage to die. But God proves his love for us in that while we were still sinners Christ died for us. How much more then, since we are now justified by his Blood, will we be saved through him from the wrath. Indeed, if, while we were enemies, we were reconciled to God through the death of his Son, how much more, once reconciled, will we be saved by his life. Not only that, but we also boast of God through our Lord Jesus Christ, through whom we have now received reconciliation.

GOSPEL (ABC), JOHN 6:37–40

Jesus said to the crowds: "Everything that the Father gives me will come to me, and I will not reject anyone who comes to me, because I came down from heaven not to do my own will but the will of the one who sent me. And this is the will of the one who sent me, that I should not lose anything of what he gave me, but that I should raise it on the last day. For this is the will of my Father, that everyone who sees the Son and believes in him may have eternal life, and I shall raise him on the last day."

The Hope in Which We Live

It seems fitting that the Church would set aside a day to remember all those who have died in the faith. They are our grandparents, parents and friends, distant relatives and neighbors who are bound to us not just by family or circumstance but by a faith in Jesus Christ as God incarnate. Many are the saints who passed on the faith to us; others are our brothers and sisters who shared the struggles and joy of faith. All of us were (and are) striving to walk the path Jesus laid out for us. And all of us share the hope that Paul talks about in the Letter to the Romans. This hope lies in the certainty that God loves us; it is made manifest in the knowledge that Christ died for us, even though we were sinners; and it is confirmed in the Holy Spirit who is given to us as an advocate of truth, guiding the Church through its history. And our hope remains with us as we look forward to the day when we shall see God face to face, and all those who have gone before us will be there waiting.

The readings here are suggestions only. Any readings from the liturgical Masses for the Dead, numbers 1011–1016, may be used today.

The Souls of the Just

The glorious vision from the Book of Wisdom describes both the sorrow of the living and the delight of the faithful dead who have been found worthy to stand before God, even though they had suffered on earth. The writer of Wisdom understands that those who remain alive can see only the death of the one they loved; they are unaware of the glories of eternal life. Indeed, for the chosen ones of God, there is only God's grace, mercy, and love. They have no need for anything else. We who are left behind place our trust in God and find comfort in the words of our responsorial psalm: "Though I walk in the dark valley, I fear no evil for you are with me," and "Only goodness and kindness follow me, and I will dwell in the house of the Lord for years to come."

Raised Up on the Last Day

In one of the most comforting passages of John's Gospel, Jesus makes two important claims: "I will not reject anyone who comes to me," and I will not lose anything of what [the Father] gave me." What does that mean for us? It means that no matter what we've done, if we turn to Jesus with a sincere heart and ask for help, he will take us in. And once he has taken us in, he will never lose us. The only way that bond can be broken is if we walk away. The very last promise, "I will raise him up on the last day," brings the point home. Not even death can separate us from the love of God in Jesus.

Good News for All of Us

In many places, November 2 marks the beginning of a tradition known as "Novembering"—remembering those in the family who have died over the past year. In our church we prepare a memorial display where people can bring pictures of their loved ones and members of the community who have died. Some put a simple flower down. One student brought in her father's favorite candy to remember him. In Mexican culture, *Dia de los Muertos* or the Day of the Dead spans both All Saints' and All Souls' days and includes singing, parades, traditional foods, and prayers that show respect for the dead and affirm the life they had. Such displays are a comfort to those who grieve and a way of remembering those who have passed. We see similar displays of pictures, candles, and names at the sites of mass tragedies such as 9/11 or the Boston Marathon bombing. We also see them in simple crosses at the site of a traffic fatality. Remembering the dead keeps them with us as we move on with our lives. In the deep heart of our faith, we believe that God has not lost these souls but holds them where he needs them held and that on the day of resurrection, we shall see them again.

Questions for Reflection and Discussion

> *What are some of the ways you remember people who have died in your family? Do you pray for them or ask them to pray for you?*

> *Do you have any trait that reminds people of past members of your family?*

Related Journey of Faith Lesson

M1, "Conversion: A Lifelong Process"

Themes

Death
   Q2, "What Is Faith?"
   Q16, "Eschatology: The 'Last Things'"
Life
   Q15, "The Saints"
   M1, "Conversion: A Lifelong Process"
Remembrance
   Q8, "Catholic Prayers and Practices"
   Q9, "The Mass"

READING 1 (ABC), EZEKIEL 47:1–2, 8–9, 12

The angel brought me back to the entrance of the temple, and I saw water flowing out from beneath the threshold of the temple toward the east, for the façade of the temple was toward the east; the water flowed down from the southern side of the temple, south of the altar. He led me outside by the north gate, and around to the outer gate facing the east, where I saw water trickling from the southern side. He said to me, "This water flows into the eastern district down upon the Arabah, and empties into the sea, the salt waters, which it makes fresh. Wherever the river flows, every sort of living creature that can multiply shall live, and there shall be abundant fish, for wherever this water comes the sea shall be made fresh. Along both banks of the river, fruit trees of every kind shall grow; their leaves shall not fade, nor their fruit fail. Every month they shall bear fresh fruit, for they shall be watered by the flow from the sanctuary. Their fruit shall serve for food, and their leaves for medicine."

PSALM 46:2–3, 5–6, 8–9

READING (ABC), 1 CORINTHIANS 3:9C–11, 16–17

Brothers and sisters: You are God's building. According to the grace of God given to me, like a wise master builder I laid a foundation, and another is building upon it. But each one must be careful how he builds upon it, for no one can lay a foundation other than the one that is there, namely, Jesus Christ. Do you not know that you are the temple of God, and that the Spirit of God dwells in you? If anyone destroys God's temple, God will destroy that person; for the temple of God, which you are, is holy.

GOSPEL (ABC), JOHN 2:13–22

Since the Passover of the Jews was near, Jesus went up to Jerusalem. He found in the temple area those who sold oxen, sheep, and doves, as well as the money-changers seated there. He made a whip out of cords and drove them all out of the temple area, with the sheep and oxen, and spilled the coins of the money-changers and overturned their tables, and to those who sold doves he said, "Take these out of here, and stop making my Father's house a marketplace." His disciples recalled the words of Scripture, *Zeal for your house will consume me.* At this the Jews answered and said to him, "What sign can you show us for doing this?" Jesus answered and said to them, "Destroy this temple and in three days I will raise it up." The Jews said, "This temple has been under construction for forty-six years, and you will raise it up in three days?" But he was speaking about the temple of his Body. Therefore, when he was raised from the dead, his disciples remembered that he had said this, and they came to believe the Scripture and the word Jesus had spoken.

Heaven and Earth Meet

As Catholics we believe God is everywhere. People report feeling close to God on mountains, in forests, by the ocean, and even in their rooms with a lit candle and music playing softly. Those individual encounters with God are important. But throughout the history of worship in many religions, the gathering of the faith community for prayer and liturgy holds special significance. Churches, synagogues, and mosques invite the faithful to come together as one people in humility before God. Even the architecture of such buildings suggests a holy place where heaven and earth meet. Spires draw the eye up to heaven; domes suggest heaven is bending to meet earth. And in both cases the interior presents a place out of the ordinary hustle and bustle of life. Is it any wonder that people over the ages have given gold and silver or just some of their hard-earned money to help create something beautiful?

Today we celebrate the dedication of the Lateran Basilica whose full name is the Cathedral of the Most Holy Savior and of Sts. John the Baptist and the Evangelist in the Lateran. It is the Cathedral Church of Rome, the oldest basilica in the Western world, and the seat of the Roman pontiff. It is the Mother Church for all Catholics. In choosing to give St. John Lateran a feast day of its own, the Church celebrates the unity of Catholics everywhere, who despite differences in culture, race, political preference, geography, and economic disparity, all gather at the table of the Lord to remember the Good News and receive Christ in the Eucharist. One Lord, one faith, one baptism, one God and this Mother Church belong to all of us.

A River Flowing with Life

Ezekiel's vision places the heavenly temple (his vision of God's dwelling place) in the center with a river flowing from it. There is a similar vision at the end of the Book of Revelation. Both speak to the abundance of life that God brings to the faithful. Both also represent a restoration to paradise as it was before the fall of Adam and Eve. The vision returns us to the garden where we first encountered God. We can only hope to do better this time.

You Are God's Building

In his Letter to the Corinthians, Paul presents a different perspective. "You are God's building." We can hear that in two ways. First, God's spirit dwells in us because of the sacrifice of Christ and we must be careful not to destroy our bodies through sin. Second, we can understand that God is building us even now through prayer, sacraments, the example of the saints, and living mentors who guide us in the spiritual life. Either way, God has given our lives in a sacred trust that we might go back to him having done as much with the gifts he gave us as we can.

Good News for All of Us

When Jesus overturns the tables of the money lenders in the temple courtyard, he is saying something important about God's house—it's not a business; it's not a place where people go to see and be seen. It is a house of prayer for everyone, rich and poor, black and white. As he does frequently in John's Gospel, Jesus goes on to talk about a different temple, and the people don't understand his meaning. Jesus' body is a temple that will be put to death by the authorities. In his promise to raise it up, Jesus confounds those listening because they think he means a temple of stone. Even the disciples didn't get it. But they remembered after the resurrection. And all of us know that Jesus himself will be a source of faith for the many generations that follow. He is the reason for our hope, and we gather in our churches on Sundays to remember that.

Questions for Reflections and Discussion

> Even the simplest churches have beauty in the quality of furnishings or the focal points to which we are drawn. In your role as a "temple of the Holy Spirit," what is beautiful in you? What draws people to you?

> What is the Church for you? Is it a place of prayer, challenge, comfort, or something else?

Related Journey of Faith Lesson

Q11, "Places in a Catholic Church"

Themes

Church
    Q11, "Places in a Catholic Church"
    Q13, "The Church as Community"
    M2, "The Role of the Laity"
Holiness
    Q15, "The Saints"
    M3, "Your Spiritual Gifts"
    M5, "Our Call to Holiness"
Salvation
    M1, "Conversion: A Lifelong Process"

Gathering Prayers

Gathering Prayers During Inquiry

Prayer

Good and gracious God, something has drawn us here to share with one another our search for you. We long to know you. We long to see where you have been present in our lives and in our hearts. Give us the grace to help each other grow in faith as we travel this way together. Be present to us now, O Lord, our God. Amen.

Prayer

Loving God, we gather to share the life we find with you. We gather to find your presence in this community of faith, your Church. Give us courage to ask questions and voice doubts. Also give us an open heart and mind to see the life you offer us as a part of this communion of souls. Never let us give up searching for you. Amen.

Prayer

Lord of all, as we come to know more about you, we see your presence in all creation and we share the awe and wonder that comes from knowing you created us in love and that you desire nothing more than that we become one with you. Fill our hearts with prayer, our lives with service, and our souls with longing. Amen.

Prayer

Gracious God, Father of our Lord, Jesus Christ, as we continue to walk with you and each other in this journey, help us follow Jesus more closely and know you by knowing him. May Jesus be with us as we commit to the next step of living our faith in the Catholic Church. May that step fill us with joy and peace and may we never cease coming to you with praise and gratitude. We pray this through Christ, our Lord. Amen.

Gathering Prayers During Catechumenate

Prayer

God of all nations, your word is life. Bless us now as we gather to reflect on sacred Scripture. In these words, let us find your truth. Help us to know you not only with our minds, but also with our hearts. When our learning is finished, bring us into your presence rejoicing. We pray this through Christ, our Lord. Amen.

Prayer

Draw near to us, O Lord, in these passages from Scripture. May our hearts grow in the desire to know you in these stories and to see ourselves as part of them. Jesus, speak to us as you spoke to those who followed you. Open the Scriptures to us as you did to the disciples on the road to Emmaus that we might recognize our presence in our lives. Amen.

Prayer

Eternal God, our hearts are hungry for your word. Teach us the story of Jesus and let us know it as our story. Give us ears to hear what you have to say to us. Always and forever be our guide and comfort us as we make our way in this journey to life in your Church. And Lord, teach us to bring your Good News to others along the way. Amen.

Prayer

Good and gracious God, this time of learning has challenged us as we have listened to your Scriptures more deeply than ever before. As we begin following your footsteps to the cross, let your words so fill us so our every longing might be for you. Increase our faith in you and help us know we do not walk alone, for you are always with us. May our discipleship be fruitful now and forever. Amen.

Gathering Prayers During Lent

Prayer

Compassionate and loving God, in Jesus you entered human experience. You were tempted and didn't despair, betrayed and didn't turn to hate, killed and spoke words of forgiveness. Be with us now in our desert experience so we can learn to walk in our trials as you did, clinging to the faith that you will us through it all. Amen.

Prayer

Lord Jesus, be the living water in the dryness of our lives. Be our sight when we are blind. Hear our prayer as we place our faith in you and in your Church. Let the communion of saints walk with us on this journey. Above all, Lord, let us know you in the depths of our hearts even as you know us. Amen.

Prayer

Jesus, our Savior, to whom else can we go? You are the source of eternal life for us. With you, death loses its sting and we await the resurrection that faith in you promises. Give us hope to walk in dark places and strength to follow faithfully in your path to the radiant light of your presence. Amen.

Prayer

Jesus, Lord of all, we sing out your praise with the rest of the crowd and then follow you to your death, uncertain, afraid that our hopes have died with you. We see where they have laid you and wonder if our lives will ever be the same. But in you we trust. You make all things new. Give us the confidence to believe with our whole being as we wait in hope for you. Amen.

Gathering Prayers During Mystagogy

Prayer

Glorious God, Lord Jesus—like the women at the tomb, we saw only emptiness at first but then you appeared Mary Magdalene and to your disciples. You opened our hearts and filled them with joy. We now recognize you not only by the wounds in your body, but by the miracle of your rising. Be with us now as we walk into your light. Amen.

Prayer

Gracious Lord, as we come together to reflect on the mystery of your passion, death, and resurrection, we pray to be filled with your Good News. Help us share it with everyone we meet. Help us live it out in every facet of our lives. And when our lives are over, grant us to live in your presence forever. Amen.

Prayer

Jesus, you call to us to follow in your path and be your disciples. Teach us the way of truth and light. Let us be your hands, your feet, your compassion in the world. Let us see your face in all we meet and be your face to all we meet. Give us grace not to waver in our commitment to you. Amen.

Prayer

Blessed are you, Lord, our God, ruler of the universe. In this OCIA journey, we have traveled far together. We have given support and comfort to one another. As we come together these last times, strengthen our resolve to be a light on the path for each other and to carry that light out into the world. We pray this through Christ, our Lord. Amen.

Dismissal Prayers

Dismissal Prayers During Inquiry

Prayer

Merciful God, we have begun this journey of faith together. We are grateful for the companions on our way, for the openness with which we receive one another, and most of all, for your love that brought us here. As we leave today, fill our hearts with a desire to know you even more and, when we return, let it be with joy and eagerness. Amen.

Prayer

God of all people, sometimes questions and doubts fill our minds and we can only ask, listen, and reflect on the response. Be patient with us as we hesitate and seek. Continue to call our names so we might find our way in the dark. We know we are never alone when we are with you and one another. Be present to us in our searching for you. Amen.

Prayer

Faithful God, the stories of our journey to faith bring us together in the great story of your salvation. Help us bear witness to your presence as we leave here today. Give us courage to continue the path if the way gets harder, to support one another, and to reach out in prayer to you whenever we are able. Amen.

Prayer

We give you praise, O God, for your faithful presence in our lives. Your Holy Spirit moved us to seek you in new and different ways. Walk with us as we commit ourselves to go deeper into your mystery. Draw us closer to you with the stories of your presence, the grace of your peace, and the love you expressed through your Son, Jesus Christ. We long to see you face to face. Amen.

Dismissal Prayers During Catechumenate

Prayer

God, Father of us all, the stories of faith in your sacred Scripture tell us the story of your presence to your people from the moment of creation to the resurrection of Jesus and even now. Give us insight to learn from them and faith to see them not just as stories of people who lived a long time ago but also as stories that speak to us of your presence so many centuries later. Help us to share what we are learning with others. Amen.

Prayer

Open our minds and heart, O Lord, to learn the truth of your love for us. Let us see in these Scriptures the evidence that you have cared for us and called us from the very beginning of our lives. When questions and doubt seek to overcome us, let us remember that you have the words of life. Amen.

Prayer

Good and gracious Lord, we are hungry for your grace and truth. We long to hear your voice calling us in every place in our lives. Now that we have shared your words in sacred Scripture, let them so fill us that we try to live them in our lives and thus give honor to you. Amen.

Prayer

Loving God, we leave this gathering ready to take the next step of following your Son, our Lord Jesus Christ, into the story of his life, death, and resurrection. We thank you for being with us since the beginning. Be present to us now as we begin to learn what discipleship really means. Watch over us as we place our trust in you. Amen.

Dismissal Prayers During Lent

Prayer

Loving Jesus, when you were tempted in the desert, you spoke only of trust in God the Father. We may be tempted many times in this journey. As we go on our way today, give us the confidence to trust God as you did and feel his presence when we find ourselves in a desert place. Amen.

Prayer

God of all, we are thirsty for your peace and presence in our lives. Through the Incarnation, you walked among your people as Jesus Christ. You reminded us that you are living water and light to the blind. Help us remember that you are with us still in your body, the Church. Help us see the signs of your presence in every place we go and in every person we meet. Amen.

Prayer

Lord, we will continue to walk with you this Lent and throughout the rest of our lives. Give us your grace to follow your path and not our own. Give us strength and courage to face what lies ahead. Fill us with your life that we might enter into eternal life when we see you at the end. We pray all these things in your holy name. Amen.

Prayer

Jesus, our Brother and Savior, we are about to make a final commitment to live our lives as disciples. We are eager to follow your path, proclaim your Good News, and witness to your love by our actions. We are filled with gratitude that you have brought us this far. Let us rejoice in this new step in faith. Amen.

Dismissal Prayers During Mystagogy

Prayer

Jesus, Lord of life, you have risen into our broken world and brought grace and healing with your presence. In your life, we have become a new creation, a people set apart to do your will and a witness of your presence to all we meet. Pour out your grace on us that we may live into that new life with faith in you always. Amen.

Prayer

Gracious God, source of all good things, as we reflect on what it means to be your daughters and sons, we know we will face dark times and difficult paths and that the way will not always be easy. When that happens, fill us with the desire to bring our troubled hearts to the cross of Jesus so he might take them up, calm our fears, and send us out rejoicing once more. Amen.

Prayer

Brother, Jesus, we are new at being your disciples. Like Peter, Andrew, James, John, Mary Magdalene, the woman at the well, and countless others, we strive to do your will. Please give us courage us to do what is right. Forgive us when we fail. Have mercy on our efforts to please you. But above all, let us never forget that you love us and that our only good rests in becoming one with you. Amen.

Prayer

Loving God, our hope and light, we have shared a journey of faith with one another. Our stories have joined the stories of the prophets and people of the Old Testament and those of the early followers of Jesus. We have come to know that they are all one story of your divine grace breaking into our imperfect world and making something holy of us. We praise you for this miracle now and forevermore. Amen.

Thematic Index

Numerals in bold type refer to pages in this book.

Numerals preceded by a letter refer to lessons from the *Journey of Faith* program from Liguori Publications:
Q = Inquiry; C = Catechumenate; E = Enlightenment and Purification; M = Mystagogy.
Samples of the *Journey of Faith* lesson references are listed in this thematic index.

Example: Advent...**5–6, 10–17, 22**, Q11.
References to Advent may be found in *Breaking Open the Word, Year C,* on pages 5–6, 10–17, and 22.
Further information may be found in the *Journey of Faith Inquiry* lesson number 11.

www.ingramcontent.com/pod-product-compliance
Lightning Source LLC
LaVergne TN
LVHW070058080426

835508LV00032B/3488